BRIAN CARTER

THE
LIKE
ECONOMY

HOW BUSINESSES ARE
MAKING MONEY WITH FACEBOOK

que®

800 East 96th Street,
Indianapolis, Indiana 46240 USA

The Like Economy: How Businesses Are Making Money with Facebook

ISBN-13: 978-0-7897-4906-2

ISBN-10: 0-7897-4906-8

Library of Congress Cataloging-in-Publication data is on file.

Printed in the United States of America

First Printing: December 2011

Trademarks

All terms mentioned in this book that are known to be trademarks or service marks have been appropriately capitalized. Que Publishing cannot attest to the accuracy of this information. Use of a term in this book should not be regarded as affecting the validity of any trademark or service mark.

Warning and Disclaimer

Every effort has been made to make this book as complete and as accurate as possible, but no warranty or fitness is implied. The information provided is on an "as is" basis. The author and the publisher shall have neither liability nor responsibility to any person or entity with respect to any loss or damages arising from the information contained in this book or programs accompanying it.

Bulk Sales

Que Publishing offers excellent discounts on this book when ordered in quantity for bulk purchases or special sales. For more information, please contact

U.S. Corporate and Government Sales
1-800-382-3419
corpsales@pearsontechgroup.com

For sales outside of the U.S., please contact

International Sales
international@pearson.com

CONTENTS AT A GLANCE

TABLE OF CONTENTS

About the Author

Brian Carter is known as one of the elite Internet marketing experts in the world. His hands-on business experience, cutting-edge insights, and background in improv and stand-up comedy results in a speaker and trainer who leaves every audience not only entertained, but armed with powerful tactics and strategies.

Brian has 12 years experience with Google, Twitter, and Facebook marketing, both as a consultant and marketing agency director. He has trained and managed Gen X and Gen Y employees, in addition to the more than 5,000 students of his FanReach Facebook marketing online course. He is a social media keynote speaker who combines entertainment, comedy, and education into hilarious event experiences.

Brian develops strategies and builds search visibility and social marketing for companies of all sizes, including well-known entities such as Universal Studios, the U.S. Army, Hardee's, and Carl's Jr. He has been quoted and profiled by *Information Week, U.S. News & World Report, The Wall Street Journal,* and *Entrepreneur Magazine.*

Brian writes for two of the most popular marketing blogs, Search Engine Journal and AllFacebook, and his combined readership exceeds 100,000 people. He has more than 30,000 Twitter followers and an overall reach of more than 50,000 fans through Facebook, LinkedIn, and his other marketing channels. A speaker and trainer for top marketing conferences that include Socialize, SEOmoz, SMX, Pubcon, and the American Marketing Association, Brian is one of the nation's leading experts in Internet marketing.

Dedication

I'd like to dedicate this book to my parents and my wife, who've all made me a much better person than I would have been otherwise. I should also mention our dogs Seratonin and Brad Pitt, as well as our cats Larry and Little B, for telling me when to stop writing and share some love. Finally, this book is dedicated to the reader who thoroughly tests the ideas in this book for his own business until he gets the results he wants.

Acknowledgments

This book is not the work of one person. No good book is. The best business books stand on the shoulders of giants and require the contributions of many people and the backing of lots of good data. I've done everything I could to ensure it would be a good and highly useful book. While trying to avoid thanking every person I've ever met or bought coffee from, I do feel I should acknowledge those who had a part in shaping me and this book.

This book is not only about my businesses, my clients, or my students, but rests on the work of many companies, clients, agencies, and third-party analytics services:

- Some of the insights about how people use Facebook pages come from PageLever, which at the time of my writing had data on a broad swath of Facebook pages containing a total of 400 million fans.

- I can't name all the clients or businesses involved in what I've learned due to non-disclosure agreements, but I can thank agencies such as Epic Media Group, Epic Marketplace, BlitzLocal, Pertnear, Fuel Interactive, and JB Chicago. And my own direct clients have been amazing. I'm blessed to get to work with so many awesome clients and exciting businesses.

- Facebook marketing is, relative to other channels, quite young. Certain authors I've never met in person have played a huge role in developing some of my best practices, many of which have proven to transfer effectively. These include Claude Hopkins, Robert Cialdini, Patrick Lencioni, David Ogilvy, Harry Beckwith, Steven Levitt, Stephen Dubner, Marcus Buckingham, and David Keirsey.

- Although I also thank them in Chapter 12 ("FaceMessage: Achieving Other Corporate Goals on Facebook"), the PR folks who helped me get a better understanding of PR's modern role in social media should be thanked here as well: Sally Falkow, Carrie Bugbee, Adele Cehrs, Li Evans, Chase McMichael, and Chris Brubaker. And here's an extra special thanks to Adele Cehrs for spending even more time with me discussing Facebook PR tactics.

- Thank you to Barry Tubwell, who helped me on the FanReach Facebook Marketing course. Our course exposed us to many students and businesses who ran with our ideas and best practices and came back with more diverse experiences and affirmative results. I want to give special thanks to some of the our most active students and peers: Corey McNeil, Jason Morris, Heather Dopson, Victoria Edwards, Joe Hyde, Nickolus Cunningham, Mark Ellingson, Eliot Rosenthal, Bachir

Salamat, Crystal Curtis, Brendan Mark, Joey Lowe, Yasmin Khayat Mitchell, and Martin Maybruck. My sincere apologies for anybody I may have left out. Our student community has been incredible, and that experience taught me a lot in itself about the value of Facebook Groups.

- Last, but obviously not least, thanks to Katherine Bull and the Pearson Education team who helped make this book a reality. This was my first time working with a traditional publishing company, and their professionalism made it a smooth, enjoyable process. Thanks to Brandon Prebynski for his killer feedback. And, of course, thanks to my wife, Lynda, who had *plenty* to say about it and made this a much better book as a result.

We Want to Hear from You!

As the reader of this book, *you* are our most important critic and commentator. We value your opinion and want to know what we're doing right, what we could do better, what areas you'd like to see us publish in, and any other words of wisdom you're willing to pass our way.

As an editor-in-chief for Que Publishing, I welcome your comments. You can email or write me directly to let me know what you did or didn't like about this book—as well as what we can do to make our books better.

Please note that I cannot help you with technical problems related to the topic of this book. We do have a User Services group, however, where I will forward specific technical questions related to the book.

When you write, please be sure to include this book's title and author as well as your name, email address, and phone number. I will carefully review your comments and share them with the author and editors who worked on the book.

Email: feedback@quepublishing.com

Mail: Greg Wiegand
            Editor-in-Chief
            Que Publishing
            800 East 96th Street
            Indianapolis, IN 46240 USA

Reader Services

Visit our website and register this book at quepublishing.com/register for convenient access to any updates, downloads, or errata that might be available for this book.

1

The Like Effect: The Power of Positive Marketing

Facebook is a marketing tool unlike any the world has seen before. Facebook marketing is different because positivity is part of its DNA. The act of liking has far-reaching impact and a quantifiable effect on commerce.

Facebook likes

- Decrease marketing costs.
- Increase sales.
- Give you control of the customer conversation.
- Prove people are paying attention.
- Solidify customer loyalty.
- Create evangelistic customers who sell for you and defend you against critics.

Let's look at each of those in detail.

Likes Decrease Costs and Increase Profits

When more people like your ads, your click cost decreases and so does the cost to acquire each fan. When more of your page fans like your page posts

- You get more visibility and loyalty from each fan.

- Cost per impression decreases.

- Cost per customer decreases.

- The lifetime value of your customer increases.

ChompOn, a company that provides a white-label platform for Groupon-like deal websites, gathered data from numerous e-commerce stores to try to figure out how much revenue a company can expect on average from each person who likes a page. They found the value of each like to be $8.00 (see Figure 1.1).[1]

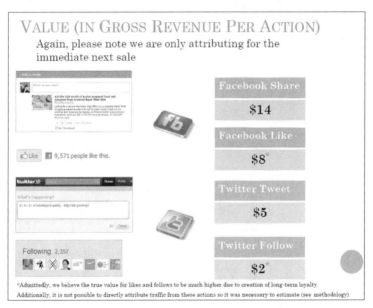

Figure 1.1   *ChompOn's study of the e-commerce value of social actions.*

Likes Increase Sales

Facebook likes build you a captive audience of potential customers. Likes on your Facebook page posts increase fans' desire to buy and increase the percentage of potential customers who actually buy. According to data from Razorfish, Econsultancy.com, and Social Media Today, 34.66% of Facebook fans will consider

1. http://www.chompon.com/chompon_social_action_value.pdf

the brand when they're in the market for one of the brand's products or services. And 33.92% of fans recommend the brand to their friends. In both of these cases, Facebook is 10% more influential than Twitter.[2]

Have you heard the axiom that customers make their buying decisions emotionally and then justify them with logic afterwards? What's more persuasive than a social platform that helps you harness potential customers' enthusiasm for what they already love and elevate it to new heights? Facebook's ability to leverage customer emotion is unparalleled.

Likes Give You Control of the Customer Conversation

A like creates a connection between a person and your Facebook page. You base that page on your major brand promise or dream. The person becomes a *fan*. More than half of Facebook users follow 2–5 brands, one-fifth follow 5–10 brands, and one-eighth follow 10 or more (see Figure 1.2).[3] As an administrator of that page, you lead these fans' conversations. You own the space where they discuss their dreams and goals. You hear what they like and dislike, and you gain market intelligence. It's an incredibly low-cost way to get great insights about your customers.

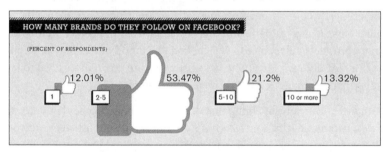

Figure 1.2   *GetSatisfaction's infographic shows how many brands Facebook users follow.*

Likes Prove People Are Paying Attention

In this age of TV, Internet, handheld devices, and digital signage, the battle for customers' attention is the first one you must win. Consumers are barraged by thousands of marketing messages a day.[4] Getting their attention for even 30 seconds of that day is a victory in the war for their business. When you run a Facebook page

2. http://blog.getsatisfaction.com/2011/06/29/what-makes-people-follow-brands/?view=socialstudies

3. http://www.allfacebook.com/infographic-why-we-follow-brands-on-facebook-2011-07

4. The number that's widely quoted is 3,000 marketing messages per day. It's often attributed to SymphonyIRI, but that number is not on their public website. It seems believable that the real number could be from a few hundred to several thousand, depending on how much time you spend surfing advertising-laden websites, how many hours you watch TV, how many subway train ads you see, and so on.

and post into people's news streams, every like and comment proves that they still see you and you're still relevant to them. You're still in the game to get more business from them.

Likes Solidify Loyalty

In an increasingly competitive social media environment, you and your competitors swim in the same sea of messages, logos, and videos. Posting messages that engage your customers means you're creating frequent micro-connections on an emotional level. Many people don't even talk to their families as often as they interact with Facebook pages. By engaging them repeatedly, you create in them a habit of loyalty.

Despite rumors to the contrary, the West is not necessarily headed for an apocalypse of disloyalty. Job tenures are slightly higher than they were in the 1980s,[5] divorce rates are lower than they were in the 1970s, and fewer married people are having affairs.[6] If you want customer loyalty, people will not naturally resist it. Only invisibility or dissatisfaction lead to disloyalty. You can control your visibility and your quality.

Loyalty increases profitability by decreasing the cost of new customer acquisition. Customer loyalty comes from customer satisfaction. Companies with outstanding customer experiences outperform others by about 15% in people's willingness to buy more products, reluctance to switch, and likelihood of recommendations to others.[7] But loyalty varies by industry—customers are much more loyal to banks and supermarkets than they are to cinemas and hotels.[8]

Case studies are already emerging that demonstrate how Facebook marketers can increase customer loyalty. The *Harvard Business Review* published a study of how the Houston cafe and bakery chain Dessert Gallery found its best customers by getting them into its Facebook page and interacting with them. It harnessed the power of these superfans who were more loyal and evangelistic. Compared to the company's typical customers, these superfans were 41% more loyal, had a 14% higher emotional attachment, and spent 45% more of their dining-out dollars at Dessert Gallery.[9]

---

5. http://www.ebri.org/pdf/notespdf/EBRI_Notes_12-Dec10.Tenure-CEHCS.pdf

6. http://blogs.wsj.com/economics/2010/08/31/amid-downturn-divorce-and-infidelity-decrease/?mod=e2tw

7. http://experiencematters.wordpress.com/2009/06/25/customer-experience-boosts-revenue/

8. http://tutor2u.net/blog/index.php/economics/comments/barriers-to-entry-how-important-is-customer-loyalty/

9. http://hbr.org/2010/03/one-cafe-chains-facebook-experiment/ar/1

Likes Create Evangelistic Customers

Happy customers, impassioned by positive discussions on your page, write spontaneous testimonials about your company. These happy, vocal customers turn fans who are potential customers into first-time buyers. And your most active fans will fight back against your critics, creating a fan page immune system that repels brand attacks.

Among decision-makers reluctant to use Facebook, one of the biggest fears is that public critiques will hurt the brand. But when you grow fans based on what they love and get them to engage daily with posts they like, the like effect creates a positivity that makes "Negative Nellies" feel outnumbered and abnormal. People are less likely to boo when they expect they'll be shouted down. Granted, you don't want people with valid complaints to be ignored, but you do want issues resolved civilly and without public relations fallout.

Think about it. When a customer presents a negative, what's more persuasive: the company defending itself or another fan taking your side? If you respond diplomatically, apologize, and fix the problem, *and* your superfans speak out on your behalf, the complainant has nowhere to go. Potential crisis averted. And, perhaps, previous critic converted.

There's No Dislike Button

It's easy to like a post or a comment. But if you don't like a post or comment on Facebook, there's no dislike button. The only way to "dislike" is to explain your objection in a comment. If people don't like your critical comment, they won't click Like on that comment. Facebook seems to be set up to support the old adage "If you don't have something nice to say, don't say anything at all."

If you say something nice or constructive, people who like your comment will grow in your affection. It always feels good to be liked, and you notice who specifically liked what you said. Bonds between people are strengthened by this positivity. We like people more when they like our posts and comments, and we're more likely to like their posts in return after they've liked ours.

This may be why you don't see as many rants on Facebook as on other social networks. Even posts that have lots of negative comments might not be seen by as many people as they would on another social network because Facebook often shows only a few of the comments under a post. You have to click to see more. The emphasis, when a post is collapsed, is on the number of people who have interacted with it. It's more obvious how interactive the post is than what people have said.

I like that Facebook is biased toward the positive because human nature is to complain rather than spread satisfaction. One study found that 75% of people will tell others about a bad experience with a product but only 42% will recommend a product they like.[10] This has always been the ugly downside of word-of-mouth marketing. By making it easier to be positive than negative, Facebook might have finally corrected that prejudice. It's not that human nature is wrong because spreading warnings helps us survive and avoid catastrophes, but we already have the 24/7 cable news channels for that (and people have taken advantage of it as well with false rumors and urban legends). Facebook serves another function, which is to bring "like" people closer together.

Can You Do Fear-Based Marketing on Facebook?

Marketers have long had to make the choice between negative and positive marketing. Political ads are some of the most negative. The biggest consumer goods brands often keep it positive and light-hearted. But in one day, a TV viewer can see one deodorant commercial that demonstrates that your man-stink will destroy a beautiful moment (negative), while another suggests that the right body spray will drive women so crazy they'll be forced to tackle you (positive, if you're in your 20s).

You can show how sad and lonely the balding man is *before* or how many women want to stroke his new hair *after*, or even show both. TV commercials ask us: Are you afraid of oily or dry skin? Are you afraid of impotence? Are you afraid of getting into a car wreck? Are you afraid you'll never be able to retire? Some marketers choose to play on those fears. I'm not making a value judgment here because if consumers are ignoring real risks, it's a legitimate service for a company to get their attention and help them solve the problem.

Facebook's positive like effect makes that approach more difficult. Because Facebook shows liked posts to more people than posts that aren't liked and because it's easier to click Like than write a negative comment, positive messages will always reach more people on Facebook than negative ones. It's something to keep in mind when you extend other marketing campaigns to Facebook. They can like a clever video that plays on fear, but the conversation is more likely to continue when you evoke the positive side of the coin.

Google and Wikipedia "Like" the Like Button

How successful has the Like button been? So successful that two of the best-known names in the modern web space—Google and Wikipedia—are copying it.

Google has scrambled to catch up with Facebook, and in late March 2011 it debuted the +1 button, which it defines as a public stamp of approval. You can see "plus ones" in Google search results, ads, and your Google profile. Google Plus uses

---

10. http://www.csdecisions.com/2011/03/09/managing-word-of-mouth-about-your-brand/

your Google contacts (from your Gmail, Google Buzz, and Google Reader) to tell you who has "plus-oned" things.[11] Unfortunately, it's ugly and mathematical and previous Google social media efforts have fallen flat. It's unclear at this point whether it will eventually give Facebook a run for its money.

Wikipedia's Love button, which became available in late June 2011, is a bit more cuddly. Wikipedia wants to encourage more new editors to join and has recognized that, for them, negativity and criticism is a bit too common. They found that editors were demotivated by widespread disdain from more experienced editors.[12] The Love button allows editors to send kittens, stars, or beers to other editors. Editors can also create their own type of appreciation to give people chocolate, leprechauns, or bacon.

What does this mean for Facebook? When two of the other biggest names on the Internet are copying you, you know you have a winner.

Facebook Is About Passions and Interests

When people create their personal profiles, they type in the things they like. Here are some of the kinds of things people like:

- Books
- Movies
- TV shows
- Bands
- Sports
- Hobbies
- Activities

When you use ads to get fans for pages, often you target these likes, which are called *precise interests* in the advertising platform. With these ads, you capture a fan base that likes things related to what you sell. For example

- A pet supply store can find fans who've noted in their profiles which breeds they like (which are almost certainly the animals they own).
- A running store can capture fans who like running and marathons.
- A digital marketing service can target people who like AdWords, AllFacebook, Mashable, and Techcrunch.

---

11. http://www.google.com/+1/button/

12. http://blog.wikimedia.org/2011/06/24/wikilove-an-experiment-in-appreciation/

- A financial services firm can build a fan base of people who like investing and retirement.

- A local beauty salon can attract folks who like beauty, fitness, facials, and manicures.

Then, you get these new fans of yours talking about their interests and passions, and they can get each other excited. You show them how your company helps them reach their goals and dreams. They love you for it and then buy what you offer. That's how Facebook marketing works.

How Often Do Facebookers Like Things?

Generally speaking, Facebookers like more than they share, post, or update:

- On an average day, 26% of Facebook's members like someone else's content.

- Commenting is the second-most popular activity, with 22% doing so daily.

- Overall, 72% of men and 82% of women like Facebook content with some frequency, and only 28% of men and 18% of women never like anything.

- As for the super-users, 20% of women and 9% of men like multiple times daily.[13]

Also on the average day

- 15% of Facebook users update their own statuses.

- 20% comment on another user's photos.

- 10% send another user a private message.

Frequency of "liking" content on Facebook by age

% of Facebook users in each age group who "like" content on Facebook with the following frequency. For instance, 31% of Facebook users ages 18-22 "like" content on Facebook several times a day.

	All SNS Users	Age 18-22	Age 23-35	Age 36-49	Age 50-65	Age 65+
Several times a day	15%	31%	17%	12%	7%	9%
About once per day	10%	13%	11%	12%	5%	5%
3-5 days per week	11%	12%	14%	11%	6%	3%
1-2 Days per week	15%	14%	19%	13%	13%	9%
Every few weeks	10%	3%	10%	10%	15%	12%
Less often	17%	13%	17%	13%	24%	27%
Never	22%	13%	13%	30%	30%	36%
N (weighted)	936	156	307	236	184	54

Source: Pew Research Center's Internet & American Life Social Network Site survey conducted on landline and cell phone between October 20-November 28, 2010. N for full sample 2,255 and margin of error is +/- 2.3 percentage points. N for Facebook users=877 and margin of error is +/- 3.6 percentage points.

Figure 1.3   *The Pew Research Center's findings on how often Facebook users like.*

---

13. http://www.pewinternet.org/Reports/2011/Technology-and-social-networks.aspx

Facebook Users Are More Trusting

In 2011, the Pew Research Center found that, when accounting for all other factors—such as age, education level, and race—Facebook users are 43% more likely than other Internet users to say that "most people can be trusted." That's actually *up* from 32% in 2009. Compared with people who don't use the Internet at all, Facebook users were three times more trusting.[14] By the way, who's not using the Internet at all? People too busy fixing their moonshine stills? "Don't use that thar Internet. It'll suck yer soul raht outta yer ahhz!"

Facebook Groups: Off-the-Charts Positivity

On Facebook, people can like and comment on the posts they see. You don't see all your friends' posts or the posts of all pages you've liked, but if you're in a Facebook Group, you do get notified about every post and comment from every member. As a result, Group members keep coming back and commenting, liking, and posting. This can create a perpetual motion engagement machine—some groups require more stoking of the conversational fire, but some virtually none. Earlier I talked about how liking leads to more liking, but leading page fans requires more sustained effort, while a Group of a few hundred people can post, like, and comment without your intervention for months on end.

At the end of 2010, I was invited into a very active Group on the topic of social media. It's a secret, invitation-only Group, and its members are opinionated and often inappropriate. If I told you about it, I'd have to kill all my readers, so just take my word for it. This Group currently has almost 9,000 posts and most posts get 15–25 comments. On a typical day, I get about eight notifications from this Group. And I probably comment at least three times a day.

Seeing how sticky (how often people go back to it) this Group was, I started an experiment. I created a Group for horse owners. I don't own a horse, but I knew that this was an affordable ad target and I wanted to see what these horse lovers would do in a Group. I paid $84.77 to bring in about 200 horse owners. Five months later, they had grown their own membership by 45% and made 2,313 posts. In another Group where I am 1 of 813 members, a typical month saw 2,677 posts.

What all Facebook Groups normally share is that their members are extremely enthusiastic. They constantly communicate about their passion, and they help each other with problems. Because of that outlet and the help, they're incredibly grateful for their Groups. If you create a Group for consumers in your niche, you'll have their gratitude, an ear on their conversations, and the ability to insert your own messages whenever you want.

---

14. http://hosted.ap.org/dynamic/stories/U/US_TEC_PEW_SOCIAL_NETWORKS?SITE=
    NYSAR&SECTION=HOME&TEMPLATE=DEFAULT

There is a drawback to Groups, however, which is why some people use Facebook pages instead. Only the most enthusiastic folks will welcome that many notifications. Others can get annoyed and leave. Groups are best used for small, super-fanatic purposes, as an add-on to your main Facebook page.

Facebook Page Brag Boards

On Facebook, it's pretty easy to get people to show off what they're proud of. Whether it's a fish they caught, their beloved pet, their kid's report card, or the best photo they've taken recently, people will post those things to an active Facebook page without even being asked to (especially if you're growing an enthusiastic fan base with Facebook ads based on consumer passions). If you actually request this kind of post, you'll get an avalanche of responses.

Easy Testimonials

Some businesses like to post quotes from happy customers (see Figure 1.4). When you get them, which happens spontaneously when you satisfy customers and are active on Facebook, ask for permission to use the quote and then post it on your website, email it to people, maybe even put it on a billboard! My preference is to take a screenshot and post it in the Facebook format, which adds a layer of third-party credibility.

Katherine Smith
Hi Brian - I just want to say thank you so much for providing such great content. The information on fanreach is fantastic. I just paid $1,000 for another course on Facebook to learn more only to have it provide very little value and have just received my refund. I am glad to have found your website and resources.

Figure 1.4   *An unasked-for testimonial from the FanReach Facebook Group.*

I Just Posted to Say "I Love You"

Stevie Wonder should write a new song about how many page fans and Group members will spontaneously post or comment how much they love your page, your Group, your company, or the other fans. I've felt that kind of affection for Facebook communities myself.

It makes sense. Think about it: If you spend day after day with other people who already share one interest with you and you gradually come to know their challenges, heartbreaks, and victories, isn't that the same recipe used to make tear-jerking movies? And what keeps you engaged with your favorite sports team? You come to love these people. Or like them strongly. Or at least you love their thumbnail pictures. It's human nature and there is even science to support it in the next section.

Emotions on Facebook Are Contagious

Scientist Adam D. I. Kramer, at the 2011 meeting of the Society for Personality and Social Psychology, presented his conclusions[15] from a study of Facebook posts by 1 million people and their 150 million friends. He found the following:

- People who used emotionally loaded words in their posts sparked similar emotions in later Facebook posts by friends for up to three days.

- When people used positive words, their friends used more positive words and their friends used fewer negative words.

That means a mostly positive Facebook page can prevent critical posts and comments and prevent the negativity of critics without any extra action being taken. Any potential critic will be more reluctant to complain when he sees a culture of appreciation on your page.

Gross National Happiness

Economists measure countries' gross national product, but Kramer also created an application based on Facebook data that tracks *gross national happiness* (see Figure 1.5).[16] It analyzes all the words used each day for positivity and negativity and then compares them to measure people's overall happiness for that day. He has plotted this data since October 2007. It's not surprising that happiness and positivity spike on holidays, but it's interesting that negativity also spikes then, though not nearly as much as positivity.

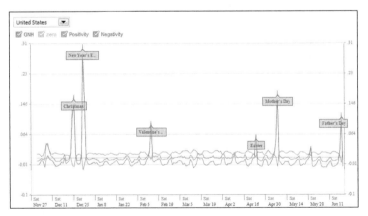

Figure 1.5   *Gross national happiness.*

15. http://www.mercurynews.com/business/ci_18183052?IADID=Search-www.mercurynews.com-www.mercurynews.com&nclick_check=1

16. http://apps.facebook.com/gnh_index/

For more, see how they've analyzed word categories and what their usage says about how many friends you have and what time of day you post them on Facebook.[17]

By the way, Kramer works for Facebook. His job title is Data Scientist. Facebook founder Mark Zuckerberg studied psychology at Harvard, so I'd say these guys are digital psychologists. I doubt it's a coincidence that Facebook has grown so rapidly or that people spend more time on it than any other website. In my opinion, this psychological savvy is Facebook's biggest competitive advantage, and if no other social network ever catches up to it, that may be the reason.

There's a saying, the source of which I can't find, that goes something like this: "I hated high school and I loved college. I thought life would be like college, but turns out it's more like high school." Many of us have found that to be true. The popularity contests, cliques, politics, gossip, and exclusion that run rampant in high schools, and that some college cultures try to deactivate, also seems to run much of adult life and business. It seems to me that the Google folks are more like college academics, while Facebook—understanding the powerful forces of high school—built them right into its social network.

Google's most essential technology, PageRank, is based on how academic papers references each other. Facebook is based on what people like. Who do you think will win in the real world, the *social* world?

---

17. http://www.facebook.com/notes/facebook-data-team/whats-on-your-mind/477517358858

2

You Can't Tell a Facebook by Its Cover: The Case for Facebook Marketing

There are a lot of myths about Facebook, Facebook marketing, and social media. In this chapter, I discuss some all-too-common misconceptions, why Facebook Marketing is worth doing, and why now is the time to get started.

I've seen real businesses make real profits from doing Facebook marketing. I've developed best practices based on real case studies and tests, taught them, and seen the businesses of my students get profits, too. I'm a true believer in Facebook Marketing...now. But I was not back in early 2010.

Let's set the scene: The 2009 holiday season had just passed at the digital marketing agency where I ran the search and social department. We had launched a lot of the springtime search strategies we'd previously found effective and were talking about how to get our clients into social media. With Google search engine rankings and AdWords advertising, we were getting one of our biggest clients in the range of 300%–900% return on investment. This client was forward-thinking and wanted to get into social media before any of its competitors did.

I was, like most social media experts at the time, drinking the Twitter Kool-Aid and wanted this client to try that first. The social media industry had already seen companies profit from Twitter but not Facebook—but the client insisted on Facebook. Our policy was to keep the client happy, and I couldn't say for sure that Facebook wouldn't work—so guess what happened?

We started trying to figure out how to get results with Facebook. We had no idea what we were doing and made a lot of mistakes, but we grew its fan base, we ran some contests, and the client was thrilled. Some time after I had left the agency to start my own consulting practice, I checked back in and found out the client had made revenue from it!

Later I worked on dozens of diverse projects, including a local hospitality company and numerous e-commerce stores; grew hundreds of thousands of fans for several national Fortune 1000 promotions and a Hollywood movie debut; and taught interns and marketing coordinators how to engage fans and persuade them to buy. I saw some companies get revenue from fans while others didn't, and still others were using Facebook for non-revenue purposes, which I discuss in a later chapter.

By then, I felt I had learned enough to begin teaching best practices. I released a free online Facebook marketing training course in November 2010 (www.fbm101.com) and by January 2011, another teacher and I had grown it into a paid course called FanReach. By March, the businesses, consultants, and agencies who had become our students began telling us their own stories of profit from Facebook marketing. It was a successful formula, and I was ecstatic.

The facts had convinced me, in less than a year that my first impressions of Facebook marketing were incorrect. I had harbored a theory—shared by others— that Facebook didn't work. But I tested that theory and found profits instead. I kept on testing and found a bunch of methods that other businesses have been able to reproduce. Since then, more stats and case studies have surfaced to support the profitability and value of Facebook marketing. But as you'll see, Facebook's momentum is so strong that companies were going to start using it whether they knew what the result would be or not.

So, now I have some big claims to make:

Why Facebook Marketing Is So Important

Facebook Is the Biggest Thing Since Google and Might Be Bigger Than Google

By 2006, somewhere between 70% and 90% of the traffic to most websites was from Google.[1] A huge industry sprung up around Google's multibillion-dollar AdWords advertising platform, and search engine optimization (SEO), the process of trying to improve a website's ranking in Google searches, was a $14.6 billion dollar industry by 2009. That's a lot of money. And most people jumped on the Google train. Since 2007, 90% of companies have engaged in SEO or Google AdWords advertising.[2] In 2010, AdWords revenues were $28 billion.[3] It shot upward like a 13-year-old basketball player, and Facebook advertising is likely to grow the same way.

2010 was a year of hypergrowth for Facebook, to the tune of $1.86 billion. As with Google, most of its revenue came from advertising. At least 60% of that ad revenue came from smaller companies. That's important because what works for gargantuan companies often doesn't work for smaller companies. There are only 500 Fortune 500 companies (pretty obvious, right?), while 99.7% of all U.S. businesses are smaller firms.[4] But clearly, smaller companies thought Facebook was worth doing, too.

Facebook's 2011 revenues are expected by eMarketer.com to total at least $4 billion.[5] So Facebook could be the next Google, in terms of Internet marketing dominance. It seems plausible because everyone's using it. According to Compete.com, Facebook visits have increased by close to 33% in 2011. Alexa.com places Facebook as the number-two most visited site on the Web behind Google (ahead of YouTube, and Twitter is only number 11). Facebook is the largest display ad (ads with graphics, as opposed to text ads) platform in the world.[6] Display ads are a staple of the Internet marketing world, so they've staked quite a claim.

What's more, it looks like Facebook is growing faster than Google did. If you compare Google to Facebook in the first few years after introducing their respective ad networks, Facebook is receiving twice as much revenue as Google did.[7] And this value is transferring to companies that market on Facebook. The average revenue value of a Facebook share is $14, says daily deal provider Chompon.

Google has released several competing products (Buzz and Google+), and former Google CEO Eric Schmidt, not long before he stepped down for founder Larry Page to return as CEO, admitted he should have pushed harder for ways to adapt to the rise of Facebook.[8] A similar thing happened to Microsoft in regards to search engines when Google was transforming from David into Goliath. Microsoft's efforts to recapture search share—including Bing and the billions of dollars spent on TV ads—fell flat, and they still get only 13% of Internet searches, which is one-fifth of

---

1. http://www.skrenta.com/2006/12/googles_true_search_market_sha.html

2. http://seo.tv/news/sempo-search-engine-marketing-report-seo-industry-market-growth.html

3. http://en.wikipedia.org/wiki/AdWords

4. http://adage.com/article/digital/estimate-facebook-books-1-86b-2010-advertising-muscles-google-turf/148236/

5. http://www.emarketer.com/blog/index.php/quick-stat/

6. http://www.comscore.com/Press_Events/Press_Releases/2011/5/U.S._Online_Display_Advertising_Market_Delivers_1.1_Trillion_Impressions_in_Q1_2011

7. http://socialfresh.com/facebook-ad-network-growth-vs-google/

8. http://latimesblogs.latimes.com/technology/2011/06/googles-eric-schmidt-says-he-didnt-push-hard-enough-to-do-a-deal-with-facebook.html

what Google receives.[9] Similarly, Google's attempts to horn in on Facebook's users have fallen flat. Google Buzz was a big deal for about three months, but now no one uses it. Google+ is newsworthy now, but there's no reason to believe it will steal away a significant portion of Facebook users. It's not clear Google will be able to compete in the social media space.

The Facebook Ad Platform Is the Most Powerful Marketing Tool in History

The power of a solid marketing campaign is measured by the following:

- How many people you can reach

- How specifically you can target the right potential customers

- How affordable it is to reach those specific customers

Some companies also look at the direct profitability of their marketing, but not all, and some cannot measure it accurately—so I did not include that in the criteria.

Facebook reaches more than 730 million people worldwide, and more than 151 million Americans. This allows companies to target more specifically along more parameters than any other online platform and is more affordable than any other advertising option. It provides the potential reach of TV and radio with even better targeting and cheaper pricing than Google AdWords. What this means is that every business owner is empowered by Facebook advertising to a revolutionary degree.

Google Dooms You to Price Wars, Whereas Facebook Creates Loyalty and Increases Your Value

Google (search) marketing excels at cashing in on searchers who are ready to buy. But these buyers are met by competing advertisers fighting on price and an overwhelming list of options on noisy search results pages. Price wars doom industries to lower profits and leave customers fewer suppliers whose quality and customer service tends to decrease as a result of the lower profits.

Facebook allows you to capture ideal prospects regardless of how soon they're going to buy, make an impression on them, and build a relationship with them. Getting potential customers more cheaply and reaching these new fans over and over with your Facebook page means you have a big advantage over companies that are only marketing on Google. And being able to market based on your value, rather than price, empowers companies to deliver quality products and services.

---

9. http://news.cnet.com/8301-1023_3-20042928-93.html

Facebook Fans Are the New Email Subscribers

For years, Internet marketers have agreed that email lists are the most profitable form of online marketing. People opt in and you can contact them repeatedly at no extra cost. Similarly, you can get people to like your Facebook page and then market to them repeatedly. You can grow a Facebook fan base for as little as $0.10 a fan, while most businesses have trouble acquiring quality email subscribers for less than $5.00. I discuss all the advantages of fans over emails in Chapter 4, "FaceBucks: Five Ways Businesses Achieve Profits with Facebook."

Facebook Is Heir to the Browsing Empire Yahoo! Lost

In the old days of the Internet, there were two major Internet experiences: browsing through Yahoo!'s directory and searching with Google. Over time, people switched to Google.

Consider that one of the currently most recommended strategies to increase traffic to your website is to create content (such as blog posts, videos, and infographics) that users will share with others. About 10% of all traffic to websites comes from people sharing website links via social media (that's 300 million people and 7 billion page views per month). People aren't just searching for websites—they're recommending them and discovering them through friends. As Figure 2.1 shows, 38% of that traffic comes from people sharing content on Facebook (Twitter is only 11%).[10]

Source of Sharing Traffic

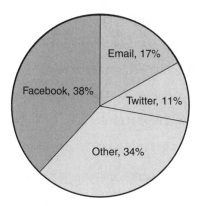

Figure 2.1   *Sources of Traffic from Shared Web Content*

---

10. http://techcrunch.com/2011/06/06/sharethis-facebook-38-percent-traffic/

Some major websites, such as NHL.com, get as much traffic from Facebook as Google. Facebook and Google are neck and neck in terms of number of visits.[11]

But, people spend more time on Facebook than any other website.[12] That means they find more value in browsing Facebook than any other site. They look for interesting things to interrupt their day when they're bored.

If you think about how human beings communicated before the Internet existed, it shouldn't be a surprise that Facebook could rival or overshadow Google—finding things through friends has always been more common than searching through a card catalogue or encyclopedia. Facebook stands on the shoulders of the age-old human desire to enjoy each other while sharing news, stories, and ideas.

I think I can say this, as a life-long nerd: Google is the way a nerd would organize the Internet. Facebook is the way everybody else would. There's a saying that most of us who went to college were surprised to find out that life was a lot more like high school than college. Life is filled with cliques and popularity and politics and unfairness—it's not Plato's Republic. Facebook is more like high school and more like real life than Google.

Myths and Misconceptions About Facebook for Business

There are a number of common Facebook marketing myths and objections, some of which I used to think were true. Facebook is part of social media, and there are also some myths about social media that carry over to Facebook:

- Social media users don't buy products.
- Social media users don't buy soon enough, and the sales cycle is too long.
- Twitter is the only social media channel worth using.
- The real power of social media comes from influencers.
- Facebook is just for college students.
- People don't click on ads (not even on Google).

Let's take a look at each of these misconceptions in detail.

---

11. http://siteanalytics.compete.com/facebook.com+google.com/

12. http://searchengineland.com/facebook-passes-google-in-time-spent-who-should-care-50263

Social Media Users Don't Buy Products

Most of the people who make this claim are search marketers with a direct marketing approach. Some are people who've done Facebook marketing poorly; didn't get results; and then made the leap to direct marketing, assuming that no one can make money on Facebook.

Many marketers visualize the process of turning a potential buyer into a customer as a funnel. It's called a *sales funnel* or *conversion funnel* (see Figure 2.2). At the top of the funnel are people just becoming aware of your brand and what you offer. At the bottom, they decide to buy and may even recommend your brand to others.

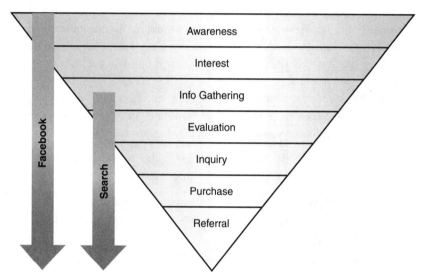

Figure 2.2   *A typical sales funnel.*

Here's a description of the steps involved:

1. **Awareness**—The consumer becomes aware of what you offer and/or of her need for what you offer. The biggest channels for this are TV, radio, print advertising, and Facebook

2. **Interest**—The consumer becomes interested.

3. **Information gathering**—The consumer looks at your website for more info.

4. **Evaluation**—The consumer compares your offer to other companies that supply the same thing. This is often where Google search marketing starts.

5. **Inquiry**—The consumer asks you for more information.

6. **Commitment**—The consumer becomes a customer by purchasing.

7. **Referral**—The consumer is so satisfied that she recommends you to others.

At each step, the consumer becomes more ready to buy. She may not really be serious about buying until she begins comparing companies and making inquiries. Plus, the number of people who make it to each next step is smaller. For example, if there are 100 people right now in step 4 evaluating you versus your competitors, each company is going to get only a portion of those customers, so each company has fewer customers commit in step 6.

Search marketers use AdWords and SEO primarily to get the attention of buyers who are most ready to buy—often in the evaluation stage. A higher percentage of the people in the evaluation stage will buy than those in the awareness stage. There's a cost to getting search visitors—either you pay for the ad or you invest in SEO to increase your website's rankings. If you invest only in the visitors who are ready to buy, you pay less, more of them buy, and so it's easier to achieve profits. But it also limits your exposure and how many sales you can make because you're not hitting the mass of people at the top of the funnel. In other words, you're only doing demand fulfillment; you're doing nothing to generate new demand.

Some of these search experts have come to believe that it's unwise to target prospects who are not looking to buy right now. But if this were true:

- No company would be spending money on TV, radio, or print ads (because it's often impossible to track the profitability of these advertising channels).

- The entire field of PR wouldn't exist (because they change perception but who knows what sales they generate).

- No e-commerce company would care about acquiring a bigger email subscriber list (because those people aren't necessarily ready to buy).

What about when you read something in the news that makes you want a new product? What about the things your friends buy that you want, too? What about impulse purchases? Impulse purchases don't require information gathering and don't involve evaluating the competition. The demand-fulfillment marketing perspective leaves out the majority of consumers.

Certainly, any case studies of companies who profit from social media would dispel this myth.

One of the best-known case studies for social media profits comes from Dell. Its @DellOutlet account constantly sends messages about deals on its refurbished computers to its 1.5 million followers. By the end of 2009, Dell had raked in more than $6.5 million from this Twitter account alone.

Similarly, there are case studies of companies who are profitable on Facebook:

- I published several such case studies on the blog "Search Engine Journal" early in 2011.[13] The return on investments (ROIs) range from 300% to 6500%.

- Our FanReach training course[14] includes interviews with five businesses that have achieved positive ROI from Facebook marketing.

- A number of my clients required me to sign a non-disclosure agreement because they're concerned about their competitors reading about their successes and copying them. So I can't give their successes in detail. That said, one company received hundreds of sales from its first post of a discount offer. Another company gets more than $5 per Facebook visitor from e-commerce sales, and its cost per fan was less than $0.10. A local well-known fast food franchise garnered $65,000 in new food sales after changing only one thing: It promoted something to its fan base.

As you can see from Figure 2.3, Chompon found that for its customers, daily deal companies, the average gross revenue from a Facebook Like (fan) was $8 (compared to $5 for a Twitter follower).[15] They don't make money from every fan, but when they average it out, it comes out to $8 per fan. Most Likes (fans) cost less than $2 each via Facebook advertising. That's at least a 400% ROI. These ROI numbers are comparable to what I've seen achieved with Google advertising, which is the gold standard in profitable online marketing.

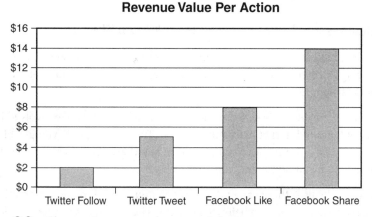

Figure 2.3   *Chompon's revenue value per social action.*

13. http://www.searchenginejournal.com/facebook-marketing-roi-3-case-studies/28254/

14. http://fanreach.net/

15. http://techcrunch.com/2011/02/18/facebook-shares-are-worth-almost-three-times-more-than-tweets-for-e-commerce/ and http://www.chompon.com/chompon_social_action_value.pdf

Social Media Users Don't Buy Soon Enough and the Sales Cycle Is Too Long

Every potential customer goes through a process that begins with his awareness of a need and ends with a purchase. Some companies never did marketing before Google, so they advertise only to the end of the sales cycle, and don't know how to effectively market to top-of-the-funnel consumers.

Some marketing executives are now accustomed to spreadsheets comparing the performance of each digital marketing channel and quickly cutting anything that doesn't immediately demonstrate profits. These folks believe that marketing that doesn't achieve profits within a month or two just doesn't work and never will work. But for companies with competitive advantages beyond price (for example, a unique product or outstanding customer service), acquiring potential customers before it's time for the buying decision is both smart and necessary.

That's not to say you can't get immediate profits. I've worked with companies that have treated Facebook advertising as a direct marketing channel, sent traffic directly to their e-commerce websites, and achieved profits. Sometimes Facebook can be a profitable direct marketing channel, but not always.

People who've been marketing for more than 10 years see things differently. While they acknowledge the accuracy of numbers we get from digital marketing, they know that marketing before the Internet was successful, too. Part of that success was because they got their message out to people at all stages of the buying cycle, not just at the end.

Most Businesses Do Better on Facebook Than They Think

One of the biggest and least discussed problems in Internet marketing is accurately attributing credit for sales to web traffic sources. That's a mouthful. Let me put that in everyday language.

People come to your website from a lot of other websites. If you're involved in a variety of types of Internet marketing, such as Twitter, Facebook, Google, blogging, and more, then any one buyer could be from anywhere. And users from each of these sources behave differently on your website.

There's a geeky little thing call *multi-touchpoint analytics*. It maps out exactly which websites a customer went to before he bought. The customer's journey can look something like this:

1. Became aware of brand on Facebook.

2. Visited the website's blog.

3. Clicked on a Google ad.

4. Came back to the site.

5. Entered email to become a lead.

6. Came back through Facebook.

7. Came back through Google.

8. Bought something.

Most website analytics only pinpoint the last traffic source right before the sale. This is called *last-click analytics*. If you searched Google right before you bought, the analytics tells the company that Google is responsible for the sale. But was it, really?

If you first became aware of something via Facebook and later wanted to see it again, you probably Googled it. That means that when you were ready to buy, you reached the site via Google. Facebook doesn't get any credit with last-click analytics. But should it?

The answer depends on whether your goal is more ROI or more volume. Here's the difference:

- The early awareness ("first-click") touchpoints, such as Facebook, TV, print ads, or PR, help generate more awareness. Many of your customers first heard of you through these top-of-the-funnel media. If they had never been aware of you before, they might never have known to Google you.

- The final sale ("last-click") touchpoints such as Google help increase profits but can diminish your total number of sales because fewer consumers find out about you in the first place.

Facebook also has technical issues that result in its getting less credit than it deserves. Whenever anyone leaves Facebook, he goes through a series of redirects that appear to be part of the reason that Facebook isn't always counted as a traffic source in web analytics. In Chapter 13, "Face-alytics: Analyzing Your Facebook Results," I explain how you can ensure that more of your Facebook visitors get counted as such.

The upshot: In most companies' analytics, Google is stealing some of the credit from Facebook. I discuss ways to combat this and get a better picture of your Internet marketing in Chapter 13.

Twitter Is the Only Social Media Channel Worth Using

I spent a lot of my professional and personal time on Twitter in 2009. Back when some of the biggest users had fewer than 100,000 followers, I had 30,000 myself. I was micro-famous and I was proud of it. I was a micro-important micro-celebrity. Twitter is a powerful social networking tool and helped launch my speaking and training career. But it has serious limits, as I discuss next.

Twitter Is Much Smaller Than Facebook

Twitter has, at most, 5% of the number of users Facebook has (some estimates put it at just 20 million active users, and there are fewer than 2 million who follow more than 500 people).[16] If you want to reach most consumers, you can't do it on Twitter. The influence of Twitter users is felt mainly by other Twitter users. Most mainstream people think Twitter is weird—do you blame them? It's short and looks geeky with all those @ and # symbols.

As you can see in Figure 2.4, Facebook is the most popular and mainstream of the major social websites. It makes sense that smaller sites have more specific audiences. LinkedIn is mainly professional and skews toward higher income brackets.

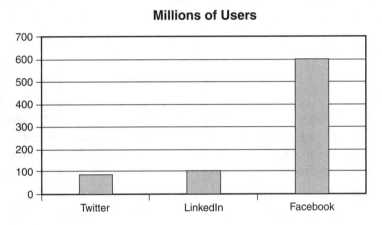

Millions of Users

Figure 2.4   *Comparison of the number of users on popular social media sites.*

Twitter Content Is Less Exciting Than Facebook

Twitter is text-based. If you want to show photos or videos, you have to link to them. Facebook shows photos and videos.

Twitter Conversations Are Hard to Maintain

You can't comment on a tweet. You can reply to it, but conversations are not organized. You're not notified when someone replies to you. It's almost impossible to have a discussion between more than two or three people. You need a hashtag to do that, which is also limited and requires a bit more Twitter experience to see and respond to. Facebook posts and comments are well organized, visible, and easy to

16. http://www.businessinsider.com/chart-of-the-day-how-many-users-does-twitter-really-have-2011-3

participate in. Facebook Groups have the speed of Twitter but are more organized and sticky (they keep people coming back because of the automatic notifications).

Twitter Has Less Power Than It Used To

In mid-2010, after seeing less response from Twitter myself, I polled a number of Twitter users who each had tens of thousands of fans. They shared with me that the number of clicks they received to their blogs and websites dropped dramatically starting in late 2009. This is when many celebrities began to adopt Twitter and the composition of the audience started to change. Prior to that, Twitter was a smaller, very open, and enthusiastic community. Networking was strong and great relationships were formed. As Twitter grew, the exclusiveness of those communities decreased. People's attention was diverted by more people and more tweets, and many of these people now also use Facebook.

Twitter Users Are Weird

Twitter is most popular with tech geeks, celebrities, journalists, and bloggers. They are not a representative cross-section of the population. In other words, Twitter users are statistically abnormal. If you want to reach a lot of the population, or want to appeal to mainstream interests, Facebook is a much better place to do that. When you listen to social media experts talk about Twitter, keep in mind that many of them, like I did, take pride in being the first to use new websites and services. My experience of being pushed into Facebook by a client helped me see that, although Twitter was important to me as a blogger and speaker, it was not as powerful an option for most of my clients.

That said, you can see that Twitter has great power and potential in the context of media and PR. If you want to network with bloggers, journalists, and writers, Twitter is a great place to do that. When I conduct training on business-to-business (B2B) social media, I always include a section on using Twitter for networking with the media. I discuss Facebook PR in Chapter 12, "FaceMessage: Achieving Other Corporate Goals on Facebook."

The Questionable Power of Social Media Influencers

Twitter aficionados love to talk about the power of *influencers*. What's an influencer? Someone with a large number of Twitter followers and blog subscribers. The theory is that businesses should pay these influencers to endorse their products. Some bloggers have demanded that companies give them cars and pay for their trips to conferences in exchange for endorsing a product. The website Klout has made a name for itself (and attracted $10 million in financing) attempting to measure online influence, amid much controversy because it seems too easy to artificially raise your Klout score. But there's simply no proof that influencers produce results for the companies that pay them. It's a beautiful theory, but I haven't seen any case studies proving it works.

In fact, some anecdotal information from the agency JB Chicago indicates conversion rates from Twitter influencers may be half those from Facebook pages.[17]

It's nice that Klout at least divides people into topics of influence. I checked out my Klout profile, and supposedly I am influential not only about SEO and social media, which makes sense, but also airports! This likely comes from the tweets I make while I'm in airports. It gets boring on layovers. And I've complained about flight delays or cancellations. But should an airline give me free first class upgrades for this? Am I likely to be able to help Southwest or Virgin Airlines with its next campaign? As far as the airline knows, yes, it should give me the first class upgrade. (Just kidding.) Even with 30,000+ Twitter followers, realistically I'm not going to reach a huge number of airline customers. There are much better ways in social media for companies to reach their target audiences, and in the targeting section of Chapter 9, "The Face of Advertising: How to Capitalize on the Most Powerful Marketing Tool," you'll see why.

For the topics I do have real influence in, like social media, does it make sense for companies to leverage my influence to market their products and services? Sure, I've helped companies by blogging about them, since my blog posts can reach hundreds of thousands of people in that niche. There might be some real ROI there for them.

But what if no one is tweeting or blogging about your industry? In my social media training projects, I sometimes work with companies in obscure niches like digital signage or pipe fitting manufacturing. They follow the typical social media advice to listen first, but there's no existing conversation for them to join. They have to create the groups and the conversations they want. Facebook marketing empowers you to create communities—you target potential buyers, gather fans and group members affordably, and keep them engaged long-term.

What does the research say? Stanford researchers suggest an idea contrary to Klout's model: that the best way to spread your ideas is through easily influenced people, who in turn influence other easily influenced people.[18] And you probably won't be surprised to learn that a Harvard Business School study found that the most influential people are the hardest to influence.[19] Ever try to influence the loudest guy in the room? Yeah, good luck. The middle status users are the most viral group. Perhaps focusing on the influencees is a better idea. Facebook does a much better job of this than Twitter because you can reach a more representative section of the general population, gather them, and lead the conversation until a good percentage of them buy from you. That's what the rest of this book teaches you how to do.

---

17. http://www.allfacebook.com/how-dish-network-got-a-1200-roi-on-facebook-2011-09

18. https://www.gsb.stanford.edu/facseminars/events/marketing/documents/mktg_03_08_dodds_paper1.pdf

19. http://www.hbs.edu/research/pdf/09-123.pdf

Regardless of the approach, you need to reach people with your message, and the Facebook ad platform excels at allowing you to target exactly whom you want to reach.

Facebook Is Just for Kids

Most people know that when Facebook began, it was mainly for college students. Now, however, less than 25% of Facebook users are between 18 and 24. In fact, now more than 50% of Facebook users are between the ages of 25 and 54, and 25% of Facebook users are over the age of 45.

Facebook by the Numbers (June 1, 2011):

- Facebook has almost 750 million users.

- Facebook has nearly 100 billion photos; 6 billion are uploaded per month.

- An average user has 130 friends.

- People spend 700 billion minutes per month on Facebook.

- The average Facebook user visits 40 times per month; 23 minutes per site visit.

- It has been translated into 70 languages.

- More than 250 million people access Facebook via mobile phone.

- 20 million Facebook apps are downloaded each day.

- Facebook has mirrored real-world diversity since 2009.[20]

Gender (United States)

- Male 45% versus female 55%

Age (United States)

- Under 13: 0.5%

- 14–17: 9.7%

- 18–24: 24.5%

- 25–34: 23.7%

- 35–44: 16.7%

- 45–54: 12.6%

- 55–64: 7.7%

- 65+: 4.6%

20. http://www.facebook.com/notes/facebook-data-team/how-diverse-is-facebook/205925658858

And according to a survey by the U.S. White House, their fans over the age of 50 were much more likely to connect with them on Facebook than Twitter. In addition, 50% of their Facebook respondents were over 50, but only 32% of their Twitter respondents were over 50.[21]

Top Five Countries, Number of Users, and Market Penetration

- United States: 149,352,140 (48%)[22]
- United Kingdom: 29,499,240 (47%)
- Turkey: 28,897,540 (37%)
- Indonesia: 37,865,680 (15%)
- India: 26,624,620 (2%)

Between 37% and 57% of each U.S. state's population is on Facebook.

Sample Interest Target Audience Sizes (U.S. Only)

When you create a Facebook ad, as you define various target audiences, Facebook gives you the number of users it estimates you can reach with that ad. Here are some samples for various interests people have listed in their Facebook profiles:

- Running: 2,146,820
- *Star Wars*: 1,980,480
- Jewelry: 500,400
- Barack Obama: 448,100
- Exercise and fitness: 288,360
- Home improvement: 240,840
- Republican party: 195,940
- Live music: 125,220
- Oprah Winfrey: 117,660
- Marketing: 106,200
- Advertising: 76,780
- Watches: 10,860

---

21. http://www.whitehouse.gov/blog/2011/06/10/what-our-facebook-fans-and-twitter-followers-told-us
22. http://www.socialbakers.com/

People Don't Click On Ads

Google made $28 billion in 2010, and most of its income is from advertisers using its AdWords platform. Google charges advertisers only when people click on its ads. Google makes a fortune because *people do click on ads*. Many AdWords advertisers make profits from people who do click on their ads and then buy something from their websites. Facebook made $740 million in 2009, made $1.86 billion in 2010, and will make well over $4 billion in 2011 also because people do click on ads.

The misconception that ads are irrelevant makes a little sense because only about 12% of clicks on any Google search results page are on the paid ads; the rest of the people click on what are called *natural* search results. People click on Facebook ads even less often because they're highly engaged with other parts of the Facebook experience. But if, as an advertiser, you pay only when people click, that's completely acceptable.

Who Harbors These Misconceptions and Why?

Unless you're talking to businesses or consultants who have specific experience marketing and advertising with Facebook, the opinions you get are as valuable as the salesman at the Ford dealership sharing his opinions on Hondas. Consider the source.

SEO and AdWords (search marketing) experts see the Internet through the eyes of search marketing. It's the only way they know, and it's how they make their money. If they choose not to learn social media marketing, they may view it as a threat to their livelihood.

TV, radio, and print advertising experts similarly can have a conflict of interest when speaking about Facebook marketing because their clients have a limited budget and they don't want them spending their money on things they can't get paid to manage. There's a phenomenon that happens with consultants—whatever they get paid for is usually "the best thing the client could spend their money on."

Public relations experts primarily are focused on changing consumer perceptions, enhancing branding, and clarifying brand positioning. These are top-of-the-sale-funnel activities. For them, the influencer concept is one way to attempt that. They also typically do not have room in their budgets for advertising and don't have experience running online advertising, so they might not see the value. Many of the tactics in this book don't fit their goals because they aren't looking directly for sales and profits. But I've worked with social media PR experts, and I discuss some of the ways they've adapted Facebook to traditional PR strategies in Chapter 12, because they're a valuable addition to your other marketing and selling activities.

Some **bloggers** make money from sponsorships and advertisements on their blogs. They might also make money from strategy consulting. Their main interest is in getting attention and readership. Using Twitter to announce new blog posts and network with other bloggers is an important part of their success. Facebook has not fit into their plans over the last four years, so they have little to no experience with it as a business marketing platform. They are beginning to use Facebook to get the word out about their blog posts, but this is new to many bloggers and they still tend to rely on Twitter more.

Some Businesses Profit on Facebook, and Some Don't

One reason for the perception that Facebook marketing isn't profitable for every business is that many businesses are doing it poorly. There are numerous pitfalls in Facebook marketing, the best practices are still being developed, and most businesses haven't taken any sort of training to learn the best practices that have been discovered.

Common Mistakes

The average business that leaps onto Facebook without preparation falls prey to these mistakes:

- They create a Facebook page with a page name that might hinder them later but that can't be changed.

- They assign an untrained intern or marketing coordinator to handle everything. As Mitch Joel says, hiring someone for Facebook marketing simply because they have used Facebook is like hiring an electrician whose sole qualification is that they've turned on lights before.

- They try to get fans for free.

- They go for quantity rather than quality when it comes to fans.

- They talk too much about themselves in their posts.

- They don't get much response from their page posts (less than 0.5% feedback rate).

A surprising number of companies are growing the fan counts for their Facebook pages but don't have the plan or the people in place to interact with those fans. Many don't realize that, because their fans haven't been interacting with their posts,

Facebook has stopped showing the posts to as much as 90% of those fans. And this only gets worse over time—the average Facebook page with more than one million fans actually reaches less than 3% of those fans with its posts. All of this can be fixed or prevented with training.

Facebook marketing is a multistep process, and businesses are not doing all the steps well yet. Some businesses are skipping entire steps and then wondering why they aren't getting the results they want.

Success Stories

Although some companies struggle with Facebook, other businesses are having success. In my experience, that's because they are:

- Taking Facebook marketing training courses (or reading a book like this one!)
- Attracting fans who might really be prospects for their offerings
- Posting in a way that fans find interesting
- Getting lots of likes and comments on their posts
- Remaining visible to their fans
- Incentivizing fans to go their website and buy
- Getting sales from fans

It's important to understand that throughout history, companies have lost money on every type of marketing that exists, just as various companies have *made* money on every type of marketing. Sometimes, a new channel like AdWords or SEO has rocketed a previously unknown company into the top five for its industry—and Facebook marketing is now doing that for some companies.

Whether your marketing succeeds or fails depends on many factors (I cover the pitfalls and how to avoid them in Chapter 5, "How Not to Fall on Your Face: Six Mistakes That Block Facebook Profitability"). And if your business is so new that you haven't made any money online yet from any marketing channel, the first questions are:

- Do people really want what you offer?
- Can you reach those people affordably?
- Is your website set up to maximize the number of people who buy?

Here's What Facebook Marketing Successes and Failures Do Differently

In this book, I teach you how to maximize your Facebook marketing profits with best practices that include

- Creating a high-quality fan base
- Securing and optimizing an advertising budget
- Focusing on your customers, not on your company
- Using effective calls to action in advertising and posts
- Tracking your metrics and optimizing for better results

Facebook's Strengths: Advantages for Your Business

Throughout this chapter I've tried to make the case as to why I believe Facebook is such a powerful marketing tool. Whether you're a business owner with doubts, or a marketer who needs to make the case to your colleagues or supervisors, you need to have a clear idea of why Facebook is so promising for most businesses.

Here's a summary of Facebook's strengths:

- Facebook is the biggest social network in terms of users and time spent.
- Facebook lets you share multimedia with your audience.
- Facebook is more compelling and stickier than Twitter.
- Facebook advertising is extremely targeted.
- Facebook fans are dramatically cheaper to acquire than emails.
- Facebook pages give you perpetually free visibility to your target audience.
- Facebook advertising is significantly cheaper than Google AdWords.
- Facebook helps you reach your potential customers before your competitors do.
- Facebook empowers you to lead conversations and create loyalty.
- Facebook does your dishes and always leaves the toilet seat down.

Okay, maybe not the last one.

3

FaceFirst: How Facebook Fits Into Your Business and Other Marketing Efforts

Facebook is part of social media, and there are a lot of conflicting voices in social media. Some social media gurus suggest that social media will turn your business inside out and change everything. This kind of talk gets them attention but creates anxiety for business owners, CEOs, and CMOs. And these attention-grabbing pronouncements might not even be true. So let's examine whether there's substance to these social media theories and then evaluate which social media approaches are worth doing, which ones it could hurt us to neglect, and which ones are risky to even attempt.

Later in the chapter, we look at how Facebook can best fit in with your other marketing and advertising campaigns. My contention is that social media shouldn't cause a messy revolution in your existing business but should help empower you to do even better what you're already good at. We also discuss how to plug it in to get those results.

How Is Social Media Supposedly Changing Business?

People have been tweeting, blogging, conferencing, and writing books about social media for the last four years. That's long enough to develop myths and sacred cows. Bloggers and authors say social media is changing business in four main ways:

- Conversation
- Transparency
- Availability
- Marketing

Conversation

Social media bloggers say the following:

- We're switching from selling to relationship building.
- We're switching from monologues to dialogues.
- We're switching from large campaigns to smaller actions and brief conversations.
- We need more interaction between departments and business units.

Are they right?

Because of Twitter, Facebook, and third-party review sites, consumers really do have a louder and more public voice than ever before. There are more of these voices, and companies are interacting with them more. Your relationships with your customers are critical. I explain how to use Facebook effectively for customer interaction in Chapter 11, "Talking Till You're Blue in the Face: How to Get More Likes and Comments" and Chapter 12, "FaceMessage: Achieving Other Corporate Goals on Facebook."

But we don't need to eliminate revenue generation just because we're building deeper relationships with customers. Consumer interaction in social media will not always lead immediately to a sale, but we don't need to give up on profit strategies. Ways to use Facebook to increase revenue are discussed throughout this book.

Thousands of miniature conversations can be very time-consuming. Personal conversations with all your customers can be impractical for you. Fortunately, it can be more effective on Facebook to start conversations than micromanage them. Asking 10,000 people a question to get them talking to each other is easier than your trying to talk one-on-one to 10,000 people. All this has to work at scale, so leveraging customers' desire to interact with each other is a smart way to go.

For those of you in larger companies, because social media crosses so many traditional departmental lines, departments must communicate more frequently and effectively. Without improved communication, your Facebook results will be significantly reduced.

Transparency, Honesty, and Trust

Social media bloggers say the following:

- We're switching from controlling the brand image to being honest.
- We need to make brands less formal and more human.
- Employees can now just be themselves.
- More people can talk about your brand online, and you have to monitor that because bad news travels faster and farther.
- The balance of power and control has shifted to the consumer.
- You can't hide anything from consumers.
- Consumers need to trust you.

Are they right?

I saw companies trying to hide facts from the public before social media became mainstream. Certain hotels had serious quality and customer service issues, made public by unhappy hotel guests in TripAdvisor reviews. Their first instinct wasn't to improve their product. These companies saw reviewers as a problem to be silenced. Often the resort's head of marketing was the first to hear about these reputation issues but had no control over hotel management and customer service—the best place to solve this sort of problem. It's perceived as marketing's job to get guests to book rooms, but management's quality control issues blocked their success.

It's best to have a quality product that makes customers happy; then social media can turn this into a lot more sales because positive testimonials and reviews help sell you to fans who are still just potential buyers.

But some of the social media bloggers' points mentioned previously are ridiculous. Yes, certain companies can be more personal and give public faces to employees, but other companies cannot. If you have a formal kind of customer who wants a professional relationship—if, for example, you're a bank or an investment firm—then cool surfer dude talk is inappropriate. Do financial services customers want to see an update about their investment advisor getting drunk and watching football? Does a defendant want to see her defense attorney goofing off? Does a grieving widow want to work with a funeral director who tweets about how he's out singing karaoke? There can be an advantage to being quirky, but it also limits your appeal and revenue.

Take it from me, I know: I have a background in comedy, and I found that I have to be very selective about how I "get personal" and let my hair down.

When I began to promote myself and my services with social media, I used a lot of humor and quirkiness in the marketing that people saw first, before they knew anything else about me. I thought it would disarm them and make a stronger connection. But I found that some potential customers took it differently—they didn't believe I take my work seriously and they assumed I wouldn't take their marketing seriously either. In fact, some people seem to believe that funny people can't be effective at anything but humor.

So I switched it up and now start with a serious professional image. People are reassured by my expertise and earnestness, and they hire me. Later, if some of my humor comes out, it enhances the connection. Authenticity becomes a value added. This makes sense because relationships grow and deepen individually. Every real relationship is unique.

But you can't really do that same variable response in public social media because a personal response to one customer might look weird to another one who has yet to connect with you. On the public stage of social media, there might never be a good time to reveal your inner goof because new/potential customers will always be watching you interact with the established folks.

It's a tricky tightrope to walk if you want to be informal. There will probably always be a level of formality in social media. We're never going to be BFFs with our customers. Sure, maybe a surfboard company should be informal with each of their thousands of customers, but it doesn't work for all businesses. And besides, if you treat everyone with the same informality, isn't that just a different way to be impersonal? Somewhere, in a big city (probably in California), I know someone is disagreeing with this. They're wrong.

Availability and Responsiveness

Social media bloggers say the following:

- We're switching from hard-to-reach to available everywhere.

- Customers and businesses are easier to reach.

- We need to eliminate the excuse that just because an employee isn't in customer service, he can't help the consumer.

- We need to increase the percentage of employees who talk to the public.

- We must "go real-time."

- Companies are expanding the staff they've devoted to social media; there are now dozens of employees in Fortune 500 social media departments.

Social media is definitely a communication tool that's here to stay, and it does require a different approach and often new employees. But it's foolish to think that any and every employee should speak to the public on your behalf. Some employees just don't communicate well in any context, and some who are very effective in person don't communicate as well in a written format.

Customer service personnel receive specific training on how to deal professionally with a variety of situations, and public relations people are steeped in the company's brand and have spent hours planning how to represent the company. Any employee who's going to do social media publicly should have both of those types of training. Some social media employees can reveal their personalities to a degree, but that personality shouldn't be at odds with your brand.

It's important to respond to customers in social media quickly, but if "going real-time" means making communications mistakes, you're creating a bigger problem than you're solving. Social media employees need to know when to delay a response and talk it over with the appropriate co-worker or supervisor. We've seen social media representatives with several big companies reply in the heat of the moment and the brands suffered negative media coverage as a result.

Marketing

Social media bloggers say the following:

- Consumers spend a lot of time in social media and you have to be there to get their attention—it's a new place to market.

- In social media, it's easier to get customers to sell your ideas.

- Start-ups with no funds for marketing can instead leverage labor and time to get business from social media.

- Social media means we don't have to advertise anymore.

There are a lot of people using social media, and Facebook is the most popular social website. It is without question one of the most important places to market online. The word-of-mouth advantage listed is just one reason.

Some marketers have a strong anti-advertising bias. Should you do Facebook marketing without advertising? In my experience, that's a difficult road to take. Businesses often underestimate the cost of that labor and don't realize that fans who come from free tactics might not be qualified as good potential customers. Facebook advertising is very affordable and highly targeted. Social media means we don't have to do advertising anymore? It would make as little sense to say that now that we have such a powerful advertising platform in Facebook, we don't have to do PR anymore!

Evaluating Social Media Experts

There are many voices in the social media space. This is a new type of marketing, with no standardized credentials. There's no way to be sure a so-called expert knows what he's talking about. Whom should you trust?

I've developed two key questions for you to consider about each expert:

- What specific measurable results has this expert helped companies achieve?

- What types of businesses has he worked with?

I have deliberately not included questions like whether he has written a book, whether he speaks at conferences, how many Twitter followers he has, or what his Klout score is. Some of the most effective social media consultants I know have written no book, don't speak, and don't look that impressive on Twitter.

And your business is unique. There are a lot of different kinds of businesses with different goals. Coca-Cola has different goals and resources from the local dentist, so they won't succeed with the same tactics. Any guru can tell them to listen and engage, but if you want more specific ways to get quantifiable results for your unique business, work with one of the following:

- **Industry expert**—If you want deep experience, get someone who has gotten social media results for businesses of your type and size.

- **Social marketing expert**—If you want broad experience, get someone who has gotten social media results for businesses of all types and sizes.

What Businesses That Profit from Facebook Do

Most companies that generate revenue from Facebook do not radically change their business. They simply add Facebook to what they're already doing well. Facebook becomes a new marketing and advertising channel for them. They do better customer service by responding to customers on Facebook.

Can Facebook Change Your Business?

Without question, Facebook can improve your business in the following ways:

- I've seen struggling start-ups for whom Google AdWords advertising didn't work instead make new profits from Facebook advertising.

- I've seen businesses that already did brisk business through AdWords increase their overall revenue with Facebook.

- I've seen businesses deal with customer service issues on their Facebook pages in a way that impressed other fans.

- I've seen ecstatic customers write comments that led potential customers to make their first purchase.

- I've seen fans bring in more fans for free and Group members bring in new Group members.

For years, businesses moved their marketing and advertising spends from print, radio, and TV to Google. Now companies are moving their budgets from Google to Facebook. Many even split their funds between the two.

How Can Facebook Fit In to Businesses in Different Ways?

Facebook can be used a number of ways, depending on your goals:

- **If you sell products online**—You can use Facebook advertising, with or without fans, to get more customers.

- **If you're business-to-business**—You can use Facebook advertising to generate leads from new prospects. You can have a lead fill out a form on your website or on a custom Facebook tab on your page.

- **If you want to improve customer service**—You can find and deal with issues more quickly and in a more personable way. You can show other potential customers how you deal with complaints and what level of satisfaction they can expect.

- **If you want more customer awareness and media attention**—You can expand your reach and distribution with both Facebook ads and Facebook page fans. You can distribute your messages in a multimedia format.

How Do You Synch Up Your Other Marketing Efforts with Your Facebook Campaigns?

Unless you do all your marketing yourself (and my condolences if you do), you have multiple role players. You might have multiple departments, consultants, and specialists, or you might be an agency that specializes in one channel and works with other agencies. Each party can either cooperate to achieve corporate goals or act like a petty fiefdom fighting the others and diminishing overall results. Sometimes these are called *silos* to emphasize how independent their power and operation can be.

Social media leads to more role overlap and creates more potential turf wars than ever before, so consider how Facebook will work with your other departments, role players, and specialists. Create a task force with representatives from each group to outline how they can quickly and constructively communicate.

Facebook + Print, Web, and Email

If you're already producing graphics for print media, web pages, email marketing, or display ads, you might be able to use these in Facebook custom tabs, advertising, and posts. Familiarize your creative team with the parameters of Facebook. For example, ad images are only 110 pixels wide and 80 pixels high. If the personnel doing advertising are different from the creative folks—and they likely are—make sure they have the leeway to adapt existing creative elements for these small image sizes. Often, simply reusing an image from another place results in a picture that's too small to really see what it is, and ad performance suffers as a result.

Another difference between graphics for Facebook and most other places is that Facebook graphics need to change more frequently. Ads burn out, so you constantly need more images. Posts are seen for a day or two at most, and then it's time to post again. Posts with images receive 50%–65% more interaction as those without images.[1]

What will you post next? If creative folks are going to be involved, they need to think ahead and provide 60–90 days' worth of images ahead of time.

Who handles choosing and buying your stock photography? Here again, the Facebook advertising and posting people might need their own access, and you'll need to budget for these stock images. Fortunately, for the advertising purposes, you need only the smallest photos, and they're the least expensive. There are also free image sources, covered in Chapter 9, "The Face of Advertising: How to Capitalize on the Most Powerful Marketing Tool."

Facebook + Google Marketing

If you're also doing AdWords, Bing, or Yahoo! pay-per-click advertising, will you use the same message from your text ads in your Facebook ads and Facebook posts? Perhaps not, but at least have the discussion about whether your high-level strategies are the same, whether the tactical implementations are similar or different, and why.

---

1. http://www.facebook.com/notes/facebook-journalists/study-how-people-are-engaging-journalists-on-facebook-best-practices/245775148767840

Vary Your Message for Each Stage of the Search Funnel

In most cases, I recommend you build your multichannel marketing strategy on the premise that consumers will hear about you on Facebook before they search for you in a search engine.

Facebook can play a mass-marketing role to spread awareness of your brand and how you solve consumers' particular problems; then search marketing can pick up consumers who are almost ready to buy. Facebook has to grab attention and interest from people who might never have heard of you, while an AdWords ad might just verify to them that your offering addresses the keyword they just searched for.

The text on your website might include keywords for search engine optimization purposes, but it could also include persuasive messages that better fit consumers in the information-gathering or evaluation stages of the buying cycle.

Testing Similar and Different Creative

I've had opportunities to test the same ad headlines simultaneously on AdWords and Facebook and found that, as usual in digital marketing, people responded differently. While promoting channels in three new cities for a national radio network, I tested ads specific to the most popular musicians the network played. For the headline, I tested just the artist's name versus "Do you like <artist>?" It turned out that usually the question worked better on Facebook but worse on AdWords, although it varied somewhat by city. Sometimes I sound like a broken record saying "test it!" to every idea a client or student of mine has, but I've often found this kind of varied result across channels, markets, geographies, and audiences. You really do need to test every variation to find out what works best.

Facebook + PR

Public relations in the social media age means managing perceptions and working with influencers. I go into much more detail about Facebook PR (along with crisis response planning and building relationships with journalists) in Chapter 12, but in terms of coordinating the work in various silos, the people doing your Facebook work need to be coordinated strategically with those doing branding, reputation management, and positioning. All your choices in the preceding three disciplines affect your how you'll craft your Facebook posts and conduct your customer service.

Facebook + Email Marketing

How often will you email your subscribers as opposed to post on your fan page? Will there be any coordination between those messages, or will they always be on different topics for different goals? While choosing your strategy here, look for opportunities to test campaigns on both channels and see what works best. See if you can learn something about which of your activities works best in email and which on a fan page.

Here are some rules of thumb for developing this coordinated strategy:

- Use email for direct sales and news.

- Very few companies email more than weekly without losing lots of subscribers, so be sparing in your use of email.

- Use Facebook posts for multimedia—especially video because email has never supported video well.

- Use Facebook posts socially to engage and look for social responses.

- Use Facebook posts to survey customers for your own research.

Are your email subscribers mostly previous customers and your Facebook fans mostly potential customers? Often this is the case. It's easier to get a previous customer to buy, and sales messages are less offensive to them. Therefore, if that describes your email subscribers, you'll be able to sell more directly to them than to your Facebook fans.

Fans can require a more introductory or educational approach, but sometimes the fans of a businesses are mostly previous customers. Just gauge this before deciding how you'll post. Most of the fan gathering techniques in Chapter 10, "FaceHook: Capturing Qualified Prospects as Fans and Group Members," pull in people who will need some familiarization with your brand and offerings first, so your Facebook posts won't be as aggressive as your emails.

Facebook + TV

Right now 18 TV shows each has more than 10 million Facebook fans.[2] TV shows do all kinds of cool things with Facebook, including

- Posting commercials and episode clips

- Posting previews of new episodes before they air

- Advertising when their new season starts

- Finding new fans by advertising to fans of similar shows

- Asking for votes when they're up for an award viewers can vote for

- Adding photos of scenes

---

2. http://fanpagelist.com/category/tv-shows/

- Creating Facebook Events if they'll be represented at events open to the public

- Reminding viewers, on the day of the show, to watch

- Posting live shows and responding in real time while the show is on

- Posting behind-the-scenes clips and special features

What about the sports we normally see only on TV or the Web? The National Hockey League (NHL) discovered more about its demographics after it delved into the Facebook Insights about its 2.2 million fans. It turns out they're younger, more affluent, and more tech savvy than fans of other major sports. The NHL's better understanding of its fans is changing the way it markets to them.

Facebook + Radio

As I mentioned earlier, Facebook can help you penetrate new markets. Tracking is difficult because Arbitron's *cume* (cumulative audience score[3]) is the standard measurement, and when you're using multiple marketing channels like billboards, search ads, Facebook ads, Facebook posts, and local events advertised locally, it's virtually impossible to isolate the effect of one channel. I decided to send Facebook ad clickers to the network's "listen online" page so that I could get them listening to the music right away. That's not the ultimate goal, which is to get them listening in their cars and showing in the cume, but it's a great, trackable first step.

HOW CUME IS CALCULATED

Arbitron estimates how many people listen to a station for a minumum of five minutes in a quarter hour and calls this *Cume Persons*. No matter how long someone listens, they're only counted once. This can also be referred to as unduplicated audience, reach, or circulation. The *Cume Rating* is a percentage of a survey population. For example, if we believe 75,000 men between the ages of 18 and 49 listen to a station, and the metro population for that demographic is 175,600, then 42.7% of them listen to that station and the Cume Rating is 42.7.[4]

Also, I had some success sending Facebook folks to event web pages and hearing that an above-average number of people showed up who had never heard of the

3. http://en.wikipedia.org/wiki/Arbitron

4. http://www.arbitron.com/downloads/purplebook.pdf

radio station before. They hadn't heard about it on the radio. I can't be sure (this is a really difficult strategy to track), but there's a very good chance these people were some of the hundreds who clicked on our Facebook ads.

Other Facebook strategies for radio include building a fan base and growing your email list. Facebook and radio seem to work synergistically because listeners feel a personal connection to the artists and the DJs, and when their curiosity is aroused, they can go to a Facebook page for more pictures and videos. If you have musicians do in-studio performances, you can post videos of that on Facebook. Having a huge listener base also means you can repeatedly tell fans about your Facebook page and grow a targeted fan base for free. This is one of the only cases in which fans not from ads are absolutely the right audience.

4

FaceBucks: Five Ways Businesses Achieve Profits with Facebook

Many businesses start working on Facebook without a clear strategy. What is your biggest goal with Facebook marketing? How does it fit into your other marketing efforts? After you get fans, what will you do with them? If revenue is your goal, have you planned out all the steps to reach that goal?

In this chapter, I discuss five ways you can use Facebook to get revenue for your business. Each of these strategic models is a sequence. They all use Facebook advertising. Some of the models use fans; some don't. One method involves an email list. Note that none of these include contests or freebies—many companies try contests, but few are satisfied with the results.

How Facebook Advertising Helps All Five Revenue Models

As you might know, advertising is the subset of marketing where you pay to place your exact marketing messages and images next to other people's content. All the Facebook marketing models in this chapter start with Facebook advertising.

Some companies try to side-step the hard cost of Facebook advertising, but in my experience, you can only avoid advertising and still succeed on Facebook if:

- You already have a substantial fan base.

- The majority of fans see your posts.

- You know for sure that those fans are legitimate potential buyers.

If you acquired a bunch of fans through contests and freebies, or if you got them with a method that didn't clarify whether they are interested in what you sell, then the portion of your fans who are real potential buyers may be quite low.

Facebook advertising gives you significant advantages over your competition. It captures an audience more affordably than any other marketing channel and helps you qualify fans as good potential buyers. Finally, it aligns you or your offering with things they already love.

For die-hard anti-advertising folks whose opposition to advertising is purely financial or those attached to organic, "no-cost" fan acquisition methods, be sure you've calculated the soft costs:

- The value of whatever you give away in contests

- The cost of employees' time spent finding fans

- Wasted labor responding to or posting for unqualified, will-never-buy fans

Include these when you determine your return on investment (ROI), and you might find they eradicate your profits.

Reaching Potential Buyers

All five of the strategies in this chapter are about generating revenue. To do that, you have to:

- Reach the right people

- With the right message

- At the right time

- With the right offer

Facebook advertising excels at helping you reach the right people. Its abilities are unparalleled in history—the average business owner has never before been able to so specifically target his ideal customers from this many people, this affordably. You can target any of more than 730 million people based on whatever combination of interests, age, gender, education, relationship status, and workplace you choose.

In the past, to reach millions of people, you had to spend more than $10,000 at a time with marketing channels that didn't allow you to select which people you would reach. You could use Google AdWords advertising to reach selective audiences, but it's at least five times as expensive as Facebook advertising, and it really only works for people who are ready to buy right now, which is a pretty limited segment.

Positive Alignment

No matter whom we're trying to reach, the way to get a lot of the right people afford-ably is to align with the things they already like. When we use interest-targeting in Facebook ads, we're finding people based on the likes, interests, and activities they've listed in their Facebook profiles. We use advertising to align the business with them and the things they like. We're sending the message, "Oh you like this thing? We spe-cialize in that! We help you with that! We will enable and empower you to do that better and get more of what you like!"

For example, if you sell minimalist running shoes, you can target people who love running or barefoot running and talk about how much your company loves it. Then you talk about how your running shoes improve performance and decrease injuries.

By aligning ourselves with things our target customers feel positive about and help-ing them get more of that, we already are transferring their passions and positive feelings onto the brand or product we're promoting.

Cheap Clicks, Cheap Fans, and Profits

There are only two things that can hurt your profits: lower revenues and higher costs. The lower you keep your advertising and marketing costs, the higher your potential profits are. There is no cheaper way to reach people than Facebook adver-tising. That means that, done properly, Facebook advertising could be your greatest source of profits.

As an example, I recently started running a few ads for my Google AdWords con-sulting services: In the last 7 days, more than 84,000 people have seen those ads and it has only cost me $33.04. In fact, I ran these ads with a phone number and phrased them purposely *not to get clicks*. I was only charged when people clicked, so this made the exposure a lot cheaper. Do you know of any other way to get seen by 84,000 people for $33.04?

Should You Try Facebook Marketing Without Fans First?

Not every business owner I've worked with wants to get Facebook fans. Are they wrong? Not necessarily. If you can profitably send people directly to your e-commerce website with Facebook ads, why shouldn't you do that? Why would we assume you need to go the fan marketing route? Although there are advantages to marketing through fans—those advantages come with the extra labor costs of marketing to fans every day. So, why not start by trying to get ad viewers to buy right away?

Facebook advertising without fans does indeed work for some businesses, but not all. I know one e-commerce business that immediately received several times in revenue what it spent on ads. But I saw another e-commerce website not even earn back half what it spent on Facebook ads. So go ahead and try it without fans, especially if your website already sells successfully with traffic from other sources like Google. But if it doesn't work, start building a fan base. You've just learned that you're going to need to spend some time marketing repeatedly to these fans before you'll get sales. This need for more time marketing to potential customers is natural when:

- They buy your type of offering infrequently.

- Your offering requires some education of the consumer.

- Consumers are very attached to getting your offering from someone else.

For example, if you sell Fords, you already know that not everyone is in the market to buy right now, right? But if you build a fan base of people who love Ford Mustangs and talk to them long enough about the newest Mustang model, some of them will eventually buy from you. The only question is how long it takes. You can decrease the time it takes for them to buy by increasing their desire for the Mustang. If you're a college trying to get new students, only a certain part of your audience is ready right now. And you might have specific enrollment deadlines that affect when people can "buy" what you offer. Over time, you can tell the story of how previous enrollees made their decision, how specific graduates are succeeding in the workforce, how much more successful college graduates are, and how much more money they make over their lifetimes.

Maybe you're an online pet store but some of your potential buyers already buy everything they need locally. You can show them the benefits of buying from you online. You can show them what inconveniences they're suffering by driving, using gas, and wasting time going to the local store. They might only buy pet supplies once a month, so you have that much time to win them over. In other words, after you have fans, you use Facebook page posts to build awareness of your brand, show the advantages of buying from you over the competition, and educate your potential buyer.

Five Facebook Revenue Strategies

Let's get into the details of each of these five revenue strategies:

- Advertising direct to e-commerce

- Advertising with email marketing

- Fan marketing for e-commerce

- Blogging for advertising revenue

- Fan marketing plus affiliate marketing

Strategy #1: Advertising Direct to e-Commerce

Advertising directly to e-commerce, as depicted in Figure 4.1, is the first strategy I suggested earlier in this chapter. If you have an e-commerce website—and especially if
you already make money from other traffic sources like Google—then test Facebook
ad traffic first. If you can get profits from this approach, fan marketing is optional.

Ad -> Purchase Monetization Path

Figure 4.1   *The ad-to-purchase path.*

I've seen this generate 300% ROI before, but I've also seen ads cost twice as much
as the revenue. You'll have to test it and see whether it works for your business. The
key is to thoroughly test everything in your advertising: headlines, images, ad copy,
interest targets, and demographics. Also try using discounts, urgency, and the other
sales tactics from Chapter 14, "FaceFluence: Turning FaceBrowsers into
FaceBuyers—13 Sales and Influence Tactics."

Disadvantages of Facebook Advertising for Direct Traffic

Even if skipping fan marketing is profitable for your company, you'll miss out on the
benefits other companies get from it. You're definitely going for short-term gain here
and, because your competitors might be growing fan bases, you're risking giving
them a competitive advantage. How would you like to be the only company in your

niche that doesn't have Facebook fans? How will customers perceive that? Will your competitors take advantage of that and call attention to it? You miss out on the social proof technique I discuss in Chapter 14. Also, studies of e-commerce data show that many sales that seem to come from Google are from people who initially heard about a brand on Facebook. Tracking this accurately is very difficult, so you may miss out on the brand awareness that leads to higher volume sales later.

Advantages of Facebook Advertising for Direct Traffic

As you can see, this strategy has the simplest diagram of the bunch, with the fewest steps. There's no relationship building outside of your normal selling and customer service. If it works, there's lower overhead and labor on your marketing. It's an easy way to start, and you can shift to fan marketing later when you're ready.

Strategy #2: Advertising and Email Marketing

Email marketing has a long and proven track record. Many marketers consider it to be the most profitable online marketing method. Let's compare it to fan marketing in Table 4.1 before continuing to discuss this model.

Table 4.1   Email Marketing Versus Fan Marketing

	Email Subscribers	Facebook Fans
How often can you contact them?	Once a week.	Up to several times per day.
How many people read them?	13%–33% of marketing emails are opened[1], and it's tough to get this above 40%.	20%–30% of fans see fan page posts, but this can be significantly increased to 50%–70% in many cases.
How many click to your website?	1%–11%.	1%–4%.
How much does each subscriber or fan cost?	Varies with how aggressively the list is grown, squeeze page conversion rate, and advertising cost. The range is from $0.20 to $20.00.	This varies a lot per niche, but the range is from $0.10 to $2.50.
Can the list grow itself through word of mouth?	Few email readers forward marketing emails to others, and even then, almost no recipients sign up to the email list themselves.	More Facebook users share posts and suggest pages to their friends and peers. Highly engaging pages can receive many additional free fans while growing a paid fan base.
Additional benefits	Very hard for other people to steal your list.	Social proof, spontaneous testimonials, protection from bad publicity.

1. http://mailchimp.com/resources/research/email-marketing-benchmarks-by-industry/

Let's make it more real by comparing the benefits of having 1,000 emails versus 1,000 fans:

- You can get fans for one-tenth the cost of email subscribers ($1,000 for the fans versus $10,000 for the emails).

- Facebook page posts get about 10 times as many impressions as emails get read—it's not that difficult to get 5,000 views from 10,000 fans, but you have to write incredible subject lines to get 3,000 people to open your email. Add in the daily versus weekly frequency, and you're getting 35,000 views versus 3,000, which is more than 10 times the exposure.

- Facebook posts bring in four times as much website traffic as emails do. Using the previous assumptions, you would get 100 visitors per post on Facebook and 150 visitors from the email, but add in the weekly versus daily factor, and it's 700 visits from Facebook versus 150 from email.

- Fan bases are likely to grow extra fans at no additional cost, but email lists don't really grow themselves. In one notable Facebook campaign, a company paid for 99,000 fans but gained another 160,000 through word-of-mouth by engaging these new fans extremely well.

Let me caution you about buying third-party email lists. The success of email marketing historically is based on people opting in to a company's private database. All the numbers quoted here are based on that model. When you buy email lists from other people, the success rate is much lower. You can buy these email lists for a lot less money, but response to them is extremely low.

Five More Reasons Why Fans Are Better Than Emails

Many people wonder if building a fan base should replace the goal of growing an email list. I think both have a place, especially if you already have proven you get profits from email marketing. If you have to choose one, however, here are some of the ways that fans provide more benefit than email subscribers:

- **Loyalty**—Email does not build a faithful community.

- **Responsiveness**—Facebook fans are more responsive.

- **Trust**—People know, like, and trust you more quickly and better through two-way conversations.

- **Viral**—Facebook events and contests are easier to pass on. Email doesn't self-promote.

- **Community**—Email doesn't build a community of raving fans who convert to customer.

At this early stage of Facebook marketing, some people are understandably more comfortable with the idea of email marketing than fan marketing—you might have viable strategic concerns about a public fan base or the extra work involved in fan engagement, or you might have an extremely effective email marketing system already tied into your customer relationship management software. Because these are all legitimate factors, I discuss how email lead generation, illustrated in Figure 4.2, fits into the Facebook marketing model.

Ad -> Email Monetization Path

Figure 4.2 *The advertising and email marketing path.*

1. **Facebook ads**—Use Facebook advertising (see Chapter 10, "FaceHook") to find people who are avid followers of the niche you've chosen and send them to a squeeze page or tab.

2. **Squeeze**—Set up a webpage or tab that is purposely very simple. Give people as few choices as possible. It's called a squeeze page because we're trying to limit their options to squeeze them into our email list. The advantage of a webpage is that it has many fewer options than a tab on a Facebook page. But often clicks to a tab within Facebook are cheaper than clicks to a webpage outside of Facebook, so it's a toss-up as to which is better.

3. **Email sign-up**—After the visitor signs up on the squeeze page, you proceed with sending out marketing emails. Anywhere from 13% to 33% of your list will…

4. **Open your email**—And from 1% to 11% of them will…

5. **Click to visit your website**—And some percentage of these will…

6. **Purchase.**

Cost of Email Acquisition

Cost per email acquisition is always the advertising CPC (cost per click) divided by the sign-up conversion rate. That means if it costs you $0.25 per click and 10% of the visitors sign up for your email list, your average cost per email is $2.50.

Getting Emails for Less

To get your emails cheaper, you have to either decrease your advertising cost or increase your sign-up conversion rate. If you incentivize your email sign-ups by giving away some free information, tips, or a video that only email subscribers get, you can increase your conversion rate to 20%–30%. Also, make sure you explain the benefits customers get as an email subscriber; your privacy policy; and how you never, ever spam. And before you begin email marketing, make sure you've read and understood the CAN-SPAM Act of 2003[2] and how to comply with it. Email spam is a federal offense, so don't even think about it.

Disadvantages of Facebook Email Lead Generation

As shown in the previous comparison, fan marketing has some significant advantages over email marketing, and fans are much cheaper to acquire than emails.

Advantages of Facebook Email Lead Generation

Email marketing has been around for more than a decade. Facebook marketing has only been around for a few years. If Facebook went out of business tomorrow, you'd still have your email list and be able to use it, but your fan base would be gone. That said, it's incredibly unlikely that a business as popular (and large) as Facebook would go belly up overnight. Could your specific page go away for some reason? The bad publicity from any one Facebook page disappearing could undermine popular trust in Facebook. If Facebook goes public, that would never be allowed to happen.

I actually worked with a company that lost its page temporarily due to a misunderstanding—the company had complained about an advertiser using its trademarks and Facebook accidentally removed the wrong page. I contacted Facebook and we had the page back in perfect shape within 48 hours. If your page is a real business or product, it's basically yours.

Previously, Facebook turned some privately owned pages into public topic pages— one example is a "wine" page with 792,000 fans that, according to Facebook policies, was too general to be a business page owned by one person. (WineGuy subsequently moved over to Wine Searcher at http://www.facebook.com/winesearcher.) The only other reason a page could be removed is for violating Facebook's policies, but if you follow those policies, you have nothing to worry about.

Strategy #3: Fan Marketing for e-Commerce

Fan marketing for e-commerce, as illustrated in Figure 4.3, is the favorite strategy of most companies that do Facebook marketing. The idea is to get fans from Facebook ads, engage them through Facebook page posts, and then get them to go to your e-commerce website to purchase.

---

2. http://en.wikipedia.org/wiki/CAN-SPAM_Act_of_2003

Fan -> Purchase Path

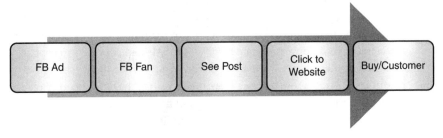

Figure 4.3   *The fan-to-purchase path.*

1. **Facebook ads**—As with all fan-capturing activities, we will use the advertising platform's unparalleled targeting abilities to wrangle the best potential buyers into your fan base.

2. **Facebook fans**—When ad viewers click Like on your ad, they immediately become a fan and will start seeing your page posts in their news feeds.

3. **Facebook page post engagement**—Write posts that make your fans want to like the post and/or comment on it. *Sell the dream* that your offering helps fulfill. Post about things that get them to go to your website. Incentivize them with discounts and other persuasion techniques.

4. **Website visit**—After they visit your website (or your Facebook page's e-commerce tab), if you've brought the right potential buyer there and if your website does a good job turning them into buyers, you'll get a...

5. **Purchase.**

Even after they purchase, these buyers can be important to your fan page. Happy buyers will spontaneously post and comment positively (and you can also ask them to post in a follow-up email or page post), and those fans who have yet to buy will see this and be more convinced that buying from you is a good idea.

Disadvantages of Fan Marketing for e-Commerce

Your website needs to do a good job turning visitors into customers; otherwise, all the money you've spent on fans will be wasted. It takes time and money to acquire fans, and it takes time and creativity to post daily in a way that gets people to respond. If you don't post at least daily, you're missing an opportunity, and if you don't post in an engaging way, the percentage of fans who see your posts decreases.

Advantages of Fan Marketing for e-Commerce

All fan marketing strategies can produce spontaneous testimonials from happy customers, friends of fans might become fans without any additional cost to you, and the number of fans you have can serve as social proof that many people think you have a good brand. Acquiring fans from ads ensures you control the quality of your fan base and that they are more likely real potential buyers, not just looky-loos and warm bodies.

e-Commerce on Facebook Itself

You can sell your products from within a Facebook tab. This is essentially the same model but with the tab substituted for the website. There are a number of carts and applications you can use for this, which I discuss in Chapter 8, "Putting Your Best Face Forward: Setting Up Your Facebook Page to Get More Fans and Sales."

Strategy #4: Fans for Blogging and Advertising Revenue

Bringing fans to your blog and then generating ad revenue, as depicted in Figure 4.4, is a great strategy for bloggers. It can also be added on to any company that has an active blog.

Fan -> AdSense Path

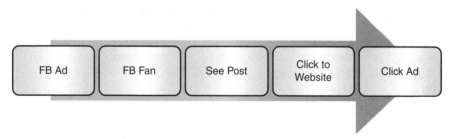

Figure 4.4   *The fan-to-blog-to-ad clicks path.*

1. **Facebook ads**—Use Facebook advertising to find people who are avid followers of your blogging topics.

2. **Facebook fans**—When ad viewers click Like on your ad, they immediately become fans and will start seeing your page posts in their news feeds.

3. **Facebook page post engagement**—Write Facebook posts that make your fans want to like and/or comment on it. You not only need clicks to the blog posts, but also likes and comments so you stay visible to

fans. You might not blog daily, but you'll want to post on Facebook daily. You can use Facebook posts to ask questions that might generate ideas for blog posts. Then you know for sure that the topic is relevant to your fan base. If you do a good job creating interesting blog posts and writing blog post titles that grab attention, there's a good chance that that alone will get you good clicks from your Facebook posts.

4. **Website visit**—After they visit your website, if you've brought the right potential buyers there and if your website has good relevant ads, you'll get...

5. **Ad clicks**—You might use Google AdSense or another advertising program. You sign up as a publisher and, in many cases, the code they give you will automatically show relevant ads for whatever page it's displayed on. If you want to make more money, you can do a bit of research about which ads earn the most money and then write on those topics specifically.

Disadvantages of Facebook Blogging with Ads

Not every subject you could write about has lucrative ads. For example, sports and celebrities are very popular topics but provide notoriously low ad revenues. Some topics are hard to monetize—for example, what company would advertise on sports topics? What are they selling? DVDs, posters, and team jerseys don't sell very well and don't provide a lot of revenue, so the ad clicks aren't valuable.

On the flip side, some products such as herbal medicines sell very well online; other niches besides health include insurance, mortgage, computers, dating, and consumer electronics. When considering a topic, think about whether there are obvious products connected to that topic that companies make good money on online.

Advantages of Facebook Blogging with Ads

You don't need a product, fulfillment, or customer service. You simply write blog posts, get your Facebook fans to interact, and make money when they click on ads.

How to Research the Most Profitable Blog and Fan Page Topics

If you are starting from scratch with no blog yet, I suggest you avail yourself of a keyword research tool. The best is Google AdWords's own keyword research tool. You need an AdWords account to use it, but that requires just a $5 one-time deposit. Type in anything and everything you would search for related to the topic, and see which keywords come back. These keywords are the most popular phrases people search for in your niche. Look at both the monthly searches and the cost per click (CPC). In AdSense, you're going to make a percentage of this CPC. You need to find keywords with both high search volume and high CPC. Then go to the Facebook advertising platform and see if you can find a good volume of people on interests related to these keywords.

For example, if you have an alternative medicine blog, you can check into keywords related to herbs, acupuncture, acupressure, massage, chiropractic, and so on. If you find that herb keywords are both popular and lucrative, check Facebook and see how many people have put "herbs" or "herbal medicine" into their profiles. If you can get thousands of cheap herbal medicine fans into a page and you have a passion for writing about herbal medicine, this could be a profitable blog for you.

Strategy #5: Fans and Affiliate Marketing

Building a fan base and making a percentage selling other people's offerings, as illustrated in Figure 4.5, can be an effective way to generate clicks. Many websites have affiliate programs, and Amazon's Associates is probably the best-known one. iTunes also has one. Affiliate programs exist in many niches. Affiliate marketing with Facebook can be accomplished with nothing more than a Facebook page—you can use a website or blog, too, but it's not required.

Fan -> Affiliate Paths

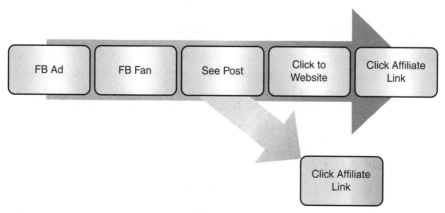

Figure 4.5   *The fan-to-affiliate revenue path.*

1. **Facebook ads**—We'll use Facebook advertising to find people who are avid followers of the niche you've chosen.

2. **Facebook fans**—When ad viewers click Like on your ad, they immediately become a fan and will start seeing your page posts in their news feeds.

3. **Facebook page post engagement**—Write posts that make your fans want to like the post and/or comment on it. You not only need clicks to affiliate links and blog posts, but also likes and comments so you stay visible to fans.

4. **Website visit**—You don't have to have a website for this model, but if you do, you'll have affiliate links on your website or blog. You'll either get clicks from there or from the links in your page posts themselves.

5. **Affiliate clicks**—After a fan clicks on an affiliate link, it's all up to that destination website to do the selling. It's better to be an affiliate of multiple companies and offerings so that you have a chance to see what works and what doesn't. Follow the principles in Chapter 6, "Facing the Facts: How to Continuously Get Better Results with the Five Steps of Optimization," to improve your results. Also, keep in mind that some sites such as Amazon will give you a percentage of sales of any product bought, even if it's not the one that initially got the buyer to the website.

Disadvantages of Fans for Affiliate Marketing

The biggest disadvantages of affiliate marketing are that you get a small portion of the revenue; that you can't control how well the company sells its products; and the fact that if you send people to a company with bad customer service, their bad experience can reflect on you and cause you problems with your fans.

Advantages of Fans for Affiliate Marketing

The biggest advantages of affiliate marketing are that you don't have to run your own company, create your own product, or manufacture or distribute anything. You don't do customer service because you can always refer people to the companies you promote. You simply get people to see and click on affiliate links and collect the money you make from what they buy.

How to Choose a Niche

There are entire books and courses on choosing the right affiliate niche. The best advice I've ever heard is to choose something you're really passionate about. If you have any hobbies or interests you've loved for years, you probably know more about them than you think and aren't likely to mind talking or writing about them for a couple more years. Also, you might have already built up some kind of social network around one of them that you can reconstruct on Facebook.

Complying with the Federal Trade Commission

The Federal Trade Commission (FTC) has become much more vigilant in watching out for hucksters who would take advantage of less savvy Internet users. If you're going to engage in promoting affiliate offers via social media, you need to read and understand all the implications of the FTC's guidelines on these matters, make sure you have a disclaimer available, and comply with FTC regulations. It would be a good idea to put a disclaimer in the Info section of your fan page explaining that fans should assume that any of your links may be affiliate links, thus you can be paid for your recommendation of them. If you want to play it safe, put "(affiliate link)" next to all the links you disseminate.

Affiliate Groups Instead of Fan Pages?

As I discuss in Chapter 8, "Putting Your Best Face Forward: Setting Up Your Facebook Page to Get More Fans and Sales," Facebook Groups are very effective for the most extreme fanatics in any niche and they are super sticky (people get notified aggressively about all comments and posts, so they tend to return much more than fans do to pages). This is why they might also be a good place to promote affiliate links. Here, though, disclosure is more difficult because Groups don't have much room for information. You will have to point out every affiliate link if you want to play it safe.

5

How Not to Fall on Your Face: Six Mistakes That Block Facebook Profitability

Some businesses make immediate profits with Facebook. Others don't and have no idea why. Some business owners assume that obstacles or lack of immediate profits mean Facebook will never work for them. It's important to have realistic expectations and look at Facebook marketing as a step-by-step process. Depending on the Facebook strategy you choose, you may be obtaining and engaging fans for a few months before you see profits. And if you make money on an e-commerce website, you'll have to get Facebook users from ads or fans from your fan page to go to your website before they'll be able to buy.

I've found six common problems—fundamental mistakes both on Facebook and corporate websites—that block companies from the Facebook revenue they seek. This chapter helps you ascertain whether any of these are to blame for your own situation and teaches you how to do a better job in each of these areas. Even if you don't have major problems in any of the six areas, you might be able to learn to do better in a few of them and increase your profits.

It's important that you first understand the revenue strategies in Chapter 4, "FaceBucks: Five Ways Businesses Achieve Profits with Facebook," which gives an overview of the steps consumers must take before they buy from you.

Here are those six mistakes and how to fix them.

1. Viability and Profitability

Profitability—the ability to earn revenue that's greater than your business costs—is just simple math, but if you don't have data, you can't do that math. For those of you experienced with e-commerce metrics, forgive the following refresher. In my work I've found that a surprising number of business owners who engage in digital marketing have not answered some of these critical questions.

 Note

Determining the viability of Facebook marketing is different for start-ups than it is for already profitable online businesses, so we'll talk about these separately.

The New Online Business

New companies with new websites or online stores have a unique problem. Until you have sales and profits, there are a lot of unknowns, including these:

- Will people buy what you offer?
- Do they trust your website?
- What percentage of web visitors buy something?
- What's your average order size?
- After your operational costs, what's your average profit per order?

If you have a new product or service that few people have ever bought or heard of, and generally speaking, no one wants it yet, you're *really* experimenting. You could do everything in this book correctly, but until enough human beings have bought what you offer, you don't know for sure that they want it. There are cheaper and easier ways to find this out than Facebook marketing—for example, surveying your friends and family or people in online discussion groups and forums if they would buy it, when they would buy it, and how much they'd paid for it. Yes, these people may not be your best target customers, but if there's something seriously wrong with your offer or approach, you may find it quicker by asking them.

Fighting the Temptation to Go Cheap

You'll find that most of the Facebook marketing methods I advocate require advertising, whether for fans or for traffic directly to your website. When you're considering spending hard cash on advertising and don't have answers to the questions in the previous section, it's tempting to start with marketing options that cost labor and time instead of cash. But it takes more work to get Facebook results with the free methods, and if you do have a serious undiscovered obstacle to your success, because it takes longer to build fans and get traffic to your site, you won't know about that obstacle for a long time.

What if you spend three months working on free methods only to discover that all the free traffic you generated was wasted because some suboptimal aspect of your website's copy or layout kept people from buying from you? Believe it or not, sometimes there are technical website problems that you'd think would have been tested and checked before but are only discovered by frustrated potential customers. *It's worth the advertising investment to spend several hundred or a few thousand dollars getting visitors to your website to answer these questions.* In other words, free can ultimately cost you more. Don't go cheap.

In summary, here are a couple steps you should take if you have no online business track record: Do market research and test your Facebook and website selling system with advertising to get direct traffic to the website.

Google AdWords Versus Facebook Advertising

For the start-up determining its online viability, the question is: Should I get this traffic from Google's AdWords service, from Facebook ads, or from somewhere else?

There's no one right answer here. My experience as a consultant and an entrepreneur is that AdWords and Facebook ads are the best, but I hear good things about the new Bing pay-per-click services. If you can afford to test more than one, do it!

How much money will you need to test them? If you think your conversion rate is 1.0% (a modest goal), you need 100 visitors for every test. But within Facebook and AdWords, you will probably run multiple tests. For example, let's say you're a chiropractor in Peoria. You might want to target people who like natural health, fitness, golf, and tennis, and you also suspect you should narrow it to people over 40 years old. You're going to run at least four ads:

- People over 40 in Peoria who like natural health

- People over 40 in Peoria who like fitness

- People over 40 in Peoria who like golf

- People over 40 in Peoria who like tennis

That means you need at least 400 clicks (100 visitors per test). Those clicks, because you haven't optimized your ad performance yet, might cost you $0.50–$1.00 a piece, so you'll need to earmark $400 to test Facebook ads. This should probably be ad traffic sent directly to your website. It might be cheaper later to get these people as fans, but then you'll have to post for a while to get them to become clients, and maybe not all of them are ready to come in for chiropractic services right now. Chiropractic service isn't an impulse buy unless you're in pain.

You could test ads that show up for AdWords or Bing keywords like "peoria chiropractor." For a business with a longer sales cycle, the AdWords or Bing test might be quicker than Facebook and help you find the conversion rate and profitability information sooner. But whether you sell action figures, which is something that fans will buy impulsively, you can probably run Facebook ads for action figure fanatics and get some sales pretty quickly.

Learning the Ad Systems While Determining Viability

Keep in mind that you're not testing whether Google, Bing, or Facebook work because they've proven themselves to work for a variety of businesses. What you're doing is running tests to see if your website or business, as it is right now, works.

If you're new to these kinds of advertising, you'll probably make mistakes in setting them up. You're at the beginning of the learning curve, so poor results can be a function of your rookie advertiser skills, not of a problem with the advertising system.

I've read articles from well-respected websites such as AdWeek claiming Facebook advertising doesn't work (often, though, they make other statements that indicate they come more from a media buying perspective and are not familiar with self-serve advertising and optimization[1]). As a consultant, I've seen so many companies new to both Facebook and AdWords make so many basic mistakes that I'm not surprised—it's because they haven't learned to use these advertising systems well yet. It's frustrating to see inaccurate generalizations made so early in the life of a new marketing channel. These are complicated self-serve advertising platforms that require both time and a tolerance for trial-and-error to learn to use effectively. If you put in the time and follow the techniques in this book, you will get much better performance and be much more likely to achieve Facebook marketing profitability.

Typically, when you first run ads for any business, even an already profitable one, you get mixed results. Some ads work well; others don't. Some Facebook targets or audiences make good customers; others don't. You keep the ones that work, learn from them, and test more things based on what you learned.

---

1. http://www.adweek.com/news/advertising-branding/report-facebook-ad-performance-abysmal-126285

Assessing and Comparing Advertising Results

Let's do a little math to compare the results (here for simplicity's sake I'll just talk about Facebook and Google):

1. Get your actual cost per click (CPC) from Facebook and Google.

2. Get the conversion rate for Google traffic and the conversion rate for Facebook traffic from your analytics.

3. Get the average order size for each.

4. Subtract your operating costs and figure out your profit for Google and Facebook.

5. Find your gross profit per click for Google and Facebook.

6. Subtract the CPC from each to get your real profit per click for each.

For example, let's say you discover that Google AdWords visitors convert 1.2% of the time and Facebook ad visitors 1.0%. The average order size is $100 from Google traffic and $110 from Facebook traffic. Your CPC from AdWords is $1.50, and your Facebook CPC is $0.50. Finally, your operating cost per order is $30. Let's do the math:

AdWords cost per customer = $120 ÷ 1.2% = $83.33

Facebook cost per customer = $50 ÷ 1.0% = $50.00

AdWords real profit per customer = $100 – 83.33 – 30 = –$13.33 (negative)

Facebook real profit per customer = $110 – 50 – 30 = $30 (positive)

All these are summarized in Table 5.1.

Table 5.1   Sample Comparison of AdWords and Facebook Advertising Profitability

Channel	Cost Per Click	Conversion Rate	Average Order Size	Ad Cost Per Customer	Operating Cost Per Customer	Profit Per Customer
AdWords	$1.50	1.2%	$100.00	$83.33	$30.00	–$13.33
Facebook	$0.50	1.0%	$110.00	$50.00	$30.00	$30.00

These results are, of course, completely hypothetical. The numbers for your business, and the profit or lack thereof, from AdWords and Facebook will be different. But you can see how the conversion rate of your website is a big factor in Internet marketing profitability—across all traffic sources, in the previous example, it might be 1.1%. Now imagine that all your conversion rates were below 1.0%. In that case you'd know that it was your website, not the traffic source, that was reducing your sales.

The Successful Online Business Now Testing Facebook Marketing

If you have a type of product or service many people offer and many have bought, you don't need to worry so much about its viability. If your business is already selling online, even better! Even so, you do need to think about how often people will need or want your produce or service, and whether Facebook marketing is the best place to market it.

For this type of business, you need to discover:

- Overall conversion rate, cost per customer, average order size, and profit per order

- Facebook advertising CPC, conversion rate, cost per customer, average order size, and profit per order

- And, perhaps, Google AdWords CPC, conversion rate, cost per customer, and average order size, profit per order

You won't really know if Facebook will be profitable for you until you test it, but some offerings are more likely to sell on Facebook than others.

Examples of Businesses Difficult to Market on Facebook

It might not be a good idea to market wedding services with Facebook because Facebook targeting isn't great for things that almost anybody could buy at anytime but that they don't buy repeatedly. There's no specific age you can target for marriage, and few people type "getting married soon" in as a Facebook profile interest. Most people will only need wedding planning services once or twice in their lifetime, so you don't want to get everybody in the world into a fan base so that maybe in five years they'll need you. Owning that prospect creates an incredibly long sales cycle.

Real estate is another tough one for fan marketing. Facebook ads have brought in significant leads for realtors, but I would think long and hard before starting a fan page to sell real estate. Is it going to contain every person in the city in which you sell real estate? What's the age? Gender? Or could it be anybody? What about people who are moving from other cities? The fan base could be almost everyone. Maybe it would work if you could target by income level, but you can't. And, you're not going to get as many repeat customers from real estate as you would in other businesses, so the long-term value of these fans isn't as high.

Figuring Out Facebook Marketing Profitability

Let's say that regardless of traffic source (Facebook, Google, and others), you've had enough web traffic to confirm that people like what you offer, trust your site, and will buy from you.

Now look at your website or ecommerce analytics. Do you have a good idea what your average conversion rate and order size are? Can you figure out what percentage of your order revenue is profit? Then you know how much you profit on each order.

Therefore, you want to figure out whether Facebook marketing will also be profitable. If you know the conversion rate and average profit per order, you can quickly figure out whether it's likely or unlikely that you'll profit from advertising. I use this a lot. I've talked to a number of businesses where, in the first conversation, we discover that advertising is way too expensive for them. The math doesn't work. Here's how you figure it out: Work backward from what cost per customer you can tolerate and what your advertising CPC needs to be to profit.

Let's say your typical e-commerce order is $150, you profit $75 per order, and your conversion rate is 1.0%. Your conversion rate is 1%, so that means 1 out of every 100 visitors will buy from you. And that means you need to pay for 100 visitors before you'll get a sale.

Because your profit is $75, you can spend $75 on advertising and still break even. For some businesses, this is fine—and some will even capture the customer at a loss—because they know or believe they'll get repeat business from that customer. If you're one of those lucky, savvy few who knows what their average customer was worth to them over the last year, you can comfortably spend even more to acquire a customer.

Now if you can spend $75 per sale and you need 100 visitors, let's divide that $75.00 by 100. We get $0.75. And that is the amount you can afford to pay per click for visitors.

Here's the equation:

Acceptable Cost Per Click = Profit Per Sale × Conversion Rate

Now all you have to do is get advertising visitors at or below that acceptable CPC. The lower you get it, the bigger your profits will be.

2. Head in the Sand: No Analytics

If you can't quantify the effects of what you're doing, how do you know if it's working? If you can't measure one technique versus another, how do you know which one works better?

Without web analytics, you can't see what Facebook users and fans are doing and, just as importantly, what they're not doing on your website. You can't diagnose problems or determine your degree of success. You have no insight.

Without a clearly quantified picture of your business, all your ideas, the new inspirations or troubleshooting fixes alike, are shots in the dark. This is a good way to waste a lot of time and money and miss out on bigger successes and profits.

As I discuss in Chapter 6, "Facing the Facts: How to Continuously Get Better Results with the Five Steps of Optimization," measurement is a critical part of improving your results. In Chapter 13, "Face-alytics: How to Track Your Facebook Results on Your Website," I discuss how to set up better web analytics and track your Facebook results in depth.

3. Too Many Hoops: The Arduous Conversion Funnel

You lose money if you make the online buying process too complicated. This is one of my favorite things to teach because it happens everywhere in online marketing. So few people grasp the 1% rule I'm going to explain here, but it's obvious after you think through the process.

The problem is when we want consumers to do things but make it too difficult for them. We make it take seven clicks to something instead of three. Our website is a Rube Goldberg machine. We assume people will go through any and all convoluted processes if they really want what we offer. The truth is that only some people want it that badly. For others, the more steps they have to go through, the more frustrated and impatient they get and the more likely they are to jump ship before they finalize a purchase. So how do we make it easier for them?

The 1% Rule: Only 1% Of People Will Do What You Ask Them to Do Online

I discovered this rule after years of poring over client website analytics and online advertising results:

- **1% CTR on AdWords ads**—Most Google AdWords optimizers look for at least a 1% click-through rate (CTR) on their Search Network ads, and this is quite easy with best practices.

- **1% sales conversion rate**—Most e-commerce sites aim to get at least 1% of their visitors to buy, and most achieve it. Some conversion optimization consultants do much better than this, but we know for sure if you aren't getting 1%, something fundamental is wrong with either the website or whom you're targeting with ads.

- **1% feedback rate**—When you ask people to like or comment on a Facebook post, usually at least 1% of those who see it will do so.

- **1% CTR on posts**—My own survey of my clients, students, and other Facebook marketers found that about 1% of people who see a post with a link in it will click on it.

- **1% traffic from email**—About 22% of email subscribers open emails and 3.7% click, so the actual percentage of emails that lead to site visits is 0.8%[2], which is pretty close to 1%.

When I was writing this book, I Googled the "one percent rule" and discovered another Internet-related example: 1% of people on the Internet create content, 9% edit or modify content, and 90% read or view it without contributing.[3]

To me, the 1% rule is about taking action. In many contexts, you should be able to count on 1% of people taking a desired action. Certainly, conversion optimization experts will tell you that you can and should optimize for better results than that. But we know that something is wrong with your set-up if less than 1% take action.

The rule doesn't quite apply to Facebook ads. The average Facebook ad does well to get a 0.1% CTR (1 out of 1,000). Google display ads have historically hovered around this click rate as well. This is because display ads are usually placed next to the actual content the user was looking for, and they look different from that content. Search ads get a higher CTR because people are actively looking for something and the ads look very much like the search results.

The Effect of the 1% Rule on Internet Sales Processes

So, if you have more than one step involved, these drop-offs add up. The longer your process is, the more people you lose. For example, if you have 10,000 people on an email list that you want to become fans of your Facebook page, only 1% will make it to the page, right? That's only 100 people. Not all of them will click Like, but the max number of fans you'll get from this email is 100. Most people, before learning the 1% rule, think that the majority of that 10,000 will become fans. Wrong!

Because every additional step loses you customers, e-commerce stores have gotten better over the years at reducing the number of steps involved in checking out. A certain number of people drop out at each step. Some businesses lose as much as half of their buyers this way. To be fair, many people put things in a cart without

---

2. http://mailchimp.com/resources/research/email-marketing-benchmarks-by-industry/

3. http://en.wikipedia.org/wiki/1%25_rule_(Internet_culture)

being sure they're going to buy, but even when you look at the last few steps, businesses can lose up to 25% of their sales by having a confusing process and too many steps.

Now consider that in 1999, Amazon created one-click ordering and patented it.[4] It's pretty amazing they were allowed to patent this, but doesn't it make sense they would try? This gives them a huge advantage at the purchasing stage. They licensed it soon after to Apple.

4. Why Should I Care? Unmotivated Customers

There are a lot of what I call "me me me" mistakes that businesses can make. All these mistakes come from not thinking about the customer as a real person and then imagining his wants, needs, and problems. We tend to think that if we get people to our page or to our website, we'll get sales. As you saw earlier, having too many steps in the process can reduce the number that buy. And, no matter how few steps remain, after you've optimized the conversion process, if you haven't thought about how to motivate people at each step, you're probably underperforming.

Why Should They Care?

One principle of marketing for results is to make sure you don't assume everyone is an avid fan who gets up every day just looking for chances to give you cash and fulfill your organizational objectives. You have to meet the customer halfway by anticipating her needs and problems and removing as many obstacles and as much friction as you can.

WIIFM?

I've heard it said many times that most people are always listening to their favorite radio station: WIIFM, which stands for What's In It For Me. Until you think and talk to them about what they want, they won't come close to giving you what you want. As renowned author and motivational speaker Zig Ziglar says, "You can have everything you want, if you'll just help enough other people get what they want."

Incentives

An incentive is something you offer someone in exchange for doing something. The prosaic donkey can be urged forward with a carrot or a stick. Incentives are the carrots. Books like *Freakonomics* are behavioral economic studies of why people do what they do. It turns out that people act in accordance with how they're incentivized. For

---

4. http://en.wikipedia.org/wiki/1-Click

example, if a salaried employee doesn't get bonuses, you may have trouble improving his performance. He is motivated only to avoid getting fired. Maybe you can incentivize him with other perks, like a better parking spot or an office with a view.

In online business, you're asking potential customers to "come this way," and incentives are the fuel that keeps them moving forward. The longer the path, the harder the path, and the less incentive you give them, the fewer customers you will get.

Keeping Their Attention and Engagement

When your potential customer is moving toward a purchase, at each step along the way, there are reasons for her to drop out. Do you still have her attention? Is the difficulty of using your website or shopping cart starting to reduce her desire for your offering? I'm sure as a web user, at some point you left a bad website because you were so frustrated that you no longer cared about what you were going to get from it or because you felt disrespected because the company didn't make the process easier for you. After you've removed the bumps and extra hoops, you still need to keep customers' eyes on the prize.

Getting More Likes

Let's say you're acquiring fans so you can later turn some into customers. Why should they like your page? Give them a reason. If they make it to your welcome tab, do they get something for liking? Even if they don't, explain why they'll love the page posts.

Getting Emails

If you're using ads to get emails and plan to use email marketing to get sales, you might need to give people a reason to give you their email addresses. Are they going to get discounts? Deals? Helpful information? A free video? A free whitepaper? What's the carrot for them to move forward?

Facebook-Specific Landing Pages on Your Website

A *landing page* is an entry point into your website from advertising. Digital marketers have learned from AdWords how effective it is to take a granular approach—from keyword to ad to landing page. As the potential customer goes through that process, you reassure him of the relevancy and importance of each step. You connect with him and show him he's in the right place.

The same approach to Facebook advertising can make customers care and stay in the sales funnel. If you targeted the right people, your ad won't seem strange to them. You might even call them out by location (Bostonians), relationship (hey, moms!), or profession (chiropractors) in the ad. Then when they reach the website, the page also makes sense, given the ad they just clicked on.

Some questions you should consider include

- Do you have at least one page on your website dedicated to sending Facebook traffic?

- Do you have a discount just for Facebook customers and a page that explains the discount to them?

- Are you targeting several different types of customers with ads? Do you have a different landing page for each?

5. You've Got the Wrong Guy: Unqualified Fan Base

All of the fan marketing tips in this book assume you do a good job targeting the right fans with your Facebook ads. If you get the wrong fans for your offering, they're not going to go much further down the road with you. They won't be interested in your posts, you won't get likes and comments, they'll stop seeing your posts, and you'll just be talking to yourself.

Here's a pretty obvious example of targeting the wrong fans (see Figure 5.1).

Figure 5.1   *How to get the wrong fans.*

I'm sure there are a few people who like AC/DC and Michael Bolton. I know—I'm one of them. Just kidding!

Chapter 9, "The Face of Advertising: How to Capitalize on the Most Powerful Marketing Tool," and Chapter 10, "FaceHook: Capturing Qualified Prospects as Fans and Group Members," discuss targeting the right audiences and getting the right customers to increase your chances of getting a positive return on your fan growth campaigns.

6. Let's Get It On: No Warm-up

Marvin Gaye said it. But I bet he didn't say it to a woman he'd just met. Well, maybe he did and maybe he could get away with it because she already knew his music. But if the average guy went up to a woman he didn't know and said that, he'd deservedly get slapped.

Everybody wants something. Your company does. A guy on a date does. A customer does. Your kids do. But when you want something from someone else, you can't just go up and ask for it. Okay, you can, but you might not get it.

Why is cold calling so difficult to do? "I don't know you, you called me during dinner, and you want me to buy something? How about respecting my time and privacy? How about acknowledging that I'm doing something important here?" That's why there's a national "do not call" list. That's why we don't like spam email and there are federal laws against it.

People using Facebook feel the same way. "Hey, I'm socializing here, could you turn down the sales voice a little bit? And get a better tie?"

As the saying goes, "Honey catches more flies than vinegar." I'm not sure if someone was really trying to catch flies with vinegar, or why they wanted to catch flies in the first place, but you get the point—people help people they like. They buy from companies that they like or that they feel obligated to.

Start with Generosity

There's this weird phenomenon—gifts inaugurate and deepen friendships. One good turn deserves another. Dating can start with a yes to the question, "Can I buy you a drink?" People fight over the check after eating. Why? Because giving creates an obligation. It's nice to give gifts and it can come from a place of love, but we also know that our gift recipient is more likely to help us in the future.

Think about it this way: It's a big, cold, cruel world. We each have limited time and resources. We can't be everybody's customer. We can't be everybody's friend. So whom do we gravitate toward? Which relationships develop and which don't?

We like the people who care about us. If you want customers, start with generosity.

Warming It Up on the Web

You've seen websites with videos and demos. These are ways to introduce people to you and your services. Have you ever signed up for a free trial? You might not think of it this way, but that's a gift. It can be a gift we've come to expect, but we appreciate the company's willingness to let us enter the relationship with them risk-free.

Warming It Up on Facebook

You'll see this theme throughout the book. In Chapter 7, "Selling the Dream: Going Beyond Benefits to Arouse Your Fans' Desire for What You Offer," I talk about how you arouse potential customers' desire. Painting the picture for them makes them more likely to give you their business. In Chapter 11, "Talking Till You're Blue in the Face: How to Get More Likes and Comments," I show how giving people interesting content can get them to give back by liking or commenting. In *FaceMessage*, I show you how to build relationships with bloggers and journalists with generous tactics. In Chapter 14, "FaceFluence: Turning FaceLookers Into FaceBuyers—13 Sales and Influence Tactics for Increased Facebook Profits," goes deeper into the hows and whys of influencing potential customers.

6

Facing the Facts: How to Continuously Get Better Results with the Five Steps of Optimization

I almost named this chapter "How to Get Better Results Than the Other Guy Who Skipped This Chapter." The goal of this chapter is to provide you with a framework for getting continuously better Facebook marketing results. What separates those who are able to improve their results from those who are just lucky—or unlucky? Optimization.

The system I present in this book is different from what you'll find other social media experts suggesting. In part, this is because of my background in direct marketing, but perhaps more accurately, I was drawn to direct marketing because of one of my strengths: I'm what the Gallup organization would call a "maximizer."[1]

---

1. http://strengths.gallup.com/110659/Homepage.aspx

Optimization is the process of improving any system's efficiency and effectiveness. It's hard to argue against improving efficiency. Should we instead try to waste more of your marketing dollars? Of course not! Should we goof off and have fun with creative pictures and videos and ideas regardless of the campaign's effect on sales? Probably not. Should we set advertising in motion and never check to see how well it's doing? Ridiculous!

On Facebook, should we get you as many fans as possible regardless of whether they're potential customers? That depends on your goal, doesn't it? If you just want to impress people with a big fan count, by all means, get as many of the cheapest fans as possible! But if your goal is more bottom-line-focused, that will affect our strategy choice and how we implement it.

Part of being efficient is being an 80-20 thinker: Let's do the 20% of things that yield 80% of results. So, the system I propose will not be using every possible aspect of Facebook for marketing. Instead, I have emphasized the tactics I've seen get clients the results they want and have deemphasized things that don't seem to help as much. To some social media experts, my system will seem too focused, not as broad as what they would suggest, but that doesn't mean you shouldn't spend more time on custom tabs, apps, or events than I've suggested.

If you find that one of those options makes sense for your specific business, just apply the optimization system I teach in this chapter to it as well. It's a scientific system focused on testing, so your own testing will assure you which tactics work best.

The Five Steps of Optimization

In 2008, I developed a five-step system for improving the output of anything, including your marketing (see Figure 6.1):

1. Clarify what your goal is.

2. Find a way to measure your goal.

3. Look at your starting point.

4. Test tactics that move you toward the goal.

5. Check to see what worked and what didn't, then adapt your next moves accordingly.

Most people do some of these steps, but not all—and missing one of these steps is enough to ensure you take too long to evolve, possibly losing the leadership position in your niche. Companies that use all five of these steps consistently get better results than their competitors.

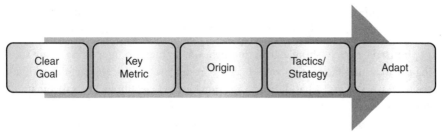

Figure 6.1 *The Five Steps of Optimization*

I created this process while working with a keynote speaking mentor who asked me some tough questions: "What is the fundamental thing you teach? What is the strength or system you can help people most with?" I felt that it was optimization.

As I looked back over my Internet marketing work since 1999, I saw a pattern. With every new channel, tactic, or tool I learned, I instinctively created a system around it or added it to an existing system to get more results; then I tried to make the system more efficient and effective. I tested things, kept what worked, and threw out what didn't. I did this with search engine optimization (SEO), pay-per-click advertising, and more.

I optimize my driving—what's the quickest route? How do I safely get around these other drivers, even the ones who don't want me to get around them? How do I get there quickest without getting a ticket? How do I do all this without provoking road rage in anyone else? I like to joke that I even tried to optimize my wife, but she didn't like that. It turns out that wives are often much better at optimizing their husbands.

In search engine optimization, your goal is to attract website visitors who will find, in your website, what they seek. You can use Google AdWords tools to see which search phrases people use and how many people type them in per month. You can measure how well you're doing with Google Analytics. You can find out exactly which search phrases are already bringing people to your website.

My question was: What can I do to SEO my website and get more visitors? I learned from other SEO experts that each search phrase has a different degree of competition. Stronger sites like the New York Times and Yahoo! could dominate all top 10 search results and leave me little chance of showing up and getting traffic. But my site could certainly rank for less competitive phrases. By comparing the keywords that already brought traffic into my main website to the data collected by Google, I was able to calibrate the level of competition I needed to target. To find keywords I thought I could rank in the top 10 for, I created an equation calibrated to my website's level of authority. Then I wrote about 20 articles, 1 per keyword. And it worked—within weeks, I was getting a lot more traffic and making good money from the Google ads I showed on my website. So I farmed out the job of writing to other writers and paid them 50% of the advertising revenue earned from their articles; at one point my site was in the top 10,000 of all sites online.

I optimized by establishing a goal, finding a way to measure it, looking at my starting point, testing tactics that would get me from start to goal, and then checking to see what worked and what didn't. In the previous SEO example, I was fortunate enough that my first tactic (using the equation to find the right keywords) worked right away. Later when I did more AdWords pay-per-click advertising, I found myself doing a lot more optimization.

Sometimes you have to take baby steps toward your ultimate goal. In AdWords, if your goal is to maximize your advertising return on investment (ROI), you won't have success if bad setup practices prevent your ads from showing in the first place. Sometimes you have to start with a more modest goal, achieve that, and then move on to the next one. For example, a sequence of goals in AdWords might be

1. Clarify the ultimate goal—are we ultimately working toward ROI or something else?

2. Prioritize key metrics—is ROI most important, even if it diminishes sales volume?

3. Understand the offerings and customer.

4. Research which search phrases the customer is using.

5. Organize the search phrases into logical groups by topic.

6. Write ads that fit each topic.

7. Set up the account.

8. Make sure the ad is running and being seen by searchers.

9. Improve the click-through rate (CTR) and quality score.

10. Check keywords to see which are performing well for the key metric, and which aren't, and stop the ones that are subpar.

As you can see, we didn't get to optimizing for the goal until step 10.

Similarly, when you do Facebook advertising, you might use a process like this:

1. Clarify the goal: Is it to get the best fans for the least money or to get sales by driving traffic directly to the website? Or is it to just get the most brand awareness for the least money? And, no, you can't say, "all of them." Prioritize.

2. Discuss key metrics—is it cost per fan? ROI? Total number of impressions? Cost per impression?

3. Understand the offerings and the target customer.

4. Create likely lists of interests, categories, demographics, location, and other factors that will help you reach the target customer.

5. Write ads that fit each target.

6. Set up analytics for each ad to see which ads get the best results on your website.

7. Make sure the ads are running and searchers are seeing the ads.

8. Check on performance and optimize according to the selected key metric.

Just to show you how different optimizing can be depending on your answers to the previous questions, let's say your goal is to get a lot of cheap clicks or fans. You need to keep the CTR high to keep click costs low, so you'll pause ads with the lowest CTRs. But if your goal is to get a lot of impressions cheaply, you'll pause ads with high CTRs and look for lower CTR ones.

Do you see how the optimization action was opposite for different goals? That's how important clear goals and metrics are.

No matter what, you need to check performance frequently. For cheap clicks, has the CTR dropped too far because of ad burnout? For cheap impressions, has the ad stopped running?

That's a quick overview and some examples. Let's look at each of the five steps of optimization and how they apply to Facebook marketing.

Step One: Establish One Clear Goal

You've probably experienced this—there's a dramatic difference in work situations with clear goals and those without. What happens when you have one goal and your supervisor has another? What happens when a husband and wife have different goals? What happens when people in a car want to go different places?

It's simplest when you have just one goal and all stakeholders (everyone who has a say or an interest) agree on that goal. And, no matter who proposes the goal, your ultimate success requires buy-in from the highest-ranking person. This prevents a lot of frustration and increases the chance everyone will be pleased with the result.

Let's say we have a Facebook coordinator managing the company Facebook page. He's growing the fan count and the fans are interacting positively with him. If he thinks that getting people engaged and conversing is the goal, he's pretty happy. But if executives above him expect quick ROI and aren't seeing it, they might be ready to cancel the whole Facebook thing. To the Facebook coordinator, it's a success. To the executive team, it's a failure. What happened? There wasn't enough communication about the goal and how it should be measured.

What I've learned from working with a variety of clients is to get answers to questions like these before agreeing to start a project:

- Why do you want to do Facebook?

- What's your goal/What are you trying to achieve?

- When we're three to six months into this project, how will you know if it's a success?

All these questions are different ways to probe for the real goal. In a bit, I show how I get even more specific with the quantification in the next step.

Facebook Marketing Goals

What kinds of goals can you achieve with Facebook marketing? The following are a few of the most common ones.

Facebook ad goals:

- Lower cost per click

- Higher CTR

- More impressions per dollar

Facebook fan growth goals:

- More relevant fans

- Lower cost per fan

- Faster fan growth

Facebook posting goals:

- More impressions per post

- Higher feedback rate

- More comments per post

- More likes per post

Facebook web result goals:

- More clicks from posts to website or blog

- Web traffic from ads and posts that's more ready to buy

- Web traffic that's more likely to do some other task on the website, like listen to music or join a free trial

Prioritizing Goals and Reconciling Conflicts

There's nothing wrong with having more than one goal, as long as they're all clear and prioritized. For example, you might want higher profits, more sales, more fans, *and* more ads seen by more people. But sometimes the action we take to improve one can hurt others. For example, what if we find out that the best ROI comes from ads that don't deliver as many fans or sales? Is there a minimum number of fans we want to get in this project? Is there a minimum number of sales we need to get while trying to achieve the ROI goal? When we're unwilling to sacrifice any of our numbers, we might be unable to improve any of them.

There is a mathematical relationship between ROI and sales and a sweet spot in the middle. It looks like this:

- Some ads and tactics get you a lot of customers at too high a cost.

- Some ads and tactics bring in a moderate number of sales at a moderate profit.

- Some ads and tactics get you a very small number of customers at very high profits.

I've worked with some clients on a tight budget who had to maximize ROI regardless of sales volume. For Facebook skeptics, a large ROI might be more important than sales volume. If your boss is among those skeptics, showing a fast and fantastic ROI might be the only way to get the buy-in and budget to use Facebook for longer-term sales growth. I also worked with a client that spent millions and was fine with a relatively low ROI because their goal was to dominate their market by getting many more sales than their competitors. They cared more about market share than short-term profits. So, the right decision depends on your goals and resources.

Here are some examples of goals that fit well together and those that conflict:

- Typically a higher Facebook advertising CTR lowers cost per click.

- But going for more Facebook ad impressions can lower CTR, which increases cost per click and lowers the overall clicks you get.

- If you write ad copy that more stringently qualifies who will want to click on your Facebook ads, this can reduce CTR and thereby increase cost per click, but if the conversion rate improves enough, you'll increase profits.

- Decreasing your fan growth cost can, in some cases, lower fan quality. It depends on whether the audience the ad targets is really your potential customer group. For example, growing a page of *Star Trek* fans makes sense if you sell *Star Trek* memorabilia, but if you are selling tickets to a Virgin Galactic flight, only a small percentage of Trekkies will have the money to take you up on it.

- A large number of only semi-relevant fans will also either force you to use irrelevant posts to keep engagement and visibility high or lead to a larger percentage of inactive fans when you try to persuade them toward your offering.

- If you need to grow a high volume of fans in a short time period (for example, 50,000 fans in a week), you have less time to optimize, so you don't improve CTR as much as you might have and cost per fan is higher than it might have been.

Step Two: Quantify the Goal with a Key Metric

Each goal needs a corresponding key metric. Sometimes you'll see reports that have dozens of metrics, and it's very difficult to tell whether you're making progress. In fact, I've seen people create confusing reports just to hide the fact that things weren't going well. You should always know what the most important key metric is for each campaign or channel so that you can quickly see whether you're going forward or backward, or stagnating.

For each goal:

1. Define the goal.
2. Define which metric will measure your progress toward that goal.
3. Set a target number you want to achieve.

For example, you might want to do a Facebook advertising campaign with these quantified goals:

- 10,000 website visitors
- Minimum 1,000,000 ad impressions
- Minimum exposure to 100,000 unique people
- Relevant visitors only
- $0.75 cost per click
- 300% ROI from ad spend

Can you achieve all of these? If not, which one is most important? We prioritize them in the next section.

Balancing Metrics

In discussion with stakeholders, you might find that the most important thing in testing some ads is to first discover what kind of results are realistic. If you can get 200% ROI in initial testing, there's a good chance that before too long you can optimize that up to 300%. When evaluating the initial test, keep in mind that some of the things you test won't work, and these underperformers will drag down the averages, but later when you go with only what tested best, your overall results will be better.

Make sure you have a prioritized list before starting. The previous list might be revised to look something like this:

1. 200%–300% ROI from ad spend

2. 10,000 website visitors

3. Relevant visitors only

4. $0.75 cost per click

5. Minimum 1,000,000 ad impressions

6. Minimum reach of 100,000 people

Now you know that, for this project, ROI is the number-one goal, and you'll find out how close you can come to 200% ROI. As I mentioned before, you can eliminate lower ROI ads more quickly the further your average is from that goal. If stopping those ads decreases the number of clicks significantly, the test will take longer to complete.

Estimating the Likelihood of Success

Until you have experience and a certain amount of data, it's hard to estimate whether target goals are achievable. Just because I've gotten 31,000 fans for a vet supply company at $0.13 apiece doesn't mean I can guarantee fans even as low as $0.50 for a business-to-business company that sells pipe fittings.

The more a project differs from your previous experience, the less accurate your estimates will be. I've run campaigns where I was hopeful I could keep the per-fan cost under $1.00, and it turned out I was able to optimize down to $0.36 each. You just never know. Some supervisors or clients might not want to hear that, but it's the truth. I always describe new projects as *tests*. I can't tell you how many times clients ask me about a new idea and I say, "Let's test it." I can certainly guess how effective or ineffective it might turn out to be, but usually you have to run the test to find out.

Tracking

You can't optimize if you don't track your results. Make sure you choose key metrics that can be tracked and that you track them *granularly*. By granularly, I mean that you can't optimize your Facebook ROI if you know only the ROI of all your Facebook traffic together. You need to track the ROI of each ad. In Chapter 13, "Face-alytics: How to Track Your Facebook Results on Your Website," I show you how to do this step by step.

Facebook Marketing Metrics

Here are some of the most commonly used Facebook metrics. There are actually a host of Facebook advertising metrics, but some are much more important than others and more commonly used as key metrics.

Facebook advertising metrics:

- Cost per click
- Click-through rate
- Cost per impressions
- Total number of impressions
- Spend

Facebook fan growth metrics:

- Fans added per day
- Cost per fan
- Click-through rate (see Figure 6.2)
- Action/Connection rate

Facebook posting metrics:

- Impressions per post
- Feedback rate
- Comments per post
- Likes per post

1,920,420 Impressions **2,457** Clicks **1,282** Connections **0.128%** CTR **$527.54** Spent **$0.21** CPC

Date	Ad Name	Impressions	CPC	CPM	Spent	Reach	Frequency	Social Reach	Connections
Week of 09/18/2011	photography_smileguy	733,271	0.16	0.27	200.00	0	0.0	0	706
Week of 09/11/2011	photography_smileguy	211,424	0.18	0.38	80.00	52,717	4.0	1,692	249
Week of 09/18/2011	topic_iphnone_earbud	255,625	0.31	0.26	66.86	0	0.0	0	100
Week of 09/18/2011	photography_gray	99,480	0.21	0.30	29.98	0	0.0	0	71
Week of 09/18/2011	FO_V_PAGE1_BD[1]2_BD[2]0_IM4	41,903	0.34	0.60	25.32	0	0.0	0	24
Week of 09/18/2011	FO_V_PAGE1_BD[1]1_BD[2]0_IM2	35,637	0.37	0.41	14.49	0	0.0	0	24
Week of 09/11/2011	topic_iphnone_earbud	78,374	0.30	0.20	15.39	18,022	4.3	1,195	24
Week of 09/11/2011	FO_V_PAGE1_BD[1]1_BD[2]0_IM6	14,262	0.60	0.89	12.69	1,704	8.4	107	12
Week of 09/11/2011	iphone_phoneguy	110,993	0.42	0.12	12.92	11,048	10.0	721	12
Week of 09/11/2011	topic_smartphone_earbud	43,670	0.38	0.18	7.88	6,434	6.8	338	11
Week of 09/18/2011	topic_smartphone_earbud	67,826	0.40	0.19	12.74	0	0.0	0	9
Week of 09/18/2011	iphone_phoneguy	88,065	0.46	0.10	9.23	0	0.0	0	6
Week of 09/11/2011	FO_V_PAGE1_BD[1]4_BD[2]0_IM7	12,545	0.40	0.35	4.44	2,232	5.6	219	6

Figure 6.2 *An Advertising Performance Report. Here you can compare each ad's performance on metrics such as CTR. You can also export to Excel and calculate the cost per fan for each ad.*

Facebook web result metrics:

- Click-through rate from post to website
- Bounce rate of Facebook ad or post traffic
- Conversion rate of Facebook ad or post traffic
- Time on site for Facebook ad or post traffic

Step Three: Look at Where You're Starting

We're trying to figure out a route to our project's goal, and every route has at least two points. When you use Google Maps to get directions, you have to put in more than the destination—you also need the starting point. To optimize your marketing results, you have to understand what you're starting with in relation to your goal to decide which tactics or channels you should test to get there. Your starting point includes resources, obstacles, and capabilities, all of which influence your strategic decisions.

Resources

Before you drive somewhere, you had better check the gas gauge. Marketing campaigns require resources like these:

- Budget for advertising
- Number of staff and hours that staff can focus on Facebook
- Email subscribers to transform into fans
- Website traffic to convert into fans
- Budget or items for giveaways

Resources limit what you can test. If you don't have a budget allocated for advertising, you can't test Facebook advertising's ability to help you reach your goals. If your budget is small, you have to become very selective about which tests you'll run.

Resources aren't always good—sometimes they can become rationalizations for not committing fully to trying something new. If you already have a sizeable email list, you might believe that will be enough to get you a sufficient fan count and use that as a reason not to budget for ads. Most companies that go down this path quickly find out not enough email subscribers become fans.

Obstacles

Sometimes limiting factors either reduce campaign success or require clever solutions. Some of the worst obstacles I've run into include

- **Legal limits on ad copy**—The ways you can describe some health products, for example, are highly restricted. You can't claim certain natural health products can cure or treat certain conditions.

- **Multiple approvals required and slow moving bureaucracy**—Facebook moves fast and people can quickly tire of your ads. Sometimes you need to create a dozen new ads today because the old ones are burning out. An approval delay of more than a few hours could mean pausing the campaign, which might extend the project timeframe. Facebook posts can be conceived and approved 30–90 days ahead of time, and that's not a bad idea, but you'll lose the opportunity to post about breaking news and current events. To capitalize on these golden opportunities, your approval delay can't exceed a few hours.

- **Inability to agree on goals or changing goals**—Some organizations are indecisive. Politics can prevent people from taking strong positions.

Sometimes a person in authority is unable to stay on target for the entire duration of a campaign. To be fair, sometimes you learn something or something important changes, so your goals need to change. Or new stakeholders are brought into the picture before the project is complete and they have conflicting goals, but politics requires their appeasement. This can reduce the performance from the perspective of the key metric. None of these things is necessarily bad or wrong, but they can definitely reduce performance and ultimately make the project appear to be less successful than it might have.

- **Extreme skepticism from authoritative stakeholders**—Sometimes the support for Facebook marketing initiatives is less than 100%. This can lead to prematurely cancelled projects. When you're the employee, there's not much you can do about it, but if you're a consultant, you have a choice. At the beginning of the project, call it a *test* and skeptical top dogs can usually get behind that. If you're not sure the project will go through to completion, it's better to get paid 50% up-front.

- **High prioritization of goals we can't control**—Your client or boss might, for some strange reason, want all your ads to be seen 10 times by each viewer. This is not easy to control in the ad interface. Explain why you might not be able to achieve that and suggest an alternative solution.

- **Customers who are difficult to target**—There are usually ways to target most audiences, even if you have to get clever to do so, but occasionally you'll encounter an audience that simply can't be effectively targeted with Facebook. It's also hard to help companies that believe their offering is good for everyone because these companies give you no ideas how to target or connect emotionally with their potential customers.

Capabilities

Capabilities are like resources but are more talent and skill-oriented:

- How much experience does your staff have with Facebook? With social media? With Internet marketing? With Facebook advertising? With Facebook posting?

- Can they write effective ads? Headlines? Posts? Have they had any copywriting training?

- Do they have customer service experience and skills that work in a written format?

- Have they had any specific Facebook marketing or advertising training?

- Do they understand analytics, tracking and how to overcome the challenges involved in tracking social media marketing?

- Have they read any awesome books like this one? They have? Okay, then they're geniuses with loads of potential. Move along. But seriously, if an employee new to Internet marketing reads this book, he'll jump about five years ahead in experience and best practices.

Step Four: Choose Tactics to Test

What you test is up to you and should fit your goals, resources, and starting point. The more experience you have, the better it is that you invent the tests. But if you've never done this before, the following sections offer some ideas to get you started.

Ad Copy Tests

The goal of ads can be fan growth, traffic to a website, immediate purchase, or even to show page posts to fans who are ignoring your page.

Fan Growth Ad Copy Tests:

- How many precise interests have you tested? Can you think of more? Have you surveyed the likes on existing fans' profiles to get ideas?

- Have you run a demographic responder report and tested variations of your ads specifically targeted to the highest CTR buckets?

- Have you tried all the variations on no-brainer ad copy like "Click Like if you love x" versus "Do you love x? Click like now!" versus "Click LIKE now if you LOVE x?" What about other creative phrasing, capitalization, or punctuation variations?

Traffic-to-Website Ad Copy Tests:

- Have you tried super-general no-brainer text to get high CTR and low CPC and see what those profits are?

- Have you tried more restrictive, qualifying ad copy to increase conversion rate and then checked the profit on those ads?

Ad Image Tests

In my experience, testing more images can make a huge difference in your results. And vice versa, not testing more than one image means your results may not be great. For example, recently just by testing more images, I cut a campaign's cost per click from $0.96 to $0.49.

- There are usually at least four or five different images that might work for any one ad concept. Have you tried more than one?

- Have you tried zooming in and cropping differently?

- Have you tried outlining the image in an attention-grabbing color?

- Have you tried weird, unrelated images?

- Have you tried showing the image upside down?

Facebook Post Tests

I've seen studies say that longer posts work better, while other studies say shorter posts are better. I don't believe there's a one-size-fits-all formula. It's critical to find out what kinds of posts, images, and calls to action your specific audience responds best to.

- Have you tried really short text? Longer text? Capitalizing entire words you want to emphasize?

- Have you tried talking about the interests you used in advertising to get fans?

- Are you explicitly asking for likes and comments?

- Are you tying your offering or company into relevant news?

One reason it's not a bad idea to plan posts 30–90 days ahead is it forces you to sit down and write a whole bunch of ideas at once. You may reject half of them, but going into brainstorming mode is sometimes the only way to find breakthrough ideas that get great results (see Figure 6.3).

Message	Posted ▼	Impressions	Feedback
Please step away form the sandwich. ▓▓▓▓ talking...	Wednesday at 7:05pm	60,625	0.70 %
Enjoy stories & songs? We've got your chance to enjoy some...	Wednesday at 5:07pm	827	0.73 %
The ▓▓▓ Tour is making its way to Baylor University!...	Wednesday at 4:55pm	378	0.79 %
Hey Oklahoma! Who wants FREE MOVIE TICKETS? ▓▓▓▓ is...	Wednesday at 4:46pm	423	3.1 %
"Out of our ashes, we rise. You see it often in history...	Wednesday at 1:55pm	19,942	4.3 %
▓▓▓▓▓▓▓▓▓▓▓	Wednesday at 8:30am	17,494	5 %
▓▓▓▓ says you are more likely...	September 20 at 8:03pm	63,833	0.58 %
▓▓▓▓▓▓▓	September 20 at 6:35pm	227,270	0.43 %
Are you ready to ▓▓▓▓▓▓▓	September 20 at 4:31pm	1,276	0.47 %
What is your Favorite ▓▓▓▓▓▓▓	September 20 at 4:14pm	123	0 %

Figure 6.3 *Facebook's Page Insights, in the Interactions tab, show you the last 15 posts, how many impressions each received and each post's feedback rate. What can you learn from these results?*

Testing Post Types

The concept of EdgeRank comes up frequently with fan page posting. An often-ignored aspect of EdgeRank is that Facebook tracks how each fan interacts with each type of post (status versus video versus photo, and so on). For example, you might prefer the AC/DC Facebook page's video posts, while I prefer to comment on their pictures. This level of detail is important when evaluating how visible you are to your fans.

The type of post your fans prefer can be unique to that audience. For example, I worked with an action sports company and found that its fans wouldn't comment on status updates no matter what I tried, but they would click Like on cool videos. Until you're sure how your fans will react, test several posts for each type: status, picture, video, and links.

Landing Pages

It's common practice for Adwords experts to test landing pages specifically geared toward a set of ads or keywords. Do you have at least one landing page that speaks to Facebook fans directly? If you offer a Facebook-specific discount, create a landing page that welcomes fans to your site and gives you a chance to explain the discount further. You can create landing pages for specific ads or posts. You might even program something into your website to dynamically display certain text, a picture, or a video only to people who come from Facebook. The options are really limited only by your creativity, budget, content-creation capacities, and programming abilities.

Step Five: Optimize Based on Results

This is the most no-brainer of the five steps. Optimization means doing more of what worked and less of what didn't.

Look at the results of each test and ask how it performed for the key metric. If you couldn't estimate a reasonable target value for that key metric before, what would you say now? Let's say you had wanted to increase feedback rates and tried 10 different Facebook page posts. If the average result was a 0.5% feedback rate, that's a reasonable baseline. If several of them hit 1.0%, now you know it's possible, and that might become the target to beat for that metric.

Try to learn from the best performing tests. Is there something about the ones that performed poorly that's obviously different from the better performing ones? If so, theorize about what might work better and design new tests based on that.

Let's say, in that test of 10 Facebook page post approaches that you had 3 that got above a 1.0% feedback rate. What do they have in common? What do the worst ones have in common? Does this give you ideas for more posts? Try some variations on the ones above 1.0% and see whether they also perform that well.

Then, most importantly, identify the worst performing tactics and stop doing them. As Google Analytics expert Avinash Kaushik hilariously orders his audiences, "Learn to enjoy killing things!"[2] Usually, just putting a stop to the ads and posts that don't perform will dramatically improve your overall results.

When I start most new advertising campaigns, I test 8 or 10 targets. In the more challenging niches, often only 1 of these will have an exceptionally low cost per click. This immediately gives me clues about what to try more of and what to stop doing. But at the beginning, in challenging niches, I often have to dig deep for new ideas for several rounds of tests before I start to see what's going to work and what won't.

---

2. No tests were harmed in the making of this chapter.

7

Selling the Dream: Going Beyond Benefits to Arouse Your Fans' Desire for What You Offer

This chapter is about how to turn potential customers into buyers. You have gathered potential buyers into a fan base. But how do you move them from liking to buying without turning them off? What I have found is you must extrapolate from fans' likes to their goals and dreams. Their dream, in my parlance, is what they want their life or business to look like—it's a highly desirable vision. The better you understand that dream or vision, the better you can discuss it with them, or evoke it. You connect your brand and offering to that dream, letting them know you are on their side in their efforts to achieve it. This creates enthusiasm, ensures you remain visible to fans, and arouses a desire for your offerings that leads to sales.

Facebook Is Not About You: Curing the "Me Me Me" Epidemic

I've worked with a lot of companies, of all sizes. Over and over, I've found that one of the biggest obstacles to marketing success is the inability to put yourself in your customers' shoes. Many companies are accustomed to thinking about their own goals and needs rather than those of their customers'. This leads to all kinds of misguided marketing ideas that fail to achieve corporate objectives. Why? Because by not knowing who customers are and what they want, you fail to connect with them in the first place, so they don't respond to the degree you would like.

Here are some symptoms of selfish marketing:

- Using corporate/industry jargon
- Disinclination to better understand the potential customer
- Believing anyone at the company is the best example of your target customer
- Obsession with the artistic/creative parts of marketing
- Lack of interest in measuring results
- Inability to change strategies and tactics even when they're not working

Let's briefly discuss each of these symptoms, what we can learn from them, and how to reverse them.

Your Favorite Words Versus the Customers'

My years of search marketing taught me with absolute clarity that the customer's way of saying things are sometimes very different from corporate speak or industry jargon. I begin each search campaign by researching the precise search phrases used to find information related to my client's business. Google's Keyword Tool (https://adwords.google.com/select/KeywordToolExternal) provides the number of searches per month for each phrase. Often, clients suggest a phrase that they think is important but few people are using. This book is not about search marketing, but this proves you can quantify the most popular phrases in each niche. The lesson is that we need to discover the customer's language to reach him. Using our own language can limit our effectiveness.

For example, I did a social media training workshop for a group of companies that were having an ongoing debate about the best way to describe their industry. Some called it *technological integration*; some called it *unified communication*. In reality, they were a diverse group of companies with very different specialties. Some built control rooms for TV stations. Some installed audiovisual screens and sound systems for churches. Others were Department of Defense contractors who built custom A/V solutions for the government. Still others installed centrally controlled digital signage systems in casinos and malls.

But when speaking with them about their specific customers, it became clear that none of their customers were searching for "unified communication." I asked them what they actually provided and what their customers were looking for. It turns out there were a number of different groups of customers with very different needs.

When you put industry words into the Google keyword tool, it comes back with the most popular related searches. And you can compare jargon to the language your customers might use. Some of the digital signage providers were talking about "narrowcasting" even though, as you can see in Figure 7.1, 12 times as many people search Google for "digital signage" each month. In other words, the companies were obsessed with words that their customers didn't use. Yes, *narrowcasting* is a very cool word, but it doesn't help us reach the customer.

Search terms (6)		
Keyword	Competition	Global Monthly Searches ⑦
☆ digital signage		201,000
☆ unified communication		90,500
☆ narrowcasting		14,800
☆ tv station control room		36
☆ worship av equipment	-	-
☆ tv control room set up	-	-

Figure 7.1   *Comparing searches for jargon versus customer words.*

Every customer has a specific problem and need, and when you divide customers into the right groups, you see similarities in the words and phrases they use when searching for a solution. With search marketing, you learn how to meet the customer right when he's looking for that solution, and you use his own word choices to find him. You are rewarded by Google AdWords with lower click costs when you use the same words the customer typed into his search engine. As you continue to market to that customer, you can use his phrases on your website. You might introduce some of your own jargon, but only if it's helpful to the sales process and only if it doesn't confuse the customer and reduce your success rates.

Disinclination to Better Understand the Potential Customer

It seems as though you could ask someone whose livelihood depends on knowing and reaching certain people who her customer was and you would get insightful answers. But often, I hear something like "people who need what we sell." Okay, but who are those people? Are their entire lives focused on buying your products?

Probably not. Do they only wear clothing with your logos on it? Not unless they're NASCAR drivers who never change out of their jumpsuits. Do they sit in front of the TV all day filled with emptiness until your commercial comes on? I hope not!

Potential buyers are real people with real, full lives—just like you. Yet, it's amazingly difficult to think about the customer as a real person. We over-generalize them until there's nothing useful to latch onto. Should we instead force ourselves to think about only one specific person? No, because then we get lost in the idiosyncrasies that don't help us relate to a larger group. So, we need methods to make the potential customer specific enough to be real but general enough to describe a lot of them.

There are a number of ways marketers do this, including

- The 16 personality types from Meyers Briggs Type Indicator.
- The 34 strengths from Gallup, Inc.[1]
- Demographic profiles including age, gender, education, and location.
- Behavioral profiles (a variety of market research firms use their own sets of characters such as "the upwardly mobile" or "the early adopter").

Most businesses have more than one type of customer. For example, if you have both male and female customers, is the man one personality type and the woman another? I've heard several companies say their customer is "women between the ages of 25 and 55." Are all these women the same? Try telling them that. No. On second thought, don't. I want you to live to finish reading this book.

Right now, there are almost 58 million women on Facebook between the ages of 25 to 55. But the 25–34 group thinks and talks and works and dates very differently than the 45–55 age group does, doesn't it? It's obvious when you think about them as real people. And later when you run demographic reports on your Facebook ads, you'll see measurable proof of those differences.

What about getting to know where the customer lives and how that area's culture has affected her? If you've lived in different cities, you know that people talk differently in different places. And subcultures within countries use different words and have different concerns and different priorities. People in different regions have different values. Can your product be used for so many different purposes that different kinds of people use it?

If you can identify five types of people who are your best customers and then target those people, you'll do much better than if you think they're all the same or if you classify them into an unmanageable number or groups, like 25 types of customers.

---

1. http://www.strengthsquest.com/content/143324/themes-full-description.aspx

Can You Really Say, "I Am the Best Example of Our Target Customer"?

You simply are not the best example of your own target customer, and I'll tell you why: If you are in charge of marketing or you run the entire company—in other words, if you have power in a company that matters—you are, by definition, strange. And I mean that in the very best way.

By the time you've succeeded to that degree, you've achieved a lot and differentiated yourself from 99% of the world. You've become so special that you're now part of a very small target market. If you're a CEO, CMO, or director of marketing, you're the target customer for business-to-business companies that target CEOs, CMOs, and directors of marketing. The only time you are really your own best customer is when you target people with your specific occupation, age, gender, culture, and preferences. Then you can use marketing that speaks to your level of sophistication and the preferences and values of your segment. But if you are a marketer who sells consumer packaged goods, you're not the same as that customer. Even if you occasionally buy what your company offers, it might be for a different reason than most of your customers. It's safer to assume you are not your customer.

Also, marketers are intimately familiar with the company itself; its offerings, benefits, and advantages; and the quality of your customer service. Because of that, you perceive it all very differently from the way the average customer does. You're an expert on your company, but your customer is not. You have at least 40 hours per week to think about it, and probably many more. Your customer does not. This might be the first time he has heard of it!

All of this means that you need to take the time to understand his perspective before you make marketing decisions.

Obsession with the Artistic Parts of the Marketing Process, to the Detriment of Other Aspects

The creative arts in all their various incarnations—film, writing, music, art—have huge power in marketing. They're great tools for making an impact on the minds of your customers, but they are not an end in themselves. Only the biggest companies with brands worth millions of dollars can afford to think about marketing as an exercise in using art to define and underline their brand concepts. The rest of the business world needs their advertising and marketing to increase their revenues and profits. The artistic parts of the marketing process must serve that goal. If the art distracts the customer from what you want her to think or it actually conflicts with the goal, it needs to stand down.

Some advertising and marketing professionals take pride in competing and winning industry awards. Some commercials that make a big splash or impress judges also achieve the goal of increasing corporate revenues and meeting corporate goals, but not always. We can't assume that achieving one results in the other. The focus on these award-winning campaigns is potentially at odds with helping the companies that pay marketing professionals.

Let me be a bit more blunt for some of you: If you want to be an artist, quit your corporate job, move to New York or L.A., and pursue your art in its purest form. That's a very noble pursuit and I respect it. If you would rather work in marketing and advertising, can you put aside being in charge of the marketing process? You already have a critical role in that process because there are people in your company with no clue how to create art or music or choose images that make the consumer feel a specific feeling. Advertising and marketing needs you. But your company also needs money, so learn about strategy and metrics and how your art affects customers in a measurable way. I find this side of the business fascinating and satisfying: quantifiable proof of how art persuades? Beautiful. It's like Spock and Kirk mind-melding.

Lack of Interest in Measuring Results and Changing Strategies and Tactics to Get Better Results

To succeed, a business needs clear, quantified goals. Every marketing campaign either helps you accomplish those business goals or doesn't. Successful campaigns tell you what to do more of. Failures tell you what to stop doing.

This is discussed in depth in the Chapter 6, "Facing the Facts: How to Continuously Get Better Results with the Five Steps of Optimization." But it's relevant to bring it up here because if the goals and interests of marketing aren't aligned with the company, the result is marketing failure that never changes. Commit to having clear goals, appropriate key metrics, and monitoring the results of your efforts in terms of those metrics.

Facebook Is the Consumer's Playground: So Play by the Rules

People are not on Facebook specifically to shop. If they're trying to solve any one major problem, it's boredom or stress. Facebook users *want* to be interrupted, and this is a huge opportunity for us. They want to see something cool. They want to catch up with exciting things their friends, family, or peers are doing. If you want to market successfully on Facebook, you need to meet Facebook users where they are psychologically.

Businesses need to fit in on Facebook. Who in the company should do this? Some business owners don't have much Facebook experience. Anyone who doesn't

Facebook much won't have a sense of what's appropriate and what's not. Younger employees might use Facebook more, but Facebook marketing is an activity with strategies and goals. The average employee in his early 20s may "understand Facebook" but be just as ineffective at marketing on Facebook as the 55-year-old who never uses it.

Here's an analogy that might help: If you've never used Microsoft Word, you'll have a tough time even writing a letter with it. But even people highly familiar with Microsoft Word can't just sit down and write a great book. You need to understand what makes good and bad writers—you need to actually write, get feedback on your writing, and then get better at writing.

Just because you've driven a car your whole life doesn't mean you can race in the Indy 500. If we put your amateur abilities behind the wheel of a 200 mph car, you're definitely not going to win the race, and you might even go up in a blaze of glory.

Facebook marketing requires familiarity with Facebook *and* specific training. There are a huge number of misconceptions about Facebook, and there are best practices that get good results. You have to take the time to learn them. Young people don't just absorb this by being on Facebook. New Facebook marketers underperform at the beginning. It takes training and experience, just like any new marketing channel.

Do Pushy Sales Messages Turn People Off?

Sales and marketing folks learn a bunch of tactics that work in other places but turn off Facebook users. Listing benefits, giving discounts, and writing explicit calls to action are all good in Google ads or embedded in TV commercials, but they can sound dissonant in a Facebook post. An ad that goes right for the sale also might seem out of place, but this has already changed as more and more advertisers try it. There's a time and a place for hard sales tactics, even on Facebook, and there are more moderate ways to get the messages across without turning people off.

Note: I'm going to come back to this later and talk about better ways to use sales messages. One of the most profitable pages I know uses two sales posts per day and three engagement-oriented posts. But I want to emphasize engagement and selling the dream at first because some people are overly focused on getting sales right away.

Facebook Is Like a Conference: How Do You Sell at a Conference?

While speaking on selling in social media at conferences, I found a pretty good analogy to explain it:

When you go to a conference, you have speakers, workshops, and panels. Attendees come to learn. And they come to network outside the presentation rooms.

Companies also attend that want to sell things to the attendees and are given a specific place to do that. We put all the vendors in a big room. We make the sales guys stand by, preferably behind their tables. We've set a boundary. We don't want them coming up to us in the hallway outside a workshop while we're socializing with other speakers or attendees and launching into their sales pitches, and we don't want them interrupting speakers with questions that mention their products. In the same way, we don't want random sales pitches from strangers interrupting our fun and relaxing social media experience.

Something else has to come before the sales pitch: the relationship. It has to start with, "Hi. How are you? Who are you? What do we have in common? Do I like you?" On Facebook, we start relationships with consumers based on a common interest and that later leads to the purchase.

Sales Is a Journey of Four Steps

Marketing is a process, if you have goals. And we need a set of steps to follow. Fortunately, there is an age-old sales and marketing process called AIDA that fits Facebook marketing perfectly.

What Is AIDA?

AIDA is an acronym that outlines the process of effective marketing, created in 1898[2]:

- **Attention**—First, you get your consumer's attention.
- **Interest**—Then, you interest her in your company and offering.
- **Desire**—Next, you increase her desire for the product.
- **Action**—Finally, you lead her to take action (buy).

"Hot Donuts Now"

One of the best examples of AIDA is Krispy Kreme.

If you've ever been to a Krispy Kreme and eaten one of their HOT DONUTS NOW right out of the oven, your brain has been permanently altered by this proto-diabetic adventure. Just those three words increase saliva production. Every time you drive by, you look (attention) to see whether the HOT DONUTS NOW light is on. If it is, you might (interest, desire) go in and buy some (take action).

---

2. http://en.wikipedia.org/wiki/AIDA_(marketing)

Krispy Kreme has a major advantage in its selling process because our bodies already desire massive amounts of sugar. The only real obstacle to the sale is your good sense in the *desire* phase. Fortunately for Krispy Kreme, America's marketing culture does a pretty good job on a daily basis of beating down our resistance to buying stupid things. Besides, how could one donut hurt? Of course, you end up buying a dozen because it's a great deal and you probably want to buy donuts for someone else so you don't feel so guilty about the five you're going to eat in the next 90 seconds.

"I'm on a Horse"

These Old Spice ads, so popular in 2010, may be forgotten in a few years. There's no question that they're popular; most people have seen at least one and almost every-one thinks they're funny. The question is, did they increase sales of Old Spice prod-ucts? Turns out that they did, to the tune of $3.5 million.[3] They made more in sales from this awareness and interest campaign than Old Spice spent on the advertising, so it's a success.

These ads attracted with sexiness, humor, and fascinating one-take filming tech-niques. Old Spice also staged a real-time social media campaign where an actor, Isaiah Mustafa, created 186 personal videos for both celebrities and regular users.

How did Old Spice create the desire that led to the purchase of more Old Spice products? We have the data to tell us whether the purchases were from men or women. Many have argued that the ad is targeted to women (macho male actor with no shirt on, the man your man could smell like), but I think if my wife bought me Old Spice because of that commercial, it would be a bit insulting. But if you're a guy, the humor of the commercial makes it easy to buy Old Spice for yourself. It's just a joke, right? The whole macho thing was a joke. So I'm actually buying the Old Spice because it's cool and funny, because I'm cool and funny. But you already knew that.

How long will the sales from this ad last? Almost all profitable ad campaigns are temporary. You can ride a horse only for so long before it expires. (No horses were harmed in the making of the previous sentence.) Brands move from idea to idea— some work and some don't. Social media also benefits from new ideas, and their effectiveness is temporary.

Social Media Selling Is So Romantic

When I speak about sales in social media, I like to joke about how it's like romance. First, I show a slide of a college kid drinking alcohol out of a red plastic cup with the caption "Imma get drunk and take you home with me." Then I say, "Social

---

3. http://www.adweek.com/news/advertising-branding/old-spice-campaign-smells-sales-success-too-107588

media sales is less like that and more like this…" and I show a slide of a guy and a girl smelling a rose together. I pretend to be the guy, "You like that? That smells good, huh? It's so nice to be here with you." I continue, addressing the audience:

> I don't know about you, but I'm married, and I can't just go asking my wife for sex all night…every day…I DO…but…the conversion rate's not so good.

Despite the fact that conversion rate is Internet marketing jargon, people seem to get it and laugh anyway. I go on:

> So I have to take her out to dinner, take her out to movies, take out the trash. There's a lot of taking out. And then—remember AIDA? Eventually…ACTION!

If we know this in real life, why don't we act this way in business? People go to work and try to use tactics that would never work in love or marriage. If you sell like a pick-up artist, you don't get long-term relationships. What works well in marriage seems to work well in social marketing and customer service.

Here are a few guidelines you can read as both marriage and business advice:

- Put yourself in her shoes.

- Give her *what she wants* (in order to get what you want).

- Listen to her and acknowledge what you hear.

How AIDA Works on Facebook

How specifically does AIDA works on Facebook? Table 7.1 demonstrates.

Table 7.1   AIDA Without and Without Facebook Fans

	Fan Marketing	Facebook Ads, Without Fans
Attention	See ad.	See ad.
Interest	Click Like.	Click on ad.
Desire	Facebook Page posting.	Browse website.
Action	Purchase.	Purchase.

In fan marketing, we create ads to show to consumers. If one of them clicks Like on the ad, we know we have his interest and we've also captured him as page fans. Then we can increase his desire for our offerings over time by posting from the Facebook page. Eventually, he goes to our website and purchases.

If you don't use fans, you still show ads and get clicks. The consumer goes to your website, and the more desire you generate, the deeper he browses the site and more likely he is to put something in his cart. Then you get him to take the action to purchase.

How to "Sell the Dream"

In Chapter 11, "Talking Till You're Blue in the Face: How to Get More Likes and Comments," I discuss methods for getting more Likes and comments on your Facebook posts so you can stay visible to your fans. Engaging posts can also have a hypnotic effect on consumers. They keep clicking that they like things you're talking about, which is a way of continuing to say yes to you. Every yes gets them closer to buying from you.

The Desire Phase Is Critical in Fan Marketing

Because we can't constantly use strong calls to action on Facebook without clashing with the social experience, what we can do is amplify our efforts in the *arousing desire* stage of AIDA. You use Facebook posts to turn your fans into raving fanatics. And you create raving fans by selling the dream.

So what is the dream and how do we sell it? To explain that, I have to start with a classic copywriting lesson: features versus benefits.

The Features Versus the Benefits

Almost everyone new to marketing makes the rookie mistake of talking about the product rather than how it's going to benefit the buyer. "The seat in this new Volvo is 26 inches wide" is not as compelling as "The new seats are roomier and more comfortable than in any comparable car on the road." The difference is that facts and details don't matter as much as the consumer's experience. Go to the five senses: taste, touch, feel, sight, and smell. You have to be a bit more poetic to have an emotional impact on the customer. There's an old saying that people buy with their emotions and justify the purchase with logic. Make sure you're having an emotional impact.

Look at the features versus benefits in Table 7.2 and ask yourself which makes you more interested in buying:

Table 7.2   Examples of Features and Benefits

Offering	Features	Benefits
iPad2	This iPad 2 has 32GB of memory.	You can store more music and photos than you would ever want and keep about 10 movies on there at a time.
Miel fan	It has a mini-turbine and a ring heater element.	You can cook faster while using less energy.
Uggs	Sheepskin is porous and thermostatic.	Uggs keep your feet dry and close to your normal body temperature regardless of whether it's hot or cold out.
Web hosting	24×7×365 customer service.	No matter when you have a problem, we're right there to help you solve it.
SalesForce CRM	Cloud-based interface.	Your data is secure, and you can access it from any computer no matter where you go.

If you haven't written down the benefits of your offering before, you should first write down every feature you can think of and then write the corresponding benefits. After you've produced this, make sure that everyone who communicates in any form about your offerings has a copy.

The Benefits Versus the Customer's Dream

We can do even better than that and leave benefits in the dust. Let's take it to what I call the *Dream* level. Benefits are how your offering will help the customer. The dream is a vision of life or work to which she aspires. Your customers might not have thought this out specifically, but they'll recognize it when you show it to them. Read the examples in Table 7.3.

Table 7.3   Finding the Dream from the Benefits

Offering	Features	Benefits	Dream
iPhone 4	iPod and FaceTime	You can listen to your music anywhere and videophone other iPhone 4 users.	Your life is high-quality even when you travel. You can travel and still be entertained and feel close to loved ones.
Self-cleaning cat box	Self-flushing, washable litter	Clean the litter box without touching the mess, and the litter is permanent and more environmentally friendly.	Enjoy your lovable pet in a more sanitary way. Feel loved while saving the Earth.

Offering	Features	Benefits	Dream
Google AdWords advertising for small businesses	Lots of data about consumers and how they search	Reach your customers right when they're ready to buy, and improve your profits.	A profitable business that supports your lifestyle and helps you retire with a comfortable amount of money.
eHarmony dating service	29-dimension compatibility matching system	Find someone to date whom you'll actually get along with.	Find true love that lasts the rest of your life.

Keep in mind for these examples that they deal with only one or two features. There are going to be a lot more benefits and possibly other dreams. Think back to the multiple types of consumers we discussed—each type can have at least one dream different from the others.

The iPhone dream in Table 7.3 could be extended further. We're always looking for the ultimate want or need when we discover the dream we're going to sell. Here we're talking about people enjoying life and feeling close to loved ones no matter where they are. It might be part of someone's job to travel, and that leads to the end game of work, which might be a much better life later on or a better retirement. These consumers want to get the benefits of travel without suffering its traditional consequences. By the way, I believe another thing iPads, iPhones, and iPod buyers seek, and that Apple admirably delivers, is a sense that the future is at hand, that we live in exciting times and everything is new. Indeed, Apple has been shaping the future since the famous 1984 commercial in which they implied that IBM was Big Brother.

Examples of Selling the Dream

Here, drawn from my keynote speeches, are a few more examples of how you should and should not Sell the Dream.

Corona

For quite a while, Corona commercials were ridiculously simple. The sounds of waves, the backs of two people at the beach, and Corona beer bottles. Sometimes there was relationship humor. What was the message? Relaxation. Vacation. Peaceful enjoyment.

These commercials use the metaphor of a beach vacation to express what Corona does for you. And what better way could you convey what beer does? If you wanted to target the young partiers, you could do commercials the way Bud Light does—louder and funnier (think Will Ferrell in *Old School*). But if you want to convey the peaceful buzz to overworked young executives, say in their 30s, the beach is perfect.

The relaxation is the benefit. What's the dream Corona sells? First, that you could have the kind of life where you could afford a vacation like that and, second (but more implicit), that you can have a day-to-day life with little bits of relaxation, anytime you want, even without the beach.

Myrtle Beach Hotels

For a time, I worked at an agency that did the online marketing for resorts in Myrtle Beach, South Carolina. Many chose to emphasize pictures of the resorts themselves in their marketing rather than the beach. The Corona commercials made me wonder if they were missing an opportunity.

These companies try to convince people to travel down from places like Ohio and Pennsylvania for vacation. The two main attractions are the beach and the more than 100 area golf courses. After the recession hit, families were more likely to opt for the beach vacation and Dad was more likely to eschew the golf buddy trip in favor of the family beach vacation. So, in January and February, when a large percentage of summer vacations are booked and these Ohioans and Pennsylvanians are sitting in their cubicles at work while their salt-damaged cars wait in snowy parking lots, what are they dreaming about?

I think it's the beach. That's the dream they should be selling. Because most of these resorts, regardless of whether they have an indoor water park or not, are quite similar. And they compete on price as well. There are only so many competitive advantages left to seize. Social media relationship is one, and selling the dream—namely, the beach experience—is another.

Carl's Jr. and Hardee's

Carl's Jr. and Hardee's employed a cliché, much like Go Daddy does, by making commercials wherein sexy models accidentally drip burger condiments on themselves. It's arguable whether these commercials are effective, and they created some controversy that not everyone was happy about. They went even further afield to dirty sexual analogies with their Biscuit Holes commercials. Some Hardee's franchisees in particular refused to run these ads.[4] All of this is an attempt to make an impact on "young, hungry guys," as they put it.

Personally, I think they're overlooking the real dream that Carl's Jr. and Hardee's fulfill: Bacon. Bacon is the dream. You may think I'm joking, but I'm not. Bacon is powerful.

People love bacon. Audiences actually clap when I mention bacon. Well, my big news is that I'm going to Sweden next month to accept a Nobel Prize for my lifetime of work in bacon science. I discovered in my research that bacon is actually a

---

4. http://hamptonroads.com/2009/07/local-hardees-owner-will-not-air-controversial-tv-ad

fundamental element of the universe, and they're going to add it to the periodic table with the symbol Bn. It is not radioactive and is not a noble gas, but it is a noble solid. I've spoken with William Shatner because I suspected—and it turns out I was right—that *Star Trek's* Enterprise was powered not by dilithium crystals, but bacon. I mean dilithium crystals? Seriously? Bacon has 100 times the power of dilithium crystals. Okay, let's move on.

For those of you who have religious or other reasons not to eat bacon, I apologize. The point of all these ravings is that bacon is something "young, hungry guys" want, and it can actually physically arouse their desire to eat fast food (did you start salivating a little while reading about bacon?). The kind of desire Hardee's ads are currently arousing does not make you want burgers and is sowing dissension among franchisees.

12 Things People Dream About

As you can see with the dreams we've discussed, the further you go, the closer you get to a list of things that a lot of people want. These things include

- Awe
- Belonging
- Choices
- Connection
- Free Time
- Freedom

- Fun
- Love
- Luxury
- Relaxation
- Security
- Simplicity

Which of these are your customers looking for? How does your offering help them with that?

How to Figure Out Your Customer's Dream

The examples listed here suggest a process you can use to anticipate what your customers' deepest desires are. Discover that, connect it to your offering, and you've connected with them on the deepest level. That is a competitive advantage that allows you to raise prices—when you sell value and connect deeply with the customer, you can charge more than the average company, which is often forced to compete solely on price.

Of course, you do still have to deliver on those promises to keep those customers! Here's how:

1. Grab the list you made earlier of all the features and benefits of your offering.

2. Figure out what kind of ideal life or business situation these benefits lead the customer toward.

3. Determine which of the 12 things people dream about that you can help people with.

4. Find out how these dreams differ for each of your 3–5 customer types.

5. Describe in as much detail as possible what the fulfillment of these dreams looks like for people.

6. Search for as many of these words as possible in Google Images, and save the ones that best represent the fulfillment of those dreams. You will need to go back later and buy the rights to stock photos, but Google Images can be a quicker way to brainstorm it.

7. If there are image ideas that you can picture in your mind but can't find, try different search words.

This is definitely a few hours work, but don't skip it. It makes a huge difference in your relationship with fans. It gives you ad targeting ideas that bring in cheaper fans. Overall, it could be a major turning point for your company's marketing success because the lessons will apply elsewhere in your business.

How to Get Fans Thinking and Talking About the Dream

Now that you have all the information about your customers' dreams, you may know the dreams better than they do! But a key tactic for getting more comments on your Facebook posts is to ask questions, so you're going to have a huge opportunity to refine your understanding of their dreams. You can even ask them to submit pictures on various topics, further rounding out the dream for all your fans. For examples of how to write posts to specific audiences on specific dreams, see Chapter 11.

8

Putting Your Best Face Forward: Setting Up Your Facebook Page to Get More Fans and Sales

When you hear a business owner say "I'm getting a website!" most of us know what that means, more or less. But what does "I'm putting my business on Facebook" mean? Are we talking about a personal profile or timeline, a business page, a group, or something else? What does it mean to set it up right? Are there any ways to shoot yourself in the foot? What makes it look professional? What will help you get fans and increase profits? These questions are the topic of this chapter.

Pages, Groups, and Profiles: The Mad, Mad World of Facebook

Before I get into the details, let's cover some of the basics about the world of Facebook, what's in it, and how people really use it. I've trained many audiences, and the Q&A sessions have revealed that many people don't understand how Facebook works. Even people who have used it for years have misconceptions. These misunderstandings lead people to use the wrong tactics and not get the results they want. Understanding the following basics will lift you above your competition and help you get better results from Facebook.

Profile/Timeline: This is you, the person. You have a personal profile with friends, photos, and other items. When you're on your Home page, you can click on Profile in the upper-right corner and see the public view of your profile. In this book, I refer to this as a *profile* because calling it a *page* of any type (as Facebook's help screens sometimes do) gets people confused with business (fan) pages. The Timeline was announced by Mark Zuckerberg in September 2011 and will change how the profile is displayed. He calls it "the story of your life in one page."

News feed: When you log in as your profile, you first see your News Feed, which contains a list of relatively new posts. Facebook shows you posts from friends and pages you've liked. It shows a combination of Top News (the most important items, selected by the EdgeRank algorithm, explained later in this section) and all the most recent posts from all your friends and all the pages you've liked. You may also see friend activity from their apps, determined by GraphRank. Most people experience Facebook through their News Feeds and do not return to pages they've liked in the past. Figure 8.1 diagrams the typical user experience.

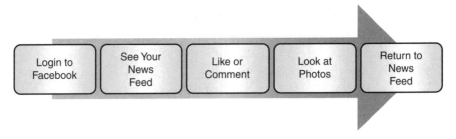

Figure 8.1   *The typical Facebook user experience.*

Ticker: The news ticker sits in the upper-right corner and shows what Facebook calls "lightweight activity." This includes virtually everything your friends and favorite pages are doing, from liking to commenting to interacting with apps.

Posts/Updates/Stories: You can post on your own Wall as yourself (as your profile). If you're an admin of a page, you can post as the page on its Wall. These posts show on your profile or page's Wall:

- Posts are seen by some friends and page fans in their News Feeds, usually according to EdgeRank.

- When a fan posts on a page's Wall, other fans do not receive those posts in their News Feeds.

- When a fan comments on a page's post, though, other fans will see those comments if they receive that page post in their News Feeds.

Figure 8.2 shows how posts go to Walls and News Feeds.

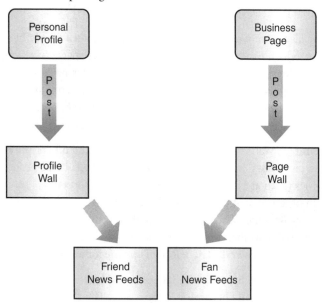

Figure 8.2   *How posts go to Walls and News Feeds.*

Status Update: A status update is a post containing only text.

Top Stories: These are posts Facebook shows you in your News Feed according to EdgeRank. Facebook believes these are the things you'll be most interested in seeing. They are denoted visually by a blue triangle in the upper-left corner.

EdgeRank: Facebook uses the EdgeRank algorithm to determine what Top Stories each person sees in her News Feed. Everyone's Facebook experience is unique and personalized. Facebook shows you posts from friends and pages whose posts you have liked or commented on in the recent past. New friends and newly liked pages are shown to you for a while, but if you don't interact with them, you will stop seeing posts from them. Most page posts reach less than 30% of the page's fans (but I will teach you how to improve that). EdgeRank also takes into account whether you interact more or less with Photos, Status Updates, and Videos. If you interact with videos from the Celtics and status updates from Kobe Bryant, you will see more Celtics videos than Celtics status updates and more Kobe status updates than Kobe videos.

GraphRank: GraphRank is a new algorithm (as of September 2011) that uses EdgeRank as well as friend lists and family lists to determine what activity a person should see. The biggest difference between GraphRank and EdgeRank is that it's used for activity from apps and your groups of friends and family may not see the same things from you. For example, if you have a list of professional contacts and they as a group like what you post from allfacebook.com, they are more likely to see those posts in their News Feeds than your family is.

Page: Also called a *fan page* or *business page*, this is a page for your business, place, institution, product, band, community, and so on. These pages have *fans*, not friends. There are six main kinds of pages and dozens of subcategories. Pages have a Wall and info and can have welcome tabs, a custom URL, photos, videos, links, discussions, and events. But data shows that fans rarely go back to the actual page after they've liked it. Pages mainly reach fans through posts.

Wall/Timeline: A Wall is a combination of your posts and others' posts. When you post in your own News Feed, you're posting on your Wall. These posts and your other activities (such as liking pages or commenting on posts) will show on your profile when others look at it. Pages also have Walls—these can be set by an administrator to show only the page's posts or also posts from fans. This will, in the future, be referred to as the Timeline for personal profiles. At this time, a Facebook page still primarily has a Wall. There is no Timeline for a Page.

Connections: Facebook has been changing the emphasis of its language to connections. Originally, you could become a fan of a page. Then Facebook shifted to likes. Now the Facebook advertising platform is using the term *connections* to refer to likes. This is a broader term because your profile friends are connections and your page fans are considered connections.

Likes: When you view a personal profile, you can find a person's likes under his Info tab. He might have typed that information into his profile (which means it can be targeted by Facebook ads), or his likes will be pages the user has clicked Like on. Likes have been the only "verb" on Facebook for a long time, but this is changing and Facebook is now allowing social apps to create new verbs. You will soon be able to *read* a book, *watch* a movie, or *listen* to music.

Like Box: Facebook makes it easy for you to add a Like Box to your website or blog that shows how many fans your page has (see Figure 8.3). It's very customizable:

You can show recent posts, show faces of fans, and specify exactly how tall and wide you want it to be. When fans see the Like Box on your website, they can easily click Like and become a fan without even visiting the page.

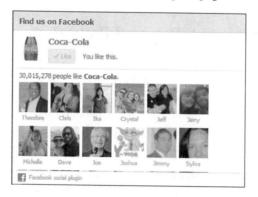

Figure 8.3 *A Like Box for Coca-Cola's Facebook page.*

Tabs: Pages and profiles have tabs, which are navigational menu items on the left side under the profile's or page's photo. Pages can be enhanced with custom welcome (or *landing*) tabs, tabs for contests, and tabs for any other special information you want to show fans. Ads can send people directly to specific page tabs.

Fan gate (Reveal tab): Your page can be set to show a welcome tab to non-fans. Otherwise, fans go to the page's Wall. What makes this tab a gate is that non-fans see one thing (like a message that says why you should like the page), and fans see another (like a thank-you, video, or discount you can see only after clicking Like).

Fans: Anyone who likes a page is considered a fan. Although Facebook replaced the Become a Fan button with the Like button, no one is eager to call their fans "likers," and marketers still call it "fan page marketing," not "like marketing." Similarly, I doubt people are going to start calling fan pages "connection pages." It's good to know both Facebook's technical terms and the preferred words of Facebook users.

Shares: You can share (repost) any post with your friends, adding your own comment to the post itself. The share goes out to friends according to EdgeRank and shows on your profile.

Facebook Groups: These have *members* and are highly engaging but very simple. Much of the functionality available on pages does not exist in Groups. But they are the ideal place for small groups of people to discuss shared interests.

Other Facebook Opportunities

Facebook also empowers you to create events, apps, questions, polls, and many other items on Facebook. This book describes a proven revenue-generating business system that focuses almost exclusively on ads and pages. Using the Pareto Principle (focusing on the 20% of activities that get you 80% of your results) means that I'm not covering these other opportunities too deeply in my system or in this book.

Can You Market with a Personal Profile?

It's critical to understand that Facebook's Terms of Service forbid you to market with a personal profile or timeline. Your personal profile can be disabled for unsolicited contact with others for promoting or advertising purposes. Not everyone gets caught at this, but understand that if you break this rule, you're taking a risk and your profile could be disabled at any time.

Do many people violate this policy? Yes. Do they all get disabled? No. But recognize that doing so is a risk and your profile could be disabled at anytime. This is why we recommend using Pages and Groups, not personal profiles.

What's Better, Pages or Groups?

Most companies start with a page because it allows them to use more of their standard branding devices, such as a larger logo space. Pages have other significant advantages, too, as shown in Table 8.1. However, Groups also can play a supplementary role for most businesses.

Table 8.1   A Comparison of the Features of Facebook Pages and Groups

	Pages	Groups
Targeting posts by language and location	Yes	No
Membership restrictions	No	Yes
User insights	Yes	No
Engagement insights	Yes	No
Like Box for websites	Yes	No
Vanity URL	Yes	No
Like button on ads	Yes	No
Main image size	200 × 600 pixels	50 × 50 pixels
Content privacy	No	Can be
Email notification	No	Yes
Red alert notifications	No	Yes
Pop-up notifications	No	Yes

Pages have these advantages:

- You get a much bigger logo image space.

- You can target your posts by location and/or language.

- You can see details on your fans' demographics and location.

- You can see details on how fans engage with your posts.

- Fans can be a lot cheaper than Group members, email subscribers, and so on.

- A page has bigger word-of-mouth potential.

- A page has detailed analytics and insights (see Figure 8.4).

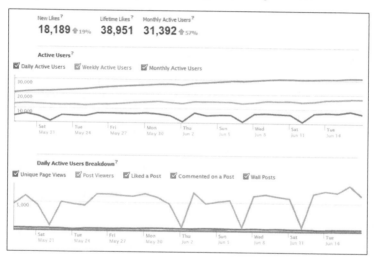

Figure 8.4 *A sample of some of the insights you get only with a Facebook page.*

Groups have these advantages:

- They can be exclusive. You must approve all join requests, even if you used an ad to send people to the Group.

- You can make the Group:

  - **Public**—Outsiders can see who is in it and what they post.

  - **Closed**—Outsiders can see who's in it but not what they've posted.

  - **Private**—Nothing is public; outsiders can't see who is in it and cannot find it in searches.

- Members are extensively notified whenever any member posts or comments. This radically increases the percentage of members who return to the Group to participate. Groups are best for the most enthusiastic segment of your page fans.

Understanding Admins for Pages and Groups

Every page and Group must have at least one personal profile who is the administrator (admin) of that page. The creator becomes the first admin. If you have someone else create it for you, make sure she adds you as an admin, too. It's a good idea to have a few backup admins, but remember that any admin can add anyone else she wants as another admin and can remove anyone else, too.

A Warning About Employees as Admins

Only employees you trust should be admins. If you have to fire an employee who is an admin, remove him as soon as possible. Firing is always an emotional time, and there's a chance he might do something retaliatory. He could remove all the admins but himself and have complete control over the page or Group. You could contact Facebook about this, but there's no guarantee they would get back to you to solve the problem. Facebook is improving their customer service, but for the most part, they're unreliable.

Page Admins

When you're a page admin, if you post on that page's Wall, the post is shown as coming from the page itself, not as from you. When an admin posts as the page, that post goes out to the News Feed of some fans but not all; who sees it is determined by EdgeRank, which is explained in depth Chapter 11, "Talking Till You're Blue In The Face: How to Get More Likes and Comments." If a non-admin fan posts on the page's Wall, that post does *not* go out to other fans' News Feeds.

Group Admins

If you post in a Group, it shows as you posting it, regardless of whether you're an admin of that Group or not.

How Do Pages and Groups Work Together?

Many companies will eventually use both Pages and Groups on Facebook. But it makes sense to start with the Page and later create some Groups. In fact, if you own a franchise, you may be organizing dozens or hundreds of pages before you consider doing something with Groups.

The priorities I recommend for companies are as follows:

1. Create a page.

2. Use Facebook ads targeted to get qualified prospects and existing customers to become fans.

3. Post to the page in a way that gets likes and comments.

4. Sell "The Dream" to increase desire for your offerings 80% of the time.

5. Post prudent calls to action 20% of the time. This is how you get fans to go to your website, read your blog, buy products, and so on.

6. Create a Group for your most fanatical segments.

Chapter 10, "FaceHook: Capturing Qualified Prospects as Fans and Group Members," talks a lot about ad click-through rate (CTR). You can take the CTR as a measurement of passion. The ads that have the highest CTRs are likely targeted to your most passionate segments. This tells you what you might want to create groups for. You can also discover Group ideas by observing which posts have the highest feedback rates. The topic of these high feedback rate posts might be good focuses for Groups.

For example, if you've been building a boxing page and find from your ads that the Manny Pacquiao interest gets a high CTR and page posts confirm that his fans are particular passionate, you can create a special group called Manny Pacquiao Fans or Manny Pacquiao Is The Best Boxer Ever.

If you're building a business-to-business (B2B) page for Internet marketers and find that your email marketing–related ads have the highest CTR, then create a Group for these folks called I Love Email Marketing. You can also announce a new group on your page to get members without paying more for ads.

Why Are Facebook Groups So Powerful?

Facebook Groups are very powerful but not widely used. Here's what you can do with Groups:

- Concentrate your most fanatic customers in one place.

- Bring influencers into a place where they'll hear about you frequently.

- Solidify your customers' emotional connection with your brand.

- Allow members to add their friends as Group members.

- Get feedback and new ideas in a private space.

- Create a secret Group for people who don't want to publicly discuss the problems your company fixes—for example, plastic surgery, addiction, weight issues, or debt.

Here are some warnings to keep in mind about Groups:

- Tell your Group members to turn off email notifications because otherwise they might get annoyed by the volume of emails and just leave.

- Some Group members will leave because they'll find the conversation too intense, but this only improves the quality of your Group because only the most enthusiastic remain.

- You can add any friend to your group without asking her first; she will immediately be a full group member and start getting notifications. You could end up with some annoyed friends, though. It's better to send someone a private message with a link to the Group and let her request to join.

Critical Mistakes to Avoid in Page Setup

When you create a page, you have to choose the page name. And when you create ads to get page fans, the page name automatically becomes the ad's headline. The only way to choose your ad headline is to send people to a URL instead of the page; however, you lose the Like button and your cost per fan goes up dramatically. I discuss this more in Chapter 10, " FaceHook: Capturing Qualified Prospects as Fans and Group Members."

Facebook doesn't allow you to change a page's name later, so let's look at the kinds of situations where a bad page name can block your efforts. Most people use their business name. This works in most cases, but sometimes it's a problem. And sometimes it keeps you from a more powerful Facebook-oriented choice.

If your business's focus is on healing a disease and you name the page after the disease, you might find fewer people liking your page. For example, you might create a page called Diabetes Is a Killer. People would love to like the cure, but they don't want to like the disease. If there's any confusion in their minds about what they're liking or if they should like it, your success rate will drop. You could solve this with a name like Cures for Diabetes or Better Solutions for Diabetes Patients.

Another thing to keep in mind when choosing page names is that your fans may prefer different words than you do. Stay away from jargon unless you're trying only to attract experts. You can use Google AdWords or other search keyword databases to explore the most used words before settling on one. You can also enter various interest-target words into the Facebook ad interface to see their reach (how many people like them).

After reading Chapter 7, "Selling the Dream: Going Beyond Benefits to Arouse Your Fans' Desire for What You Offer," you should understand that people first care about their interest and then about how you can help them go further with that interest. You have the opportunity to create a page named after an interest rather than your business. Or you can create a hybrid of the two. For example, you might have a kayaking business in New Mexico called J. R. Donnelly & Sons. Rather than calling your page J. R. Donnelly & Sons, you might call it New Mexico Kayaking Adventures, which better emphasizes what you deliver to your customers.

Before you name your page, spend some time reading Chapter 7; Chapter 9, "The Face of Advertising: How to Capitalize on the Most Powerful Marketing Tool"; and Chapter 10, "FaceHook: Capturing Qualified Prospects as Fans and Group Members."

What to Put in Your Page's Main Picture

You get to create an image for your brand Facebook page that's up to 200 pixels wide and 600 pixels high. The most obvious thing to use is your logo. Usually, these won't take up the entire height you have available, so some brands get creative with these. Consider doing one of the following:

- **Feature a fan of the week**—You can post weekly, telling people to submit images along with why they're your brand's biggest fan, and if they win, feature their image at the bottom of your page image for the week. For examples, see:

    - http://www.facebook.com/DunkinDonuts

    - http://www.facebook.com/vetdepot

    - http://www.facebook.com/nationalguard

- **Utilize an extended image that uses the five images across the top**— You'll need an image that's 830 pixels wide and that is positioned so that the things you want seen will show up in the main image and the other five. For example, you could use someone's arm stretching off to the side.

How to Get a Vanity URL

When you first get a page, it has a really ugly web address (URL) with a big long number at the end. When you get 25 fans, Facebook lets you have a better-looking URL. Just go to http://www.facebook.com/*username*/.

Are Custom Tabs Overhyped?

One of the first questions most people new to Facebook have is how can they spiff up their Facebook page. Many people are used to making creative decisions about websites and are not accustomed to the standardized look of Facebook—they want to make their Facebook page look original and branded. You can do this to a degree with custom tabs and welcome or "landing" tabs. It's definitely a best practice to create a welcome tab, and you can brand them, put videos on them, and make them look great, but there are some serious limitations to their impact, which I will explain next.

Most People Never See Your Welcome Tab

As I discussed in detail earlier in this chapter, most people never see most Facebook pages' custom tabs. Yet many companies want to create exciting, branded tabs. A number of third-party services out there will help you create custom tabs, so it's in their interests to promote doing so. But even they will admit (I've talked to several of them) that most people usually only see your posts and that if fans do come to your page, they see the Wall, which can't be customized. The main thing you can customize about the Wall is whether by default it shows only your page's posts or if it also shows fans who post on the Wall. See the Default Landing Tab option in Figure 8.5. You get to these by going to your page, clicking Edit Page, and then selecting the Manage Permissions option.

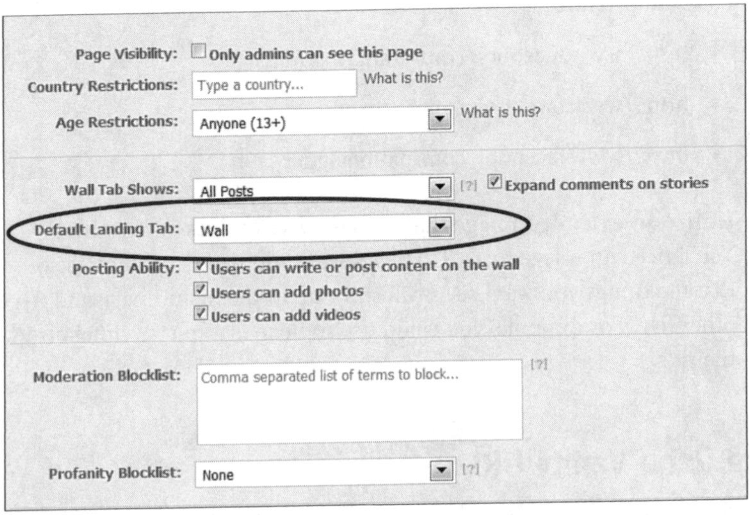

Figure 8.5 *Manage Permissions options for Facebook pages.*

After you've created custom tabs, you can select one from the Default Landing Tab option. This makes that tab the welcome or landing tab for non-fans.

Why Most People Will Never See Your Tabs

The only people who will see your custom welcome tab are those who have not yet liked your page. If a large percentage of the traffic on your Facebook page is from your website, then at least some people will see your beautiful welcome tab. But the fans you get from people clicking Like on your fan-growing ads (see Chapter 10) and the fans who click Like on a Like Box you place on your website will not see your welcome tab when they come to the page. They see your Wall. To see your welcome tab, a fan would have to click in the lefthand navigation for that tab specifically.

Figure 8.6 shows usage data from a page with a welcome tab. Look at how many go to the Wall versus the welcome tab. Almost 30 times as many people go to the Wall.

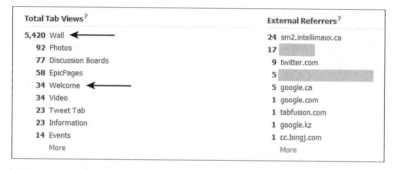

Total Tab Views[?]		External Referrers[?]	
5,420	Wall ←	24	sm2.intellimaxx.ca
92	Photos	17	
77	Discussion Boards	9	twitter.com
58	EpicPages	5	
34	Welcome ←	5	google.ca
34	Video	1	google.com
23	Tweet Tab	1	tabfusion.com
23	Information	1	google.kz
14	Events	1	cc.bingj.com
	More		More

Figure 8.6   *Page insights example of Wall versus welcome tab views.*

Chapter 11 discusses how posting is the best way to communicate with your fans. Just keep in mind that if you want a lot of your fans to see a tab, you'll have to put the link to that tab in one of your Facebook posts—and only a small percentage of those who see that post will click over to the tab.

This is not an argument against using welcome tabs. For some companies, they may be how most people like your page. But if you follow the system I outline in this book and get likes from ads, most of those people won't see your welcome tab. A welcome tab is the closest thing to a customizable front cover for your Facebook page, and because they're not that hard to create, it's worth covering your bases and creating one.

Easiest Ways to Create Welcome Tabs

The best welcome tabs are called *reveal tabs* or *fan gates*. What that means is that if you aren't a fan, you see one thing, usually a message about why you should like it (perhaps you'll get to see a video or download a whitepaper). After you become a fan, you see something different. This second view is usually a thank you, or it might be the thing you were told you had to click Like in order to see.

You can create free fan-gate welcome tabs with the following services:

- **WildFire iFrame App**—Just go to http://iframes.wildfireapp.com/, install the app, go to your page's new welcome tab, and follow the step-by-step instructions.

- **Lujure Assembly Line**—Go to http://lujure.com/tour/fangating/, sign up, log in, and create a tab. Then you're going to create the post-like version that fans see. Click on Advanced options to add the pre-like "non-fan image."

- **Fan Page Engine**—http://fanpageengine.com/

A fan gate is created from two images. For both services, you'll need a before image (pre-like) and an after image (post-like). Both of these images should be 520 pixels wide. The height is up to you, but only about the first 500 pixels will be visible before the user has to scroll down.

Here are a couple of examples of pre-like images (see Figures 8.7 and 8.8). Let's use these to talk about what goes into the pre-like portion of a fan gate.

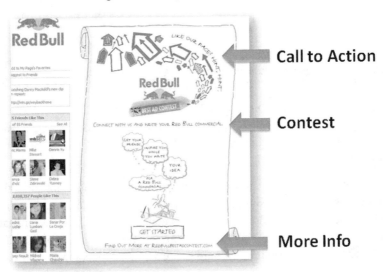

Figure 8.7   *Red Bull's welcome tab.*

Branding

Naturally, your creative folks will want to take this opportunity to represent your brand. You can see in Figures 8.7 and 8.8 that Red Bull and Backcountry.com are continuing their normal graphic identities on their welcome tabs.

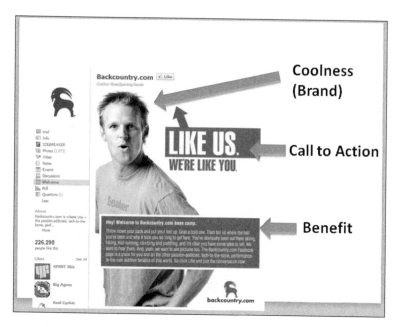

Figure 8.8 *Backcountry.com's welcome tab.*

Call to Action

The main call to action on a welcome tab is Like This Page! And of course you can phrase that however you want. Some people create an arrow that points to the Like button.

Benefits of Liking

Why should people like your page? For one thing, they'll have access to your Wall and be able to discuss things. Step back for a minute and think about the benefits they'll derive from those discussions. What's the benefit of getting news from you? What's the dream you're selling here and helping them achieve? Talk about those benefits on the pre-like page.

And do you give people something cool in the post-like view? A special video? A discount?

Other Great Uses of Custom Tabs

You can always send people to your website or blog by posting a link. And you can just as easily post a link to your tabs. What tabs might you create to send people to?

Product Info

Create a tab that features pictures, benefits, or even video of a product. Or feature several products on one tab. Put links to the products, or even put "in my cart" links that automatically put the product in a shopping cart on your website.

F-Commerce Store

Take that one step further, and use a third-party service to sell your products directly on Facebook. Fans don't even have to go to your website to complete a purchase. There are a bunch of services that help you do this:

- VendorShop: http://www.facebook.com/Vendorshop
- iFanStore: http://www.milyoni.com/products/ifanstore.php
- Payvment: http://www.payvment.com/
- ECWID: http://www.ecwid.com/
- Moluko: http://moluko.com/

Lead Generation

Chapter 4, "FaceBucks: Five Ways Businesses Achieve Profits with Facebook," discussed five revenue generation strategies, and one of them includes getting emails for email marketing. If you're a B2B marketer, this is for you. You can always send people from Facebook ads or posts to an email submission webpage, but you could alternatively set that up in a custom Facebook page tab. It's worth testing because sometimes the advertising cost per click is lower when you send traffic to a URL inside of Facebook.

Videos

You can always put a video on some of the other types of tabs discussed in this section, or you can create a tab that features multiple videos. Lujure has a template that makes it easy to put four YouTube videos into one tab.

Contests

I'm not a huge fan of contests, especially for growing fan bases, but for other business goals, they can spark participation. If you do hold a contest, you'll need somewhere to explain all the details. Speaking of Lujure templates, there's one that lets you add a video and then an email capture below that. That's a simple way to explain the contests and get entries. And when it comes to promotions on Facebook, Wildfire is the platform of choice (http://www.wildfireapp.com/). Wildfire's service starts at $5 per campaign plus $0.99 per day.

9

The Face of Advertising: How to Capitalize on the Most Powerful Marketing Tool

Facebook advertising is the most powerful marketing opportunity online—a bold statement, but I'm going to back it up. Because Facebook advertising is so much cheaper than Google AdWords, and because its targeting has many advantages over AdWords, companies that leverage it now are capitalizing on a significant advantage over their competitors. The most aggressive businesses and those that tend to lead in their industry will find the kind of edge they like in Facebook advertising.

Why Facebook Advertising Is Critically Important

Facebook advertising is from 2 to 10 times cheaper than Google AdWords, depending on your niche. It's also much less time-intensive than either Google AdWords or Facebook marketing methods that depend on manual social network activities.

What I mean by *manual activities* is this: A lot of companies just plunk some 20-something down who "knows about that Facebook stuff" and tells him to make something happen.

YOUNG PERSON: Is there a budget?

SUPERVISOR: No, we just want to see what you can do with this. It's a great opportunity!

YOUNG PERSON: Can I run ads?

SUPERVISOR: Ha ha ha, no. Just go talk to people. You, know, network! It's called social *networking*, right? Go out there and network!

YOUNG PERSON: Um, ok…

SUPERVISOR: Great! Really looking forward to what you can do with this!

YOUNG PERSON: But my friends mostly play Xbox. Don't we sell Xerox machines?

(SUPERVISOR has already left the room.)

Most of these budgetless wonder types of campaigns are doomed to failure. The social media employee can't expand his network of the right potential customers quickly. The CFO doesn't see any return on investment (ROI). Many marketing initiatives are run as tests and if revenue doesn't come back from them immediately, they don't allocate more budget.

Many of the social media workers with no budget rack their brains trying to come up with some big clever idea that's going to miraculously "go viral" and make their company famous. Big ideas are hard to come by, and most viral initiatives fail—some actually fail spectacularly and cause negative publicity for the brand.[1]

We know that less investment of time and money can mean greater profits. The biggest objection to Facebook marketing is the assumption that social users are not looking to buy. It is true that they may not be ready to buy at that moment, but many businesses, especially those that use Facebook advertising to gather their ideal customers, have seen conversion rates from Facebook traffic on par with or greater than traffic from search engines. Let me say that again.

---

1. http://www.allfacebook.com/9-secrets-to-successful-facebook-viral-marketing-2011-07

Facebook conversion rates can be on par with or greater than those from search marketing.[2] The fact is that social users are the same users who search engine marketers reach; they are just at a different point in the sales cycle. Meeting them earlier than search marketers has its advantages, and I explain those here.

Comparing Google Search Marketing with Facebook Marketing

The main differences between search marketing and Facebook marketing are

- How and who you can target
- How close people are to buying right now
- The cost of access to be able to market to potential customers over and over again

How Ready Are They to Buy Now?

Google marketing gets you the low-hanging fruit of the sales cycle. Let's say you sell shoes online. If a woman is looking to buy high-fashion shoes, by the time she decides to search "buy Prada shoes" on Google, she's already gone most of the way through the sales cycle. At this point she's just deciding on from whom to buy them. Every business that relies on this kind of marketing is stuck fighting over price in a very competitive niche, and only one or two companies can survive that kind of fight. From this perspective, having the consumer's permission to keep contacting her earlier in the sales cycle can remove you somewhat from that deadly battle.

If you start a fan page for Prada shoes and target women who like Prada shoes, you have the opportunity to build a relationship with that consumer. If you do a good job, she'll stick with you and spend more with you than with your competitors. Or you could go more global and create a fashion footwear fan page, targeting women who like all sorts of expensive shoes. Then you've grabbed a larger market and even if that customer changes her mind about the brand, you still have a good chance to sell the prospect something.

Cost of Permission Marketing

Chapter 10, "FaceHook: Capturing Qualified Prospects as Fans and Group Members," I explain the value of having permission-based customer emails or fan bases. One of the things that makes Facebook advertising so powerful is that it's attached to fan pages. It's simpler, easier, and cheaper to use Facebook ads to get

---

2. http://www.allfacebook.com/how-dish-network-got-a-1200-roi-on-facebook-2011-09

fans than to use AdWords to get people to your website to opt in to your list on a third-party email service—fewer steps is good.

It's possible to get attention from potential customers with Google AdWords ads or Facebook ads and then try to get those people to give you their emails or become fans. Let's look at your options for these two methods and what the likely costs are (see Table 9.1).

Table 9.1   Comparison of Costs for Acquiring Emails and Fans

	AdWords -> Email	AdWords -> Fan	Facebook -> Email	Facebook -> Fan
Average CPC	$2.50	$2.50	$0.50	$0.50
Average CR	20%	50%	20%	75%
Cost Per	$12.50	$5.00	$2.50	$0.66

These numbers are averages from my experience running campaigns for clients and from students of my FanReach course. Your business might have different numbers. I encourage you to do the math for your business. All you have to do is, for each channel, divide your average cost per click by your average conversion rate.

Amazingly, email acquisition through Google is from 8 to 20 times more expensive than fan acquisition through Facebook. This is because AdWords is more expensive than Facebook ads and people are more likely to click Like than give you their email.

Add to this the facts that

- You can be seen by a fan every day, but you couldn't email your subscribers daily without a lot of them unsubscribing.

- You can get 80% or more of fans to see your posts while only 20%–30% will open your emails.

The winner here is obvious, but old habits die hard. Email and Google have worked for so many businesses for so long, and so many consultants have a vested interest in selling them, that the shift cannot be instantaneous.

Facebook Ads for Different-Sized Businesses

Businesses of any size and fan count can use ads to increase their ROI. Done well, ads increase the percentage of good prospects coming to your fan page or website. As we aggregate more data about pages across Facebook, we're finding out that the biggest pages don't get as high a proportion of fans to interact with them. This is for several main reasons:

- Few fans ever return to fan pages after liking them.

- Only fans who like and comment will see that page's posts in their News Feeds.

- These big pages aren't writing posts designed to get likes and comments.

- They might not have gotten much interaction in the past, and so Facebook has completely stopped showing their posts to more than 95% of their fans.

Getting new fans based on new ads may bring in a more enthusiastic segment, if you use the techniques I teach in this book. And new fans are more likely to see your posts, no matter what, for awhile. While older fans might be gone for good, you have a grace period to write engaging posts and keep these fans interacting and seeing your posts for the long-term.

Mistakes and Misconceptions

My own experience learning to do Facebook advertising for my clients plus teaching others in the FanReach course and watching them learn has shown me that most people make many of the same mistakes when they're new to Facebook advertising. Over the next few sections, I cover these:

- Aren't demographics outdated?

- I already know how to do display ads!

- How do I target people by their interests?

"Aren't Demographics an Outdated Approach?"

If your main experience in online marketing is from search marketing (SEO and AdWords), you haven't been able to use demographics, so you might think it's antiquated. I did. When I worked mainly on search marketing in an agency and I overheard the media buyers discussing demographics, I thought, "How quaint! They can't know their customer any better than that? *We* know exactly what the consumer is searching for!"

They didn't know the why, how, or when the customer would go searching for what they offered. It turns out, however, as you run more and more Facebook ads, not only does using demographics sometimes work better than other interest targeting, but it's also an asset to be able to make your ads target a more specific audience. I had an ad related to actress Olivia Wilder targeted to men, but the responder report told me she was most popular with men ages 35–44. When I created a more refined version of this ad with those age targets, my cost per click (CPC) went down 28%.

"I Already Know How to Do Display Advertising"

You might have run display ads for years, but you might not have had demographic targeting and you certainly didn't have interest targeting, so you won't be able to use the same approach here. Also, in some display advertising situations, you work through an account executive, not a self-serve ad creation interface like Facebook or AdWords. So, you can only create a few ads and don't have the ability to test the performance of each. That plus the fact that all Facebook ads perform worse over time means you'll be creating a lot more ads and more frequently than you're used to.

Getting into the Interest Mindset

Everyone has trouble initially with trying to think about what interests their potential customer has. If you're a search marketer, it's so different from keywords—instead of what people want, it's who they are or what they like. You have to start thinking about consumers as real people, not just one of thousands who suddenly wants something specific. You're marketing a product or service, but you have to start with the interests consumers have that lead them to want your offering later.

Some people realize things like, "Oh wow, no one is going to put into their profile that they like cancer (or diabetes or depression)." Facebook is about what people like, not what they dislike, so you have to look for the positive side of every issue.

When I was learning to target ads to interests, I felt like I was learning to think sideways. It was a completely different way of thinking, and it took me several months to get comfortable with it.

How to Do Facebook Advertising

When you first start any advertising campaign, consider it a fact-finding mission. You're a scientist and it's time to go into your advertising lab, run a bunch of tests, and find out what works and what doesn't. Keep an open mind because you're likely to learn a lot about your niche, your prospects, and Facebook.

Here's the overall process:

1. Analyze.

2. Target.

3. Create.

4. Optimize.

I describe each of these steps in detail over the rest of this chapter.

1. Analyze Your Business and Customers

First understand your brand and your customers. It's easy, but not helpful, to assume you know everything there is to know about them. Assume you may have missed something about who your best prospects are. Start with doubt and do some exploring. If you were right in the first place, you won't find anything.

You can only improve your results by doing this, so if you run ads and the click-through rate response to your messages is below 0.05%, you probably haven't really figured out exactly whom you're targeting.

Who's Your Ideal Customer?

Even if you skip fan marketing and use ads just to get traffic, you still need to know whom to target. Sending the wrong people to your website reduces your results, increases your costs, and lowers your profits.

Suppose you were marketing for the singer Michael Bolton (I know you probably aren't, but bear with me), and you targeted potential fans who say they like AC/DC in their Facebook profiles. This wouldn't help Michael Bolton very much. In fact, the AC/DC fans would probably make fun of him, which would be bad for his brand. But beyond people who already say they like Michael Bolton (the most obvious target), women above the age of 50 who like music or, more specifically, adult contemporary music, might also be his ideal listeners. But how do you find this out for your company? If you've been in business for a while, you know your industry or niche and you might have some idea what kind of people your best customers are. I would say you should know this, but a surprising number of successful business owners can't tell me more than a few words about their ideal customer. Others know things about their customers, but not things they can use for targeting the ad. A lot of people struggle with this step.

Here's how to round out your understanding of your prospect:

- Have you met, talked to, or emailed with your best customers? Write down some of their names so that you're thinking about real, three-dimensional, flesh-and-blood people.

- Who's the decision maker?

- Can you reach out to more of these people and spend some time getting to know them?

- Can you find any of them on Facebook and check out their profiles? This is easiest if you already have connected with some good customers via a fan page or your profile.

- What books, movies, sports, and hobbies do they like?

- What things are similar to your offering that they also might like?

- Do many of them have the same large companies as employers?

- Are they in a specific level of school currently, or do they have a specific level of education?

- What's their marital or dating status?

- What's their age and gender?

Finding Demographic Data for Your Business

Here are several free online sources that can help you narrow down your demographics.

Clues.Yahoo.com is keyword-based. You type in a keyword related to your niche, and then it gives you back age, gender, income, and location. If you don't get results for your search, try searching for something more general.

Alexa.com gives information about the users of popular websites. Choose one of the biggest websites in your niche and get details for it. Click the Audience tab, and you'll see age, gender, education, children, browsing location (home/work/school), and visitors by country. You can get advanced demographics if you install the Alexa toolbar. This is a great example of using an incentive to get a web user to do something or opt in, which I discuss in later chapter.

Quantcast.com provides a way for sites to install code that tracks demographic data more accurately. You may want to take part in this, or you can use it to search for industry websites. But keep in mind that the data may be estimated. You can get gender, age, ethnicity, children, income, education, and website loyalty (return visits) as well as some affinity info such as movies, books, and consumer electronics.

Compete.com is another option, but its demographic data requires a paid subscription. Consider this if you don't find the data from the other three websites satisfying for your niche.

2. Target Your Audiences

After you've analyzed your target customer, you're ready to try to find (target) that person with Facebook ads. We'll talk about what kinds of targeting are available and then you might need to translate your understanding of your customer into the available targeting options.

When I talk about a *target*, I'm referring to the combination of options you use to target your potential customer. For example, you might target 25–44 year old women who like rollerblading. That's a target, and the people you've targeted are the *audience*. If they're basically the same people you've understood as your target customer, you're on the right track.

Here's how we'll do that, for each combination of ad targeting options:

- Use the Facebook ad platform to find the estimated reach (the size of the audience that target reaches).

- Look at each *precise interest* you've thought up as well as the additional interests Facebook suggests. You can also test the topics that begin with # signs but thus far I've found the click-through rate is lower and costs are higher when you use these.

- Modify age ranges and genders to discover more about the demographics for each interest. By watching the estimated reach while modifying demographics, you can find out the ages, genders, and other things about the majority of people in an interest.

Targeting Prospects with Facebook (Versus Google)

Much of what follows about brainstorming about your ideal prospects is dictated by how you can target Facebook users with the Facebook advertising platform.

In my opinion, the Facebook ad platform is one of the most powerful marketing opportunities in history. Let's take a look at how you can target with it and compare that to other channels (see Table 9.2).

Table 9.2   Comparison of Google Versus Facebook Advertising Targeting

	Facebook	Google
Precise Interests (likes)	Yes	No
Intent (searches)	No	Yes
Location	Yes	Yes
Age and gender	Yes	No
Marital status	Yes	No
Workplace	Yes	No
Education	Yes	No

Demographics targeting is available in Google's Display Network (privately held websites that have opted to show Google ads), but my experience and that of many others is that the best profits are in the Search Network (the normal Google search results pages), where demographic targeting is not available.

With Google ads and SEO, you can attract attention based on what people are looking to buy right now. Google's biggest marketing ROI advantage is your ability to meet a buyer right when he is looking to buy. Facebook has been experimenting with showing ads next to discussions about interests, which brings it closer to reach people at the point of need, but these are not yet widely available.

With Facebook marketing, you're communicating to the kind of people who generally would and will eventually buy what you offer. Google has great ROI but on a limited volume of searches. Because not everybody is actively seeking to buy at any one time, you can't affordably reach all your prospects with Google.

With Facebook ads, you can reach and—more importantly—capture the much larger world of prospects (as fans) for your offerings. The advantage here is that you can create a relationship with, affection for, and loyalty to your brand before the prospect has even compared you to your competitors.

What Is Interest Targeting?

The newest and most unique aspect of Facebook's targeting abilities is centered around likes. Traditionally, we call this *psychographics*. In other words, we're looking at what people are passionate about. This is one of the most exciting aspects of Facebook marketing, not only because it brings new and powerful tactics to marketers, but also because we can actually measure people's passion with metrics like the ad click-through rate.

For example, when we subdivide aspects of a pet supply website, we start looking at cat and dog breeds, and the ads we run reveal that people are much more apt to confirm their love for their Rottweiler than they are for their Golden Retriever. Insights like this are often surprising and inexplicable, but we can use that knowledge to make decisions that increase ROI.

Also, because cost per click and cost per fan (CPF) acquisition drop with higher click-through rates, finding the things people are most passionate about reduces our ad costs, which increases ROI—assuming these passionate people buy. See the Venn diagram in Figure 9.1.

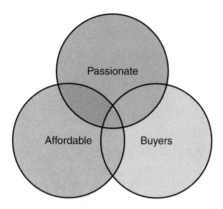

Figure 9.1   *Traits of the best Facebook customers.*

This diagram illustrates the three characteristics of the best audiences you can target with Facebook advertising:

- **Passionate** (high click-through rate), meaning you'll get fans and traffic that are...

- **Affordable**, which increases your ROI assuming that they are...

- **Buyers**, who have a good conversion rate and will buy offerings that produce profits for you.

Facebook Ad Targeting: Slicing and Dicing

You really have a huge number of options when you're targeting inside the Facebook advertising platform. For example, here's how you might slice up U.S. Facebook users who like running:

- All people in the United States over 18 who like running = 1,766,400 people.

- Men in the United States over 18 who like running = 762,180 people.

- Men over 18 in Ohio who like running = 27,660 people.

- Single men over 18 in Ohio who like running = 9,820 people.

- College graduate single men over 18 in Ohio who like running = 3,640 people.

As you can see, you can narrow your targets in a lot of ways. You can also create ads for different age groups:

- Men in the United States ages 18–25 who like running = 491,060 people.

- Men in the United States ages 26–35 who like running = 507,680 people.

- Men in the United States over age 64 who like running = 18,480 people.

Size of Targets

The estimated reach of your ad's targeting doesn't predict its performance. I've seen ads with an audience of more than 100,000 and ads reaching fewer than 5,000 both do well. The more important criteria are

- Does the ad target good prospects for you?

- Do your image and copy fit the target?

If your ad fits the target group, you can get a good click-through rate and cost per click for any size group.

3. Create Your Advertisements

Now that you've analyzed your target customer and brainstormed some ways to target audiences that contain your target customer, you're ready to create some ads.

Go to http://www.facebook.com/advertising, and click Create an Ad. You can do this while logged in to your normal account, or you can create what is called a *business account* that is not tied to your specific personal profile.

The first time you create an ad, it takes you through three screens. In the future, you'll see all this information in one screen. Then you enter your billing information, and the ad goes to Facebook for review.

Let's look at the anatomy of a Facebook ad. A Facebook ad contains

- **Destination**—Are you promoting a website? A fan page? A Facebook application?

- **Body**—The text of your ad, sometimes called *ad copy*

- **Image**—A 110×80 pixel picture

- **Targeting**

  - Location

  - Demographics

  - Interests/Categories

- Connections

- Advanced demographics

- Education and work

- **Campaign name and budget**

- **Schedule**

- **Pricing**

  - Bidding/payment method

  - Bid

I discuss each of these components, in turn, over the next several sections.

Destination

Destination is where the ad viewers will go if they click on the headline of the ad.
For website traffic, select External URL. A URL is a web address with http:// or
https:// in it. Insert the URL of the web page to which you want to send them.

For growing your fan base, choose the name of the page (see Figure 9.2). If you
don't see it, you're not an administrator (admin) and you need to get admin rights
to the page (find out who is an administrator of the page and get him to add you as
an administrator) before creating ads. This option is critical because without it,
there is no Like button on the ad and fans will be 5–10 times more expensive.

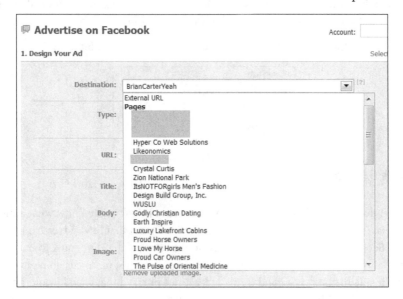

Figure 9.2   *Choosing a destination URL or Facebook page.*

Images and Ad Copy

This is the part that advertising people call "the creative." Creative is a noun they use to describe the graphic and linguistic elements that help persuade people to take action.

Your ad picture and text should fit the audience you're targeting as much as possible. They should either identify with or like the creative choice you're making. This could be really simple. For example, if you target people who love flying airplanes your ad copy says, "Hey if you love flying airplanes, click here!" next to a photo of someone happily flying an airplane, there's a good chance you're going to get the response you want.

Keep in mind that the platform is called *Face*book. It made sense when I discovered that close-up images of faces get more clicks. People connect emotionally with other people. Studies of people viewing ads show we're hard-wired to look at faces. If the face is too small to see in your ad, it won't work. You only have 110 horizontal pixels and 80 vertical pixels to work with. You might need to crop out extraneous detail and zoom in on the face.

Simplicity and personalization are the way to win. Personalize the message to the target and keep the wording simple. The simpler and more consistent you are with the targeting you've chosen, the higher the click-through rate. The higher the ad's click-through rate, the lower the cost per click. But if you use an image of something tangential and write copy that's long and complicated, your click-through rate goes down and your cost per click goes up. The best way to think about it is to assume that your ad might be viewed for 3–5 seconds. If it can't be understood and agreed to in that timeframe, it probably won't get a good enough response.

Here's an ad that I think asks too complicated a question (see Figure 9.3).

Figure 9.3 *Confusing ad copy.*

First, I don't think I like any media teams because I don't really know what a media team is. Is it a marketing agency? (Turns out it's a team that buys advertising for you.) Second, if you're going to ask me about two opposites, I'm going to have to think about it. I'm not sure, so I'm not clicking Like. Plus, no one is going to think that "inside the box" is a good thing, at least not phrased that way. I would rephrase this ad to something like: "Click Like if you need both conventional and innovative media buying ideas!"

Also, this ad's image is a QR code, but it's ugly and didn't grab my attention. I think QR codes are overhyped—most people have never heard of them. It was the "Like" that grabbed my attention. Instead, I'd use an image here that supports the question positively. A modest picture of two smiling female twins wearing opposite colors is one way to grab attention and mirror the question.

Keep in mind that if you want to test multiple images and copy for the same target at the same time, you'll need to put them into different campaigns. If you have multiple ads for the exact same target in one campaign, Facebook will not naturally rotate them for you the way AdWords does. Instead it tends to favor one ad.

WHERE TO FIND IMAGES FOR FACEBOOK ADS

Make sure you have the right to use the image you put in your ads. Facebook's Terms require you not to violate anyone else's trademarks or copyrights. Violating that policy could lead to your entire Facebook profile being disabled.

Here are some places you can go for paid or free images:

- http://www.istockphoto.com/
- http://us.fotolia.com/
- http://www.dreamstime.com/

Internal or Client Creative Approval

Typically, the bigger the company, the more control it exercises over the content of advertising.

If you are creating Facebook ads on behalf of a large company, you might not have any control whatsoever over the ad images or ad copy. In this case, your work is to be creative and skillful in your targeting to see if that will improve performance and lower costs.

If you are allowed to make suggestions but required to get explicit approval for all images and ad copy, be sure to submit much more than you actually need. Often, the people doing the approvals feel they need to disapprove of something; otherwise, they're not doing their job.

In both cases, it's a good idea to try to educate the ad approval people and the directors and executives up the marketing and advertising chain. The key concepts they should understand that will help them decide to give you more control so you can get better results are

Ad burnout: Many media buyers are accustomed to setting up ads and running them as-is for long periods of time. In other marketing channels, this works. On Google, ad performance can actually improve over time. On Facebook, it gets worse over time.

Personalization: Facebook ads perform better when you divide people by interests, demographics, and other factors and write ads personalized to them. This requires more images and ad copy than other advertising channels.

Test Both CPC and CPM Bidding

You can choose to bid (how you're going to pay for your ads) either CPC (per click) or CPM (*cost per mille*, or per thousand ad views). With CPC, you pay for each click. With CPM, you pay for all impressions (ad views) regardless of whether they're clicked on or not.

It used to be that if you had a high enough click-through rate, CPM bidding was always the cheapest way to go. Now it varies with the niche, so it's always best to test both. Seeing the actual CPC performance of ads is easy if you're bidding CPC, but if you want to see your cost per click for a CPM bid ad, you'll have to run an advertising report and calculate it in Excel.

A Warning About Putting Multiple Interests in the Same Ad

One thing to keep in mind is that you cannot use multiple interests in the same ad to narrow your targeting.

If you target people who like apples and running, you will also be seen by people who like running but not apples and people who like apples but not running.

Hopefully, in the future Facebook will add the ability to subdivide groups by multiple interests, but for now, if you run an ad with multiple interests, it needs to be along the same theme. Here's an example:

- Men in the United States ages 18–35 in California who like tennis = 24,000 people.

- Men in the United States ages 18–35 in California who like tennis, tennis mania, tennis club, or tennisnetcom = 46,980 people.

The image and copy (text) of your ad needs to make sense to the people you target, so more ads with fewer interests in each is better.

When Targeting Interests, Are We Targeting Fan Pages or What?

Many people have wrongly assumed that they can target the fans of other fan pages. When you target an interest in the Facebook ad platform, you are actually targeting people who've put these words into their Facebook profiles, not people who've liked those pages.

Not only does Facebook help make this abundantly clear, you can also easily prove this by typing in something like Hardee's as an interest and comparing that estimated reach to the number of fans on the Hardee's fan page. The ad platform tells me that only 2,580 people have written Hardee's in their profiles, while currently 466,472 people like the Hardee's Facebook page.

Test Lots of Different Targets

First, test as many relevant interests as you can think of. Activities, books, movies, places, specialties, and so on can you show some examples of these test ads. I don't start with highly segmented ads. I find it's better to start by targeting with only *precise interests*, not demographic or location. Then use the responder demographics report (which I explain in the section, "Optimizing Your Campaigns and Ads," later in this chapter) to tell you where to focus. But, of course, if your business serves a limited location, you'll want to start with that.

Figure 9.4 is an example of a fan-growing ad targeted only to interests:

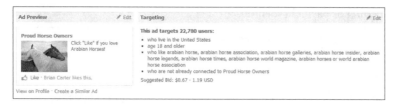

Figure 9.4   *An interest-targeted Facebook ad.*

How to Brainstorm More Interest Targets

It sounds easy to come up with more precise interests, but at some point you'll run out of ideas. Here are some more places to look when you're stumped:

- Check out affinities on Quantcast.com for big websites in the niche.

- Look at the interests on any existing fans' profiles.

- Think about the interests as keywords and use the Google Wonder Wheel. Search Google and then click More Search Tools and Wonder Wheel, as well as Google Sets (http://labs.google.com/sets) to look for related searches.

Campaign Name and Budget

How do you organize your ads? AdWords has an advantage over Facebook ads here, with the concept of AdGroups, which allow you to test showing multiple ads for the same search results.

With Facebook, you need different campaigns when

- You want to test multiple ads for the same target.
- You want to allocate a specific daily budget to certain ads versus others.
- You have specific starting and ending dates for certain ads.

Often, I have a test campaign where I run ads first, using CPC pricing. After I find ads that have a click-through rate above 0.2%, I create a similar ad using CPM pricing and put it in another campaign. I then check back later and see what the actual CPC of each ad is.

Schedule

This is simply when you want the campaign to start and end. For many campaigns, you won't have an end date.

Pricing

The bidding or payment methods are

- **Pay for impressions (CPM)**—You pay for each 1,000 impressions (although you are charged in smaller increments), regardless of whether you get clicks.
- **Pay for clicks (CPC)**—You pay only when ad viewers click Like.

It's almost always best to choose CPC pricing. When you're first testing ads, if your clickthrough rate is low, you'll be glad you're only paying when you get clicks or likes. If you choose CPM and have a low clickthrough rate, you still pay for the ad views. After you find some high clickthrough rate ads (above 0.2% CTR), you can test that and CPM as well and see which one is cheaper.

Max Bid and Suggested Bid

Bidding often causes some confusion for new advertisers. They see a high suggested bid, start calculating costs, and assume they won't be able to afford Facebook advertising.

The suggested bid is not the amount you will pay—it's the maximum amount you're *willing* to pay. Yes, you could be charged as much as your bid, but what determines the actual cost per click is mostly the click-through rate (see Figure 9.5).

Connections ?	Clicks ?	CTR ?	Bid ?	Price ?
4	7	0.394%	$0.88 CPC	$0.07 CPC
107	148	0.675%	$2.21 CPC	$0.05 CPC
380	489	0.569%	$1.91 CPC	$0.05 CPC
0	0	0.000%	$0.88 CPC	$0.00 CPC
704	855	0.469%	$2.02 CPC	$0.10 CPC
86	99	0.368%	$2.00 CPC	$0.11 CPC
556	739	0.914%	$1.96 CPC	$0.05 CPC
110	169	1.213%	$2.08 CPC	$0.05 CPC
334	428	0.185%	$1.50 CPC	$0.21 CPC
52	82	0.588%	$2.06 CPC	$0.07 CPC
14	21	0.244%	$2.54 CPC	$0.14 CPC
639	901	0.817%	$2.15 CPC	$0.05 CPC

Figure 9.5   *Twelve ads with bids versus actual prices.*

As you can see here, none of these ads has an actual cost per click value anywhere close to the suggested bid. Some of them have costs that are *one-fortieth* of the suggested bid amount. These ads also have very high click-through rates, which is the main thing that drives down click costs.

When you get click-through rates above 0.2%, you usually can get CPCs below $0.25. However, some targets are more expensive, and it's not totally clear what determines this. Business to business (B2B) targets usually cost more but also usually get lower click-through rates. I believe that what drives up CPCs when click-through rates are high is the number of other advertisers going after the same target simultaneously. This also would drive up suggested bids.

Just remember that you can bid as low as you want, and this keeps your costs down. The tradeoff is you might not get as many ad views as someone that bids more. But if you're getting enough views and clicks at a lower bid, why raise it?

Naming Your Ads

There are a couple approaches to this. When you create an ad, by default it is named whatever the headline of the ad was. If you're doing fan generation ads, that means you end up with ads named Pagename1, Pagename2, Pagename3, and so on. When you go back later, you won't remember what each one is. You'll have to expand them all to see the creative (ad copy) and targeting. So a better way that takes a little more time, but not very much, is to name your ads according to the targeting and creative.

For example, if I run ads for a photography development chain, I might name the ads this way:

- Parents smiling kids (I targeted parents with interest targeting and used a photo of smiling kids)

- ALL CAN smiling guy (I targeted all of Canada and used a photo of a guy smiling while taking a picture)

- 3050F takingpicturesofkids (I targeted women between the ages of 30 and 50 with a message about taking photos of their kids)

This becomes really important later if you want to run reports because reports will give you the names of the ads but won't show the image or ad copy.

Facebook Ad Reviewers: Approvals and Disapprovals

Facebook has someone review every single ad that's submitted through its advertising platform. Ads are accepted or rejected based on Facebook's Advertising Guidelines (http://www.facebook.com/ad_guidelines.php).

Approvals and disapprovals can be inconsistent, although Facebook's service is always improving. You could submit five ads that all violate the same Facebook policy, and two might be approved. However, your ad account could be shut down at any time for violating policies, so it's better to follow the rules. Sometimes, just as in sports, they get the call wrong. Read the reasoning for the ad disapproval, and if you're certain that your ad meets Facebook guidelines, create another one and submit it again.

There was a time when you couldn't expect a Facebook ad to be approved over the weekend. It seems like Facebook has worked this problem out. Google has long used a combination of automated and manual reviewers, which Facebook will need to mimic to scale.

4. Optimizing Your Campaigns and Ads

Optimizing means making changes to your strategy or tactics to improve your key metric. In Facebook advertising, optimizing typically means checking the key metrics and pausing ads that aren't performing adequately.

To optimize, you need data. Facebook advertising reports provide critical information for improving your results.

The newest Facebook ad interface makes it hard to find cost per click if you're bidding CPM. Click the Full Report button to see that (see Figure 9.6). You can get a rough idea of a campaign's overall CPF by dividing overall spend by connections.

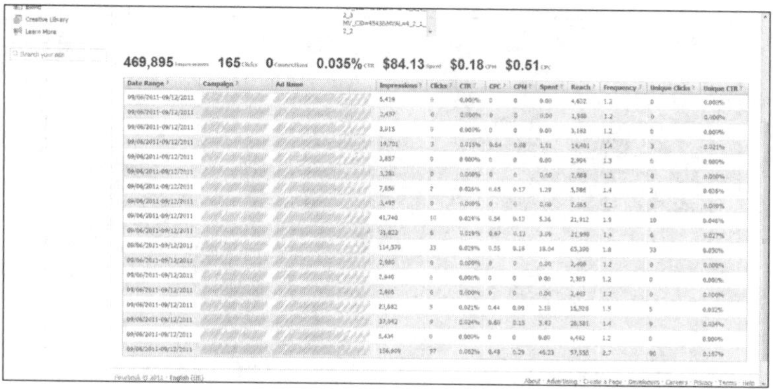

Figure 9.6 *Full Report.*

Advertising performance reports help you calculate the CPF (also called a *connection*) for each ad. You have to export it to a CSV and calculate it manually in Excel. Just divide cost by connections and you have the CPF. Now you can see which ads get you the cheapest fans. You absolutely must do it this way because no matter what an ad's click-through rate is, the percentage of clicks that are likes varies with each ad.

Responder demographics reports help you identify the demographics and locations that bring you the highest click-through rate for each ad. The column % of Clickers tells you which portion of the ad's entire audience was that particular demographic. Whenever you see a segment with a much higher than average click-through rate and the % of Clickers is above 5%, that might be a segment worth testing. Just create several new versions of the ad with the high-CTR demographic or location only, and see how they do.

Earlier I showed a general interest-targeted ad to get fans of Arabian horses. Figure 9.7 shows a responder demographic report on that ad.

Date	Campaign	Ad Name	Demographic	Bucket 1	Bucket 2	% of Impressions	% of Clickers	CTR ↑
Nov 2010	PHO - arabians	Proud Horse Owners	gender_age	F	55-64	5.483%	10.909%	2.439%
Nov 2010	PHO - arabians	Proud Horse Owners	gender_age	F	65-100	1.722%	3.182%	2.265%
Nov 2010	PHO - arabians	Proud Horse Owners	gender_age	F	45-54	13.384%	24.545%	2.248%
Nov 2010	PHO - arabians	Proud Horse Owners	gender_age	F	35-44	14.169%	25.000%	2.163%
Nov 2010	PHO - arabians	Proud Horse Owners	gender_age	M	35-44	2.112%	2.273%	1.319%
Nov 2010	PHO - arabians	Proud Horse Owners	country	US		100.000%	100.000%	1.291%
Nov 2010	PHO - arabians	Proud Horse Owners	gender_age	M	45-54	2.619%	2.273%	1.064%
Nov 2010	PHO - arabians	Proud Horse Owners	gender_age	F	25-34	17.791%	12.727%	0.877%
Dec 2010	PHO - arabians	Proud Horse Owners	region	us	South Carolina	0.924%	2.381%	0.806%
Dec 2010	PHO - arabians	Proud Horse Owners	region	us	Kansas	0.812%	2.083%	0.802%

Figure 9.7 *Responder demographics report.*

You could create another version of that ad for each line in this report. Figure 9.8 shows an example of a more specific ad.

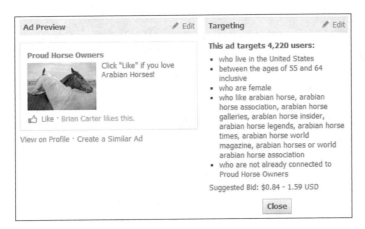

Figure 9.8 *Arabian horse fan ad with age targeting.*

As you can see, the target audience is much smaller than the original ad, but the CTR will be higher and the costs lower.

Conversions By Impression Time can give you a sense of how long after clicking an ad it takes before someone becomes a fan. If someone likes your page instantly on the ad, this SKU is called like_page_inline. If she goes to the page and then likes it, that's called like_page.

What Is Optimizing?

Optimization means taking action based on data to get better results.

The number-one activity in optimization is pausing bad ads. Bad ads are those with a cost per click or cost per fan that's higher than your target cost. To optimize in a way that improves your results, you must know what your key metric is.

The second most important optimization activity is running new test ads. Even your best ads have a finite lifetime of productivity, so you always need new blood.

If you're running a fan generation campaign, CPF is your key metric. To find this, you'll have to run the advertising performance report, export it to a spreadsheet, and calculate it. Do not try to take a shortcut here because CPC is not the only factor in cost per fan.

As I discussed in Chapter 6, "Facing the Facts: How to Continuously Get Better Results with the Five Steps of Optimization," you need to select a key metric to base your decisions on; then you'll do more of what works and less of what doesn't. As you test ads, you'll find baselines and averages for metrics like CTR, CPC, and CPF. Here's how to optimize for different goals:

- **Traffic to website**—Ideally you'll use web analytics to track individual ads and figure out the cost per lead, cost per email, or ROI of each ad. Those are the best key metrics. But if you can't do that, use CPC as your key metric. For the same ad target, you want to increase CTR by improving the image or ad copy, but ultimately, you care most about the cost per click.

- **Fan acquisition**—Your key metric is cost per fan. As discussed previously, you'll need to run advertising performance reports to check each ad's CPF.

How Do You Know If You're Doing Well?

If you're running your first ad campaigns ever, how do you know if you're doing well? And even if you've been doing it for a while, how do you know someone else out there isn't doing dramatically better with some secret techniques? Here are a few benchmarks to help you gauge this.

Click-through Rate (CTR):

- Below 0.1% is low.

- Above 0.25% is good.

- Above 0.5% is great.

Cost Per Click (CPC):

- Below $0.10 is low.

- Above $1.00 is high.

Situations in which it's hard to get CPC lower than $0.50 are

- B2B marketing

- Offerings where there aren't obviously good interests to target

- Huge audiences based only on country and demographics

I thought it would be helpful to provide an example of the rare situation in which interest targets backfired. I do work for several agencies that subcontract out Facebook fan generation work to me. One of these agencies asked me to help them grow a fan base to prepare the market for a new product that wasn't yet available. It turned out to be a nightmare campaign because of the following:

- There was nothing to sell.

- It was a totally new product that was so different from others that it was hard to find something people already knew about and liked that was related.

- It wasn't a health product, but it had health benefits. However, because of the Federal Trade Commission's (FTC's) regulations, we were very limited in the language we could use to describe it.

- The client insisted on including educational text in the ad that was so long that it lowered the click-through rate.

- We were extremely limited in our choice of images.

After testing dozens of interest targets, we discovered that we actually got our cheapest CPF by targeting the entire United States and nothing else. This probably only worked in part because few advertisers are targeting that widely, and there is a huge amount of impressions available. So there's relatively little competition to drive up price. Still, it was not a low cost per fan compared to ads that interests do work for.

Slice and Dice Your Targets

There's always a testing opportunity and potentially a performance opportunity in making your ads more targeted. The responder demographic report guides you in how to slice and dice your previous ads into more targeted ones. Run that report; sort it from highest to lowest CTR; and see what ages, genders, and locations have the highest CTR.

- Try dividing ads by location and calling that out in the ad copy: "Hey New Yorkers…."

- Divide them by age groups and genders.

As usual, watch your actual CTR and CPC, and keep the best ones.

Ad Burnout

All Facebook ads become less effective over time. The people who are likely to click on them don't need to see them too many times to do so. As time goes on, the rest of the people who haven't clicked yet are worse and worse targets. They also get tired of your image and ad copy. If you are doing fan acquisition and targeting people who are not fans of your page, then as people who click Like become fans, the only people who see your ad are people who are not fans, and fewer and fewer of them are interested in becoming fans.

Figure 9.9 shows what ad burnout looks like.

As you can see, CTR dropped over eight days from 0.168% to 0.075%—a little over half. During that time, the CPC increased from $0.19 to $0.29.

The speed that burnout happens can vary widely, from days to months. The bigger the audience you're targeting, the slower burnout will happen.

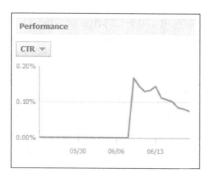

Figure 9.9 *Facebook ad burnout.*

With many ads, you can let them dip in CTR performance for a while and the CPC or CPF will still be good. But usually by the time an ad gets only 50% of the original click-through rate, you need to replace it.

Fighting Ad Burnout

It's important to understand that any ad that has performed well for you is addressing a high-quality target audience. Although your ad may be flagging, this target audience might be a lake you still want to continue to fish in. The bigger that target audience is, the more rewarding it is to keep trying to reach them with new ads.

You can combat ad burnout with these tactics:

- Change the image.
- Rewrite the copy.
- Create a promotion or something newsy to tell them about.
- Pause the ad for a few weeks and then run it again.

The smaller the target audience is, the more often you'll need to switch up ads. But also, keep in mind that if you're targeting 5,000 people, not all of them will become fans and there's only a limited number of messages you can send to them that they'll care about. There is a finite amount of results you can get from any audience.

Scheduling Your Work

How does all this ad creation and optimization look on a day-to-day basis?

The set-up phase is always more intense and time-consuming because you're trying to get a handle on demographics, interests, images, and ad copy. You'll be working on it every day until it's running smoothly. After you have data on the first ads and can review, you start to get an idea of which ad images, text, and targets are going to work and which aren't. And you get a sense of what a reasonable target value is for your key metric. Then you go into the routine of creating new ads and pausing ads that aren't working.

Also, know that some campaigns and audiences respond differently on specific days of the week. I've seen some ads do poorly on Mondays, or Fridays, or weekends, but other ads do great on those days. Don't make a snap judgment based on one day. There can be an up-and-down performance to your weekly ads, so be sure you distinguish a normal weekly performance dip from burnout.

How Often Should You Check Your Ads?

Because of the phenomenon of ad burnout, you need to keep an eye on your ads for the point where they dip below your acceptable performance threshold. If you found that you can get clicks for $0.75 each and one of your best ads starts to cost $0.85, you should consider writing a new ad to the same target. In other words, check ads as often as daily. With many campaigns, I check performance every day of the week. After I know what to expect from them, I can schedule to check them once or twice a week—whatever fits the speed with which they burn out.

How Often Should You Create New Ads?

You don't have to create new ads as often as you need to check your ads' performance. You can wait until an ad burns out and then create a new one for that same target audience. There's no advantage to creating new ones before the old ones have run their course.

The exception to this would be if you have valid reasons to run multiple ads on the same target; you'll have to run them in separate campaigns and understand that the ads might not show to the same people, so you're dividing up your impressions among these ads. And this doesn't usually work that well—often Facebook will show one or two ads and none of the others. If you're going to try multiple ads on the same targeting, put them in different campaigns.

Brainstorming to Break on Through to the Other Side

It's easy to get lazy after a while and not think of new targeting or creative ideas. With this kind of advertising, some ideas are more obvious than others. After you've tried the obvious things, how do you think of less obvious ones? I would schedule time for yourself to brainstorm either once every couple weeks or once a month. Try to be crazy on purpose. Find someone else to think crazy with and make a rule: no criticism of the ideas until later. Put your new ideas in new campaigns so you can use a smaller test budget for them.

For one campaign I ran for a vacation destination, I ran out of ideas after several months. I found it helpful to search Google News for the area to see what came up. I discovered that, once a year, the island saw a migration of a large number of a specific kind of turtle. Immediately, I tested ads targeting people who love turtles (with the normal age and location parameters the client wanted), and it turned out to be a really low cost per fan. Although you might search Google and Google Images for interest-targeting ideas at the beginning of your efforts, you might also want to create a Google Alert for certain things to catch ideas from the news.

The Relationship Between Facebook Advertising Metrics

Here's a summary of some of the core metrics you should keep an eye on:

- As the click-through rate increases, the cost per click decreases.

- The suggested bid and cost per click are not as closely related as you would expect. CTR controls the ultimate CPC to a much greater degree.

- Research is divided on whether a higher social impression percentage leads to a higher CTR. The argument is that if you see that a friend likes something, you will be more likely to take the action like it, too. I have a large body of data that disproves that.

Advertising to Existing Fans

You can also show ads to people who are already your fans. If you have a new promotion that you want them to see for multiple days, you might not want to post about that every day. You can use page posts for other things if you let fans know about the promotion through an ad.

When you're creating a Facebook ad, don't miss the section called Connections on Facebook. If you want to target fans of your page, you can choose Only people who are fans of <*your page*>.

You can slice and dice segments of your fan base with all the typical advertising targeting options. For example, if you have 20,000 fans but only want to say something to the males among them, use an ad targeted to your fan base but to men only.

Most pages only reach less than 10% of their fans with their posts. Many pages will millions of fans reach less than 3% of their fans. For more on this and where the data came from, read my AllFacebook article, "SHOCKER: 3% To 7.5% Of Fans See Your Page's Posts".[3]

---

3. http://www.allfacebook.com/shocker-3-to-7-5-of-fans-see-your-pages-posts-2011-06

If you want to reach more of them, you can first try to improve your post Feedback rates (explained in Chapter 11, "Talking Till You're Blue in the Face: How to Get More Likes and Comments"). But if you've had unengaged fans for a long time, you can have trouble reactivating them.

You can use page post story ads to get back some of these fans. Facebook will dynamically show your page's most recent post as an ad in the right sidebar, so you don't really design the ad. You don't choose the image or write ad copy. There's really nothing to creating these ads: Click Create An Ad. Then at the top, select Sponsored Stories and select Page Post Story. You don't have to do any further targeting if you don't want to. But if you do, you can segment your audience by demographics, interests, and all the other usual suspects. These ads can be expensive, sometimes up to $4 CPC, and when you see that, you'll understand why I harp on the topics of EdgeRank and keeping your fans engaged through posts.

How to Be a (Boring) Rock Star for Just $30 per Month

As I've discussed, if your ad is set to pay per click, you only pay when people click. I've also discussed how a call to action like "Click Like" or "Click Here" can get you more likes and clicks. But what if you break all the rules and don't use a call to action? What if you're boring and selfish on purpose? Then you get a bunch of impressions without paying much for clicks.

I've done this to advertise my services. I created an ad that asks people to call me (see Figure 9.10). That's a call to action that I don't get charged for.

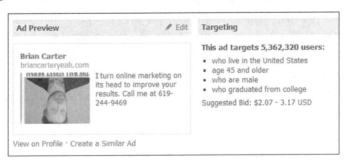

Figure 9.10   *An impression-oriented Facebook ad.*

With ads like these, in the last seven days I've reached 42,268 unique people (and on average these people saw the ad twice) for a total cost of $22.32.

The cost per thousand impressions was $0.25. How does that stack up against other impression-oriented advertising options? It's dramatically cheaper, as Table 9.3 shows.

Table 9.3   Average Cost per Thousand Impressions via Various Marketing Channels

Advertising Medium	Average CPM (Cost per Thousand Impressions)
Newspaper	$32.00
Radio	$8.00
Cable TV	$7.00
Los Angeles freeway billboard	$4.00
Facebook advertising	$0.25

This doesn't work forever; eventually your ads will stop showing if they have too low a CTR. And this happens faster when you target more competitive audiences. But every new ad gets some impressions, so you can create more. This tactic's effect can have a short shelf-life because it's not in Facebook's financial interests.

10

FaceHook: Capturing Qualified Prospects as Fans and Group Members

Fan marketing is one of the biggest innovations Facebook brings to the world of marketing, and yet it's not totally new. For decades, marketers have prized similar types of owned media for their high profitability. In this chapter, I expand on what I discussed in Chapter 9, "The Face of Advertising: How to Capitalize on the Most Powerful Marketing Tool," to explain how you can affordably gather qualified potential buyers into a page where you lead the conversation.

Why Fan Marketing Can Be So Profitable

We can break all marketing and advertising down into three types:

- **Paid media**—Includes all paid advertising, has a hard cost, and its benefits stop when you stop paying. This includes Facebook advertising, search advertising like AdWords, Yellow Pages ads, TV, and radio.

- **Earned media**—Includes press and blogger mentions. This is a function of PR and is hard to consistently achieve. Also can include shares of content posted to your fans.

- **Owned media**—Sometimes called *permission-based marketing*, this includes direct mail lists, email lists, Twitter followers, and Facebook fans. When you own a list, you can contact people repeatedly without paying any more money to AdWords or Facebook. That's why this category produces the greatest profits of the three.

Let's take a look at some examples of these three approaches in the digital marketing world.

Paid Media Versus Owned Media on Google

For many years, while Google presided as master of the Internet marketing domain, businesses had to choose between paying for Google AdWords ads or paying someone to do search engine optimization (SEO), an activity that increases your rankings for the keywords people use to find what your business offers. Some businesses have been able to run the ads effectively themselves, or they hire an AdWords consultant. If they're fortunate enough to have the cash flow, they can do both.

I like to use a real estate analogy to explain the difference: AdWords is like renting a house, and SEO is like buying a house (as long as you keep paying the mortgage, you own the house). You pay an SEO consultant to get you traffic that lasts, just as you pay your mortgage to have long-term equity. SEO gets you rankings for search phrases that deliver website traffic long after you stop paying for SEO. But with AdWords, as soon as you stop, you're no longer visible.

Paid Media Versus Owned Media on Facebook

So what's the wisest thing to do in Facebook marketing? You can choose from Facebook advertising (paid media) and Facebook fan marketing (owned media). What's the best decision? One of them? Both of them?

Let's say you have $1,000 to spend right now to grow your business, and let's assume you've mastered the Facebook advertising techniques I teach in this book.

We'll assume your ads cost $0.20 per click and the fans you gain cost $0.30 apiece. Would you prefer to get 5,000 visits to your website or 3,333 Facebook fans? Don't answer too quickly.

Let's think about the pros and cons.

Advertising to Get Website Traffic

Only a percentage of website visitors will buy from you on the first visit. What is that conversion rate (percentage of visitors that buy)? For many websites, it's close to 1%. So if you get 50 purchases from 5,000 visits, does that make you $1,000 back on your ad spend? It does if your profit per sale is greater than $20. So these numbers can definitely give you a profit.

The math in determining whether you make a profit from advertising comes from the cost per click (CPC), conversion rate, and your gross profit per sale (revenue minus operating costs). If your conversion rate and profits per sale are too low or if the CPC is too high, you might lose money on advertising. The money spent is gone, and the traffic didn't bring you enough revenue to break even. What's worse, these people who came from the ads are all gone; you can't contact them again.

Advertising to Acquire Page Fans

If you use that same money to get fans, your investment can pay off again and again. You would get 3,333 fans in this example. After you have those 3,333 fans, if you use the page posting techniques outlined in Chapter 11, "Talking Till You're Blue in the Face: How to Get More Likes and Comments," you should get 2,500 or more views of each post. You might post daily, or even five times a day (one business that makes a profit on Facebook marketing does actually post this frequently).

Do you think more than 1.5% of these fans will buy from you at some point? Our case studies suggest they will if you get good interaction and when you sell the dream. The most important advantage in paying for fans is that you can contact these people again and again.

Remember how in Chapter 5, "How Not to Fall on Your Face: Six Mistakes That Block Facebook Profitability," I talked about websites that didn't sell well? If your site's conversion rate turns out to be too low and you were running ads straight to the website (without getting fans), you can fix the issues with your website, but those people you advertised to are gone. If you were building fans all along, you can still reach them again after your website is selling better.

What's more, the exposure you get every time you post to your fans has a value. We can value the post views conservatively at $5 per 1,000 views. If you're reaching 2,500 people per post, you're getting $12.50 in value every time you post. It only takes 80 posts at that value to break even on the $1,000 you spent to acquire the fans. This is a comparative value—it's not the same as revenue in the bank, but it's repeat exposure you would have to shell out cash for otherwise.

Unwise Ways to Get Fans

The easiest way to get fans is with Facebook ads, and Facebook ads empower you to get the right fans—people who are actually likely to buy from you.

But some businesses act like they're allergic to advertising, no matter how afford-able, and they seek out alternatives. Maybe they've never run ads before, or they work in a department that has never had an advertising budget. If the social media work isn't being done by the advertising or marketing department, there might even be a perception that you're stepping on their toes. It's a good idea to have an interdepartmental meeting and get used to it because social media activity crosses over so many departments.

The Contest and Giveaway Trap

Any business can fall into the trap of contests and giveaways. While these can be use-ful when deployed intelligently with an eye for your bottom-line goals, many such efforts are poorly thought-out, are poorly planned, and leave companies with a quan-tity of untargeted fans who aren't good prospects and will never buy from them.

The best example of a bad contest idea is, unfortunately, the most prevalent. It seems like every company is giving away an iPad. If you search Google for Facebook-oriented iPad contests, you'll find more than 20,000 results. The problem with the iPad giveaway is that it does nothing to ensure that these new fans are good potential customers for you. Everyone wants a free iPad, so you get a bunch of freebie seekers who aren't necessarily your ideal customers. Freebie seekers don't care who your company is or what you offer. You might increase your fan count, and that can look impressive, but it won't do anything for your return on invest-ment (ROI). They might not respond to your posts and they might even become surly. Freebie seekers tend to respond poorly to sales messages, and at some point you're probably going to mention what you're selling, right? Plus, all these people who don't really care about what you offer will drag down your interaction statistics and make it look like you're doing a poor job with your posting.

I did see one iPad contest that made sense. Coincidentally, it was promoting a serv-ice where you could view cable TV via an iPad. The prize actually fit the service they were promoting.

In general, if you have to run a contest, you'll do better if you require some sort of task that qualifies people as good potential customers. For example, if I wanted to run a contest to give away this book to get more consulting clients, I'd ask people to tell me what their Facebook marketing goals are, and I'd select the winner based on the most interesting goal. Some people wouldn't enter because they don't have a goal—they aren't really serious, so they aren't good potential customers for my consulting business. Conversely, my respondents would be more qualified for my future marketing efforts.

Buying Fans from Companies That Get Fans for You

Many companies want more fans, and some fall for the cheap options, some of which are scams. There are two types of fan building services: consultants, like me, who are hired to use Facebook ads to get fans for companies, and the others.

The services to watch out for are the ones that quote a specific amount of fans for a specific fee ("1,000 fans for $89.95!!!"). As you'll see in this chapter, getting good fans for less than $.09 per click is difficult.

These Facebook fan-buying services use tricks that can raise your fan count but won't help you sell your products and services. Some get you fans who live all over the world, even if you do business in only one country. Some services create thousands of fake profiles—the fans you get might not even be real people.

When I help companies get fans, I never quote a price ahead of time. I might give a ballpark estimate of what I think the fans may cost, but I charge a monthly fee for my services. I also get work from agencies that do charge a specific amount per fan, and these numbers are usually $1 or more.

In other words, you get what you pay for.

Marketing 101: Targeting and Return on Investment

It would be financial suicide to market to everyone in the world, unless you sell air, water, or Coca-Cola. If you don't have millions of dollars to spend on branding, you need to learn how to think like a direct marketer. Direct marketers are obsessed with ROI, which is simply a percentage that divides gross profits by cost:

ROI (%) = (revenue − cost of marketing) / cost of marketing

For example, if you spend $1,000 on Facebook ads to get 1,000 people to your website and 10 of those people buy something for $150 each, then you get $1,500 in revenue. Subtract the $1,000 ad cost from the $1,500 and you have $500 gross profit. Divide $500 gross profit by $1,000 spent and you get a 50% ROI. But if only 5 buy, you make $750, which is $250 less than you spent. This gives you a negative 25% ROI, and you generally want a positive ROI.

There's more to this because some companies offer introductory products called *loss leaders* that they market at a negative ROI (at a loss) because they know they will later sell more profitable products to the same customers and that the customer's lifetime value to them is higher than the initial advertising investment. Game console manufacturers such as Sony and Microsoft often take losses on the consoles, particularly early in the console's life cycle, counting on game sales to make up the difference and generate profits. But other businesses prefer an immediate positive ROI.

The people who want and need what you offer (prospects, or potential buyers) are a distinct group. You can't afford to spend time or money getting unqualified prospects into your fan base or to your website. If you can target your efforts to reach the best prospects, you'll spend only what you must to acquire a customer. And if you can find affordable ways to reach these ideal prospects, you're much more likely to get a positive ROI.

Wrong Fans? Bad Return on Investment

The money you'll make from your fan base depends on whether you get the right people as fans and how much it costs to get them. Who are the right fans? They're a group of people as close to your ideal customer as possible.

I discussed five ways to make money from Facebook in Chapter 4, "FaceBucks: Five Ways Businesses Achieve Profits with Facebook," but let's take a look specifically at the fan-to-purchase path and how having the right or wrong fans affects it (see Figure 10.1).

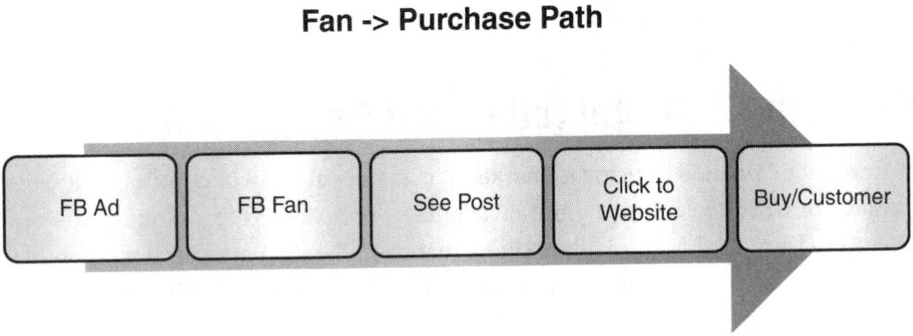

Fan -> Purchase Path

Figure 10.1 *The fan-to-purchase path.*

Forget about the first step (advertising) for a second. If you have fans, regardless of source, they have to respond to your posts to continue to see them, and they have to care about what you're marketing if you want them to go to your website and buy. So only fans who are good prospects for your business will respond, click, and buy. Makes sense, right?

But think about your existing fan base and how you got them. Are they friends and employees? People who opted in to win an iPad? How close to your ideal customer are your existing fans? If you don't use the Facebook ad platform to get highly targeted fans, your fans might be the wrong audience for your marketing.

Let's look again at the conversion path with metrics in mind (see Figure 10.2).

Fan -> Purchase Path

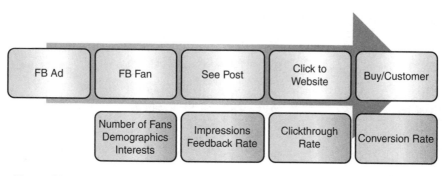

Figure 10.2   *The fan-to-purchase path with metrics.*

If you have the wrong fans, your Facebook and website metrics will show it:

- Impressions might be 40% or less of your fan base number.

- The feedback rate might be lower than 0.5% even using the engagement tactics I teach in this book.

- The click-through rate from post to website will be lower than 1%.

- The conversion rate of fans will be much lower than your website average.

Even further down the line, only the right fans will become loyal and have a high lifetime value to your business.

The math of the process shows that you must target the right people in order to achieve profitability.

A Few Fan Growth Campaign Case Studies

WebTrends says the average company gets fans for $1.07 each.[1] As you can see in Table 10.1, many of my case studies get above-average results:

---

1. How Much Does A Facebook Fan Cost? $1.07. Geoffrey A. Fowler. Wall Street Journal Blog. February 1, 2011. http://blogs.wsj.com/digits/2011/02/01/how-much-does-a-facebook-fan-cost-107/

Table 10.1   Sample Fan Growth Campaigns

Niche	Cost Per Fan	Fans Grown
Vacation rental	$0.25	5,500
Boxing	$0.003	13,300
Horse e-commerce	$0.08	24,831
Sports	$0.09	2,400
Automotive	$0.07	1,900
Parenting	$0.05	95,000
F1000 outdoors	$0.05	260,000
Pets	$0.12	13,750
Civic/Political	$0.03	6,100
F500 fast food	$1.28	300,000
Daily deal Ecommerce	$0.05	3,072
Retail photo	$0.33	5,000

WebTrends number might be right, and most companies are probably paying more per fan than I and my students have. Based on ads I've seen other companies run on Facebook, many are making the same mistakes: First, a lot of people running Facebook ads don't know what they're doing and haven't been trained. Second, they might only be using demographics targeting and not interest targeting. Third, they make their ad copy too complicated.

When I was first learning Facebook advertising for fan acquisition, I got to watch one of my mentors run a campaign to grow an outdoor e-commerce company's fan base. They had about 230,000 fans, but their main competitor had more than 500,000.

At one point when I ran reports, I found that my mentor had been able to grow his client 300,000 more fans for an overall cost of just over $0.05 per fan. He did such a good job with Facebook posting on their page that more than half of their fans came in because of friends seeing page-posting activity during his advertising campaign. The actual cost per fan (CPF) from the ads was $0.14 each, but after including the word-of-mouth fans, it was substantially cheaper. The client is now neck and neck with its competitor and both have more than 1 million fans. However, just looking at likes and comments on their posts, my mentor's page gets two to three times as much interaction from fans.

When you might be able to acquire prospects so cheaply, why would you waste labor and time on other methods that don't bring you good prospects?

I've been involved in all kinds of fan growth projects, from small business all the way up to Fortune 500, and the way to succeed is the same for all of them. In the next section, I show you how.

How to Get Cheap, Targeted Fans

Because your primary method of getting cheap, targeted fans is Facebook advertising, you'll need to employ concepts from previous chapters, such as these:

- Knowing your ideal customer's location, demographics, and psychographics
- Testing lots of different targets
- Testing different images and ad copy
- Testing both CPC and CPM bidding
- Size of targets
- Ad burnout
- How to better target ads based on reports
- How to optimize ads
- Running multiple ads on the same target
- Relationship between advertising metrics

In addition, I'm going to talk here about

- The best ad settings for cheap fan acquisition
- Tightly grouping targets with image and message
- Ad copy formulas
- Ad headline issues
- Simplicity
- How to choose images
- The key fan acquisition ad metric and how to find it
- Examples of good and bad fan acquisition ads

The Best Ad Settings for Cheap Fan Acquisition

When you create an ad, the first thing you see is a drop-down menu labeled Destination. This can be a page or a URL. When you're doing fan acquisition ads, you should choose the page here (you must be an administrator of the page to do so). If you created the page, you're the admin. If you're not, get an admin to add you.

When your destination is a page, your ad gets a Like button on it. When ad viewers click Like on this ad, they instantly become page fans. This is how more than 80% of fans are acquired cheaply.

If you make the mistake of selecting External URL and sending people to the web address for your page, you will pay 4–10 times as much for your fans. Why? Because if you select External URL, there is no Like button on your ad and the percentage of people who click Like on a page after going to its Wall or welcome tab is much lower than the percentage who click Like on an ad. You basically make them do two steps instead of one. That's the too-many-hoops error I discuss in Chapter 5, and that increases your cost per fan significantly.

Target-Ad Consistency: Tightly Grouping Targets with Image and Message

When I was growing fans for the debut of the movie *Cowboys and Aliens* (see Figure 10.3), I targeted fans of the main actors. That meant I had one ad for Daniel Craig, another for Harrison Ford, and another for Olivia Wilde. I also targeted people who like westerns. As you'll see in the following ad copy formulas, a no-brainer such as a call to action would be impossible if I tried to create one ad that covered all the actors and topics at once. The thousands of fans I grew for this movie cost, on average, about $0.25 apiece.

Figure 10.3 *Sample fan growth ad.*

Here, the name of the page actually helps qualify the fans. I targeted people who liked westerns, but this movie is a hybrid of sci-fi and western, so having the word *Aliens* in the title would prevent many of the pure western fans from clicking Like…unless they think we're talking about illegal aliens. And that would be a very different movie. But having *Cowboys* in the title helps, and despite these hindrances, the ad still brought in fans for $0.29 apiece.

An Alternative Targeting Approach

Because most people have local friends nearby, you can target friends of fans in one city at a time to increase the social percentage. Social percentage measures how often the ad shows that one of their friends already likes that thing. The friend's name on the ad acts as social proof and increases the ad viewer's trust in your brand. In some cases, a higher social percentage increases your click-through rate (CTR), and that lowers your cost per click. After you have tens of thousands of fans, you can get a good social percentage without targeting friends of fans. But social percentage doesn't always work because sometimes friends have dramatically different interests. And believe it or not, sometimes we're Facebook friends with people we don't really like but we don't want to cause any unpleasantness by unfriending them.

No-Brainer Marketing: Simplicity Gets Results

Keep in mind that Facebook users are not on Facebook to look at ads. They're catching up on the lives of their friends, playing games, and so on. If your image is attention-grabbing, you have about 5 seconds to get them to understand why they should like your page. If you write more than 10 or 20 words or try to get across several ideas at once, especially if those ideas are conflicting, your CTR will drop and your CPF will skyrocket.

Which ad would you be more likely to click Like for?

- Click Like if you love the Earth!

- The Earth is in trouble, don't you want to save it? Click Like!

In the second case, we've given them a negative idea and a guilt trip. Even if they do want to save the Earth, are they liking the saving or are they liking the trouble? That moment of confusion is enough to make them move on without taking action. It's obvious when you sit back and think about it, but the very need to think about it reduces the CTR and increases the CPC.

The cheapest fans are people we target, knowing that they already have said they like the thing we're going to ask them to like. It's a no-brainer action for them to click Like again. If you don't make them think, you have a lot better chance of getting them to take action.

Ad Copy Formulas

In keeping with both the principles of no-brainer marketing and target-to-ad consistency, the formulas here are simple:

- Click Like if you love <interest>!

- Do you love <interest>? Then Click Like below now!

- Give a thumbs up below if you LIKE <interest>!

The interest I'm referring to is whatever you've chosen as a precise interest in your ad targeting. For example, if you target people with the precise interest *market research*, write ad copy that says:

Click Like if you love Market Research!

Ad Copy Grammar, Punctuation, and Capitalization

Facebook's ad reviewers don't pay a lot of attention to how you write. They are most concerned with trademark violations. They will, however, disapprove an ad for more than one punctuation mark in a row, so you can't do the triple exclamation point. You can get away with capitalizing entire words, which is a huge advantage. A number of my tests show that capitalizing one word can increase clickthrough rate and lower cost per click. You can't do that in Google AdWords. I expect Facebook's copy guidelines to become more stringent over time, though.

Ad Headline Issues

When you target a page for fan-growth ads, the headline is always your page name. You can't change it. And if the page is too long, Facebook won't show all of it. If you created your page before you knew you'd be stuck with that, there is a clever way around this: Include some words at the top of your image.

For example, Vamplets.com manufactures and sells plush baby vampire dolls, but they named its Facebook page Vamplets. The owner felt that the people he was targeting (for example, fans of *Twilight*) wouldn't understand that they were baby vampires, so he added "Baby Vampyres" in text to the top of his image (see Figure 10.4).

Figure 10.4 *Adding an extra headline in the image.*

How to Choose Images for Fan Acquisition Ads

All the same things I discussed about Facebook ad images in Chapter 9 apply here, too.

For fan acquisition, you need a picture of the thing you've targeted, such as

- Someone doing the thing or in the place you're promoting

- A representation of the dream you're selling

- Happy faces

- Upward-trending graphs

- A picture you actually like

Choosing the right image is an art, but thankfully, you can test multiple images if you're not sure. Just remember that to test multiple ads on the exact same target at the same time, they need to be in separate campaigns.

 Note

> When you create your ad, under Connections, be sure to exclude people
> who are already fans of your page.

The Key Metric for Fan Generation and How to Find It

Cost per fan is the most important measurement in getting fans. The cheaper you can get fans, the more you can get for your budget. I'm assuming here that you're not going to go after really cheap fans who aren't relevant to your business. If we assume you're going to use sensible targets for your ads, the goal is to create and keep the ads that get you the lowest CPF.

Facebook doesn't make it easy for you to check this. Cost per fan doesn't show up in the dashboard. Cost per click, on the other hand, is easy to find if you're paying per click. To find CPF, you have to run reports and do a little math. I know! People hate that. But that's the only way to maximize your spend and get the best results. To do the math, first you have to get the raw data....

Running an Advertising Performance Report to Get the Raw Data

The idea of getting raw data from an advertising performance report sounds scary, doesn't it? It's going to be okay, though. We'll have pictures.

While you're in the advertising interface part of Facebook, on the left side is the option Reports. Click that link to see the page shown in Figure 10.5, and then follow these steps:

Figure 10.5 *Creating an advertising performance report.*

1. **Report Type**—Select Advertising Performance.

2. **Summarize By**—Select Ad if you want to compare the performance of different ads.

3. **Filter By**—If you have multiple campaigns and only want to review CPF for ads in certain campaigns, filter by Campaign and select the ones you want.

4. **Time Summary**—I often select Weekly because most ads don't burn out in less than a week, but you might want to select Daily and just look at yesterday.

5. **Date Range**—I usually just want the most recent of whatever time I chose. For weekly, I choose the most recent week.

6. **Format**—If you're doing this for the first time, just generate a webpage and see what you get. You can go back and create a spreadsheet if you want.

For a small number of ads, you can do this with just the webpage format and a calculator. For each ad, divide spent (the cost) by the number of connections (fans); that gives you cost per fan (see Figure 10.6).

CPF = Spend / Connections

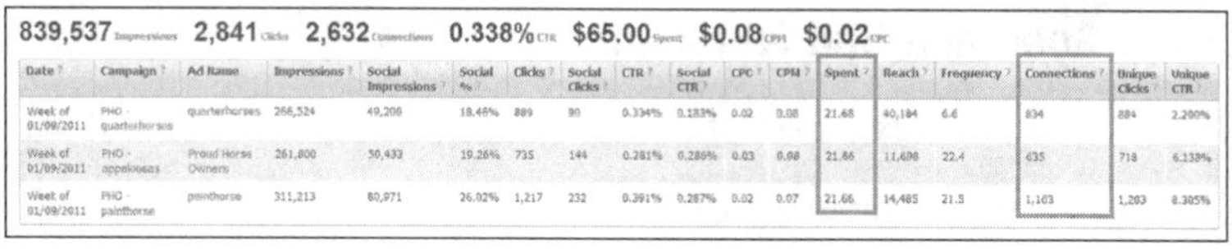

839,537 Impressions 2,841 Clicks 2,632 Connections 0.338% CTR $65.00 Spent $0.08 CPM $0.02 CPC

Date	Campaign	Ad Name	Impressions	Social Impressions	Social %	Clicks	Social Clicks	CTR	Social CTR	CPC	CPM	Spent	Reach	Frequency	Connections	Unique Clicks	Unique CTR
Week of 01/09/2011	PHO - quarterhorses	quarterhorses	266,524	49,206	18.46%	889	90	0.334%	0.183%	0.02	0.08	21.68	40,184	6.6	834	884	2.200%
Week of 01/09/2011	PHO - appaloosas	Proud Horse Owners	261,800	50,433	19.26%	735	144	0.281%	0.286%	0.03	0.08	21.66	11,698	22.4	635	718	6.133%
Week of 01/09/2011	PHO - painthorse	painthorse	311,213	80,971	26.02%	1,217	232	0.391%	0.287%	0.02	0.07	21.66	14,485	21.5	1,163	1,203	8.305%

Figure 10.6 *Finding the Spent and Connections info in the advertising performance report.*

From this report, we can pull out spend and connections and calculate the cost per fan:

- The quarter horses ad was $0.025 per fan ($21.68 divided by 834 connections).
- The Proud Horse Owners ad in the PHO—appaloosas campaign was %0.034 per fan.
- The paint horse ad was $0.019 per fan.

These are all pretty outstanding, so I wouldn't pause any of them. But usually, you have more variety in performance. You might have a few ads that generate $0.10 fans, one that costs $0.40 per fan, and another that's $1.30 per fan. At this point, you make the decision whether that's too high. After you've created 5 or 10 ads, run them, and calculated the CPF, you get a sense of what numbers are good, great, or too high. Pause the ads with CPF values that are too high.

Over time, they're going to get more expensive. Typically, we target people who are not yet page fans, and eventually everyone we're targeting that's going to become a fan already has. The rest aren't going to like the ad, so your CTR goes down and your cost goes up.

If you have a lot of ads to analyze, you can export them into a spreadsheet and use an Excel formula to get their CPF much more quickly. Just add an extra column and create a formula that divides the Spent column by the Connections column (see Figure 10.7).

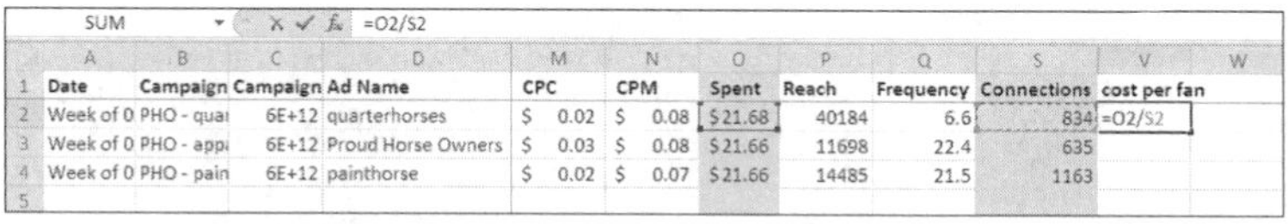

SUM =O2/S2

	A	B	C	D	M	N	O	P	Q	S	V	W
1	Date	Campaign	Campaign	Ad Name	CPC	CPM	Spent	Reach	Frequency	Connections	cost per fan	
2	Week of 0	PHO - quai	6E+12	quarterhorses	$ 0.02	$ 0.08	$21.68	40184	6.6	834	=O2/S2	
3	Week of 0	PHO - appi	6E+12	Proud Horse Owners	$ 0.03	$ 0.08	$21.66	11698	22.4	635		
4	Week of 0	PHO - pain	6E+12	painthorse	$ 0.02	$ 0.07	$21.66	14485	21.5	1163		
5												

Figure 10.7 *Creating the CPF formula in Excel.*

Then copy and paste that formula into the rest of the rows. Finally, you can sort that column so the most or least expensive fan ads are at the top.

Examples of Good and Bad Fan Acquisition Ads

Let's look at a couple of examples of what makes a good or bad Facebook ad.

The ad in Figure 10.8 resulted in $0.25 fans.

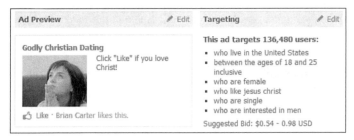

Figure 10.8 *Christian dating fan ad.*

For this ad, I targeted single women between 18 and 25 who like the interest "jesus christ" and who are interested in men. There are actually more strict Facebook guidelines for dating ads:

- You must target single people.

- You must choose Male or Female people.

- You must use Age Range and not start lower than 18.

- You must choose Interested In either Male or Female.

This turned out to be a tough group to target. The CTR turned out much lower than I expected. The problem might have been that having "dating" in the fan page name turned off some of the target group. It might have been a bit of conflict in their minds because they could say "yes, I do like that, but I'm not interested in dating on Facebook." But as with all analysis of ad success and failure, we never really know until we do another ad to confirm or disprove our theory.

The ad in Figure 10.9 brought in fans at a little over $0.03 per fan.

CTR (%)	Actions	AR (%)	Avg. CPC ($)	Avg. CPM ($)	Spent ($)
0.000%	0	0.00	0.00	0.00	0.00
0.000%	0	0.00	0.00	0.00	0.00
0.209%	81	0.19	0.05	0.10	4.45
0.319%	140	0.28	0.03	0.10	5.00
0.629%	199	0.56	0.02	0.14	5.00
0.345%	1,188	0.30	0.03	0.09	36.13

Proud Horse Owners
Click "Like" if you love quarter horses!
Like · Brian Carter likes this.

View on Profile
Edit Ad Creative

Targeting
- who live in the United States
- age 18 and older
- who are female
- who like american quarter horse, american quarter horse association, gil galyean quarter horses, olsen quarter horses, quarter horse news, quarter horses, rodrock quarter horses or ts quarter horses
- who are not already connected to Proud Horse Owners

Figure 10.9 *Quarter horses for a lot less than a quarter.*

Part of the key to high CTR is the right image. With horses, it's not easy to get the whole horse into a 110×80 image and still see much. For viewers to connect emotionally with the image, they have to be able to see it, so only the head is shown here, and this is a nice, friendly-looking horse. Also, notice that it's okay to include more than one interest in an ad if they are very similar. In this case, all the people who like these interests like quarter horses.

Notes on Business-to-Business Fan Acquisition

Business-to-business (B2B) fans are typically more expensive than business-to-consumer fans and require a different approach.

Interest targeting: People don't put enough detail in their profiles about their work, so the exact things we want to target aren't there. It's also possible, dare I say, that they just don't really love their work quite like they love their hobbies and weekend activities. You'll see this in the click-through rate.

Competition: There is more money and competition in the B2B topics, so that raises the cost no matter how good your CTR is.

Workplaces: You can target workplaces, but only the biggest employers. Small companies won't come up as options when you type them in.

That can sound discouraging, but consider this: The reason there's more money in the field is that the average customer value is much higher. B2B contracts can range from thousands to several millions of dollars. If you convert 1 out of every 100 fans to a customer, then they're worth somewhere between $10 and $1,000. You can afford to spend $5–$10 per customer if the average fan brings you $50, right?

And your Facebook fan page can also serve as a place for

- Customer service

- Answering questions from potential buyers

- Distributing new white-papers, videos, and other marketing materials

Business-to-Business Fan Generation Advertising Tips

All the same principles apply to B2B fan growth, but here are a few notes about what makes it different.

When All Else Fails, Try Targeting Widely

Sometimes too much slicing and dicing of your ad targets doesn't lower your CPC or CPF. In these cases, try going extremely wide with your targeting. I've seen situations where ads targeted to the entire country are cheaper—this was actually a business-to-consumer ad. The low cost might be because fewer companies are targeting that broadly, and it would take a lot more to increase the price of a group of 150 million people than it does in an interest target that contains 5,000 people.

Sell the Dream, Not Boredom

In creating your ad, you should still think about the dream your offering helps consumers reach and how to qualify them as good potential buyers. There's a tendency to get left-brained and boring when we market to other businesses. There's definitely a place for professionalism, but don't let that be an excuse not to stretch your creative muscles and think about more compelling messages. And if you're a smaller or newer company, you can take more risks to get attention.

11

Talking Till You're Blue in the Face: How to Get More Likes and Comments

How do we reach our fans with our messages?

This is one of the most important chapters in this book. It's hard to say one is more important than another because I've outlined a complete Facebook marketing system in these pages, so each part is necessary. But when I look at what businesses on Facebook are doing poorly and where they can improve most, how they post to their fans is near the top of the list.

This book's Facebook marketing system is a way for you to affordably get lots of fans who are likely to buy from you at some point and then how to get those people to buy. The second part of the process is the most neglected by companies. Many businesses are obsessed with increasing their fan counts but have no idea how few fans their posts are reaching. And some companies are baffled why their fans aren't buying. It's this second part—what do you do with fans once you have them—that I talk about in this chapter.

The most successful businesses on Facebook start engaging their fans with highly interactive posts as soon as they get those fans. But the ones that aren't doing a good job with interaction? It's an epidemic. It reminds me of what I've seen from many clients with their email marketing. About 95% of the businesses I've worked with that have email lists don't fully cash in on those lists. They might send out a monthly newsletter, but do you really care about the monthly email newsletters you receive? It's easy to put a subscription form on your website and collect emails, but it takes training and planning to develop an effective email marketing strategy. The same goes for Facebook page marketing—it's easy to get a lot of fans. It's even easy to get good fans with what I teach you in this book. But it takes planning and then daily posting long-term to market to those fans.

Facebook fan marketing is a marathon, not a sprint. Well, a marathon sounds really intimidating. I've never run one. Let's try again: Facebook fan marketing is like running a mile, not a 100-yard dash. There you go.

How People Use Facebook

That's such a bland section title. You probably think you already know the answer and will skip this section. You're probably wrong. Most people don't know how Facebook works. Here are some facts that might surprise you:

- Most fans never return to a page after they like it.
- Most posts by pages are seen by less than 10% of their fans.[1]
- Many fans will never see your welcome tab.
- When fans create new posts on your Facebook page, other fans don't see them.

Those facts run counter to most people's assumptions. They go to their fan page a lot, so they think their fans do, too. They assume that all their fans are seeing all their posts, which we've already discussed. They also assume their fans are seeing posts made by other fans to the page's Wall.

Your Fans See the People and Pages They Interact With

In fact, fans experience Facebook through their News Feeds. The News Feed is set by default to Top Posts, which means Facebook uses its EdgeRank and GraphRank algorithms to show people the stories it thinks they'll be interested in. How does it guess what you'll be interested in seeing? By keeping track of what posts you like and comment on. People see posts from pages and friends they've liked and comment on before.

When fans no longer see your posts, it's much harder to get them back. It's best to start engaging your fans while you're growing their numbers and never stop engaging them!

---

1. http://www.allfacebook.com/shocker-3-to-7-5-of-fans-see-your-pages-posts-2011-06

The Average Page's Posts Are Seen by Less Than 10% of Its Fans

I was fortunate to get into a beta test program with the Facebook page analytics service PageLever and speak to founder Jeff Widman. One of the most fundamental and important revelations is that pages don't reach many of their fans:

- Posts from pages with 10,000 fans reach 30%–40% of their fans.

- Posts from pages with 100,000 fans reach 20%–30% of their fans.

- Posts from pages with 1,000,000 or more fans reach 10% of their fans.

Think about what this means: at those levels, pages are reaching

- 3,000 fans

- 25,000 fans

- 100,000 fans

When you look at the chart in Figure 11.1, it shows there's a diminishing return on getting a large quantity of fans.

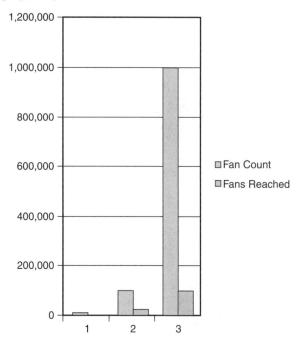

Figure 11.1 *Fan counts and actual fans reached by posts.*

There are a number of reasons for this diminishing visibility, some of which you can control:

- Many of the biggest pages have fans that are several years old.

- EdgeRank's time decay factor means that fans who don't respond to posts for many months or even a couple years probably haven't seen posts from that page for a long time.

- Most pages don't use the interaction-stimulating tactics in this chapter because these best practices were created in late 2010 and most Facebook page managers haven't had any formal training in Facebook marketing.

In April, 2011, Frito-Lay set a Guinness World Record for the most fans gained in a 24-hour period: 1.5 million.[2] They used a contest to achieve this. But was that a good thing? As it turns out, more than 50% of their comments at that time were negative.[3] And now with 2.1 million fans, they appear to average only about 1,500 likes and comments per post. The best response on any recent Frito-Lay post is about 4,000 likes and comments, and the worst is 400. What does this mean? They're probably visible to only about 300,000 fans, which means only about 13% of their fans see their posts.

If you want to know the actual math behind that, using an average feedback rate (which is the total number of likes and comments divided by how many times the post of viewed) of 0.5% and working backward from their average 1,500 likes and comments, that gives us 300,000 impressions. In reality, some of those are duplicates, so it's probably only about 250,000 fans that see their posts. Comparing 250,000 or 300,000 to their total 2.1 million fans means only about 13% of them see their posts.

Though Frito-Lay acquired 1.5 million new fans, their reach really only increased by about 100,000 fans. And a lot of those new contest-related fans were not happy with the way the contest was run.

The upshot of all this is? If you don't get your fans to like and comment on your posts, they'll stop seeing them. Imagine you spend months and hundreds or thousands of dollars getting 10,000 quality fans but in the end only 2,000 of them see your posts.

Disappointing? Definitely. But you can get much better results from the best practices in this chapter. With these techniques, you can get 50%–100% of your fans to see your posts. Although those numbers may sound extreme, I see them frequently on pages that do a great job engaging their fans. It might never be possible for pages who have millions of inactive fans—they might be better off starting over—but newer pages can achieve and maintain a very high degree of visibility to fans.

But first, let's go into more depth on EdgeRank.

---

2. http://www.pepsico.com/PressRelease/Frito-Lay-Fans-Set-Guinness-World-Record-for-Most-Fans-on-Facebook-In-24-Hours-W04282011.html

3. http://wave.wavemetrix.com/content/frito-lay-sets-world-record-facebook-likes-volume-fans-cause-problems-00775

The Mysterious EdgeRank Algorithm

Facebook determines what each person sees in his News Feed. Everyone's Facebook experience is unique and personalized. Facebook shows you posts from friends and pages whose posts you have liked or commented on in the recent past.

New friends and newly liked pages are shown to you for a while, but if you don't interact with them, you will stop seeing posts from them.

EdgeRank also takes into account whether you interact more or less with Photos, Status Updates, and Videos. If you interact with videos from the Celtics and status updates from Kobe Bryant, you will see more Celtics videos than Celtics status updates and more Kobe status updates than Kobe videos.

And now GraphRank has added a friends and family lists consideration. Your types of friends and your family may not see the same posts.

Post Metrics and Benchmarks

Anyone can see how many likes and comments each of your Facebook page's posts have received. If you're an administrator of a Facebook page, you'll see extra data about each post that your fans won't (see Figure 11.2):

Figure 11.2   *Impressions and Feedback rate are displayed to page admins beneath posts.*

Impressions

This is how many times the post was shown. This isn't a count of unique people because some people might have reloaded their page or scrolled down to see older posts and been shown your post more than once.

Feedback Rate

This is a calculation that shows how engaging your post was. Facebook adds up the number of likes and comments and divides them by the impressions count. This isn't affected by how many of your fans you reach; it's always relative to the audience that saw the post.

Sometimes a post will only go out to a very small audience but have a dramatically higher feedback rate. This means EdgeRank was highly targeted in reaching the best people for that post, but it won't make you too happy because you didn't reach many of your fans. The lesson is: Feedback rate is important but can be skewed higher when you don't reach that many people.

Generally speaking, you want to try to get a 1% or higher feedback rate. I've seen others advocate a lower goal, but all the students and businesses who've learned the methods in this chapter have been able to achieve a 1% feedback rate.

Impressions/Fan Count

This number isn't shown, but it's easy to calculate. Look at your last 5–10 posts, find the average number of impressions you're getting, and then divide that by your total number of fans.

[Average (impressions / post)] / Fan count = % of fan seeing posts

This gives you a rough idea of how many of your fans are seeing your posts. I've seen this be over 100% for some posts. I've seen pages struggle to get their average above 40%, but I've also seen a bunch of businesses using this chapter's techniques get 70%–100%.

Very new posts won't show impressions or feedback rate right away. I've seen it delayed by as much as a day or two.

Feedback Rate's Effect on Impressions

Here's the important insight: I've found by analyzing the data for hundreds of posts across dozens of pages that the higher your feedback rate is, the more of your fans you reach. The pages that struggle to get more than 30% of their fans to see their posts also have low feedback rates and probably aren't using the interaction tactics I discuss in this chapter.

Are Some of Your Fans Unreachable Forever?

Another takeaway from EdgeRank is that it includes a time decay factor. If you haven't stimulated your fans to interact with you for months and months, it can be very hard or even impossible to ever get your messages in front of them again. At this point, you need to use advertising tactics to get them back. There are a couple ways to use ads to reanimate these "dead" fans. Hey, the book wouldn't be complete without a zombie metaphor, would it? I cover those tactics in Chapter 9, "The Face of Advertising: How to Capitalize on the Most Powerful Marketing Tool."

Dancing on the EdgeRank: Increasing Response and Visibility

So now that you understand EdgeRank, why it makes sense and how it can go horribly wrong, what should you do? How do you post on Facebook in a way that ensures you can meet your objectives? Based on the experience of many companies and Facebook marketers, as well as some early data from Momentus Media,[4] I've developed some best practices that help you get more likes and comments on every post. They'll help you ensure visibility to 70% or more of your fans.

But first, let's review some of the fundamentals of Web 2.0 and social media—over the least few years, the social media industry has been working out the best ways to effectively communicate with customers online.

What the Heck Is Web 2.0?

Social media marketers began to discuss the "Web 2.0" more than five years ago[5], but one of its main lessons has yet to penetrate the minds of strategic thinkers in many companies. Table 11.1 shows some of the differences in approach that began back then.

Table 11.1   Web 1.0 Versus Web 2.0

Web 1.0	Web 2.0
Websites	Blogs, Twitter, and Facebook pages and Groups
Publishing	Participation and conversation
Reading	Reading and commenting

Think about how marketing worked in the 1980s: You advertised, had a professional PR person putting out press releases, created brochures and business cards, sent mail to snail mail lists, and went to networking meetings and conferences. By the late 1990s, we started to see business websites and email marketing. There were discussion forums, but in most of them, marketing was outlawed or heavily limited.

---

4. http://momentusmedia.com/blog/?page_id=1468

5. http://oreilly.com/web2/archive/what-is-web-20.html

In the early 2000s, we saw the birth and growth of blogging and people began to comment on blog posts and converse with each other more publicly. Amazon.com allowed reviews of books, both negative and positive, and voting on these reviews. More and more consumers' voices were heard.

By 2005, services that enabled sharing such as YouTube, Digg, Flickr, and MySpace started to take off. It became the norm to expect people not to just experience or read content, but also to respond to it. That's where Web 2.0 began. In 2006, *Time* magazine made "YOU" the person of the year, recognizing the new mass of anonymous users who create and contribute content online.[6] In fact, one of those sites was Wikipedia, initially made fun of because people thought that random nobodies couldn't create a factual encyclopedia. However, 184 sources are quoted in a Wikipedia article about its own accuracy (ironic, isn't it?) and found that despite notable temporary inaccuracies, it covers many more subjects more in-depth than any other encyclopedia.[7] It's clearly being used and referred to heavily. Despite its problems, it's not going away.

As Twitter became a hot topic among bloggers, geeks, and journalists in 2007 and 2008, social media gurus began to emerge and social media marketing became a serious topic of discussion. Some companies made mistakes and were targeted by enraged and suddenly powerful bloggers and Twitterers. In 2009, celebrities started jumping on Twitter, and in June of that year it was on the cover of *Time* magazine. Media was changing dramatically because news was sometimes broken by amateurs on Twitter rather than by major news networks. Newspapers were going out of business or experimenting with new revenue models.

As you can see, the upshot is that consumers now expect to be able to give public feedback about businesses, services, and products. And they expect to be able to read reviews from average customers. They trust less what the company says about itself and more what its customers say. Testimonials supplied by the companies themselves, ostensibly from real customers, also are considered less trustworthy than reviews on third-party websites.

The implications for businesses are dramatic. If you don't have a good product or service and if customers have valid reasons to complain, chances are that your potential buyers can find that out. You actually need to do a good job and keep your customers happy. Those companies that do an outstanding job at this get spontaneous positive word-of-mouth support from their customers.

Consider Zappos, which had more than 400 employees on Twitter way back in 2008. At that time, many companies didn't have a single person on Twitter, but Zappos encouraged more than 400 of its employees to tweet on company time, and

---

6. http://en.wikipedia.org/wiki/You_(Time_Person_of_the_Year)

7. http://en.wikipedia.org/wiki/Reliability_of_Wikipedia

its CEO was one of the most popular Twitter users in the world. Zappos sells shoes, but its main focus has been on customer happiness above all else, taking Nordstrom's legendary customer service a step further. CEO Tony Hsieh engages in some crazy practices, but they work—Zappos was acquired by Amazon for $928 million, and you can't argue with that. For example, during their four-week training, Hsieh offers employees $2,000 to quit. By incentivizing the wrong people to leave, he improved his employee base. He also likes to tell the story about late one night when he and a group wanted some pizza. He suggested they call Zappos for it. The employee didn't know Hsieh was involved but called a pizza place for them nonetheless. Crazy? Crazy smart.

So the point is: Have good offerings, make your customers happy, and expect that they're going to tell the truth about you.

Leading the Community You Create

Facebook empowers you to gather a community of potential buyers and then lead the conversation. This is better than Twitter, where conversation is too fragmented and hard to follow.

You also can use Facebook's multimedia nature to post images and videos for discussion. It's possible that the people you serve have never had a community in which to share their passions. Less connected people like that give you high click-through rates and low-cost clicks, they don't cost a lot to acquire, and they talk like crazy. Put them in a Facebook Group and you have a perpetual motion machine.

You can ask also questions and use polls to gather more information about them. I've seen businesses who were having trouble make strong sales through Facebook simply by asking and acting on the insights gained.

Formulas for Posts

There are two or three main goals for each post, and if you want, you can try all three at once!

- To get likes, say "Click Like if..." and keep the second part simple.

- To get comments, ask a question or say, "Tell me in the Comments below..." followed by whatever you want to know.

- To get clicks to your website or blog post, put the URL in the update and say, "Click this link..." and tell them why.

Here are some more details on each.

"Click Like If…"

This is a really simple formula. It's all about whether people agree with you. Choose something that you're pretty sure 60%–100% of your fans like. If you got a lot of fans from targeting a particular interest, you can be pretty sure they'll respond positively to that. Tell them to click like if they like that thing. No brainer, right?

After you have the thing you want to show them or mention to them, combine it with the following variations of the formula:

- Post a photo or video related to the dream or benefits you're selling, and make it something like "Click Like if you'd love (to have this benefit)" or "Click Like if you'd love to see yourself (living such and such dream)."

- "Click Like if you love…" (ponies, bacon, or whatever applies to your niche).

- "Click Like if you think…."

- "Click Like if you'd love to have…."

- "Click Like if you believe that…."

- "Click Like if you want…."

"Question" or "Tell me in the Comments below…"

The best questions are open-ended, which means they get fill-in-the-blank, not yes-or-no, answers. Imagine you're on a first date and the goal is to get the other person talking. The more you listen, the more likely you are to get what you want. The more you talk, the more the other person turns off and you don't get what you want.

Here are some ways to ask questions:

- "What do you think about…?" (For example, you could ask about some recent good news in the niche you're operating in. Try to avoid asking about bad news unless you're asking for people's ideas for solving problems.)

- "How do you feel about…?"

- You can actually tell people to fill in the blank if you want. For example: "My ideal work day includes _____. Fill in the blank and tell us!"

- "What happens when you…?"

- "What are your goals related to…?"

- "If you could change one thing about…, what would it be?"

- "What's your favorite thing about…?"

- "When do you feel most…?"

- "Why do you...?"

- "What's your favorite way to...?"

- "When you were younger..."

A good example of combining this comes from *SportsCenter*: "CLICK LIKE if you think the Heat can SWEEP Dallas or COMMENT as to why the Mavericks will make this a series."[8] (Obviously, that was written before game two was over.) That approach gets you likes and comments both! The formula is

> "Click Like if you think [one thing] or Comment as to why you think [the opposite]."

This is definitely a more complicated formula, but it works. The proof is in the pudding. Test it and see whether it works for your page.

"Click this link..."

If you type or paste a URL into a post, Facebook automatically pulls in the photo, page title, and description. Most people assume the page title and description are written in stone, but you can actually change them. Click on the title and rewrite it, and click on the description and rewrite that. That's a lifesaver if, for some reason, it's pulling in weird HTML formatting. And make sure you choose the thumbnail that looks more interesting or fits best with what you're sending them to. If none of the images fit, select No Thumbnail.

Don't assume that the information Facebook grabs with your URL is stimulating enough by itself. Add calls to action like these:

- "Check out this blog post because..."; then tell them what the benefits of reading it are.

- "Click here to get this discount now before it goes away!"

- "Check out our latest press release"; then make sure they know why they should care. Press releases are often "me me me" selfish information about the company that no customer cares about.

If your blog post already has a catchy, stimulating title, you might not need to get too creative with the text you add in the Facebook page post. But make sure you add a reason to click and/or a question for commenting. If you don't, that's a missed opportunity. Remember, although you want people to click to the website, you still need the Facebook post to be visible to as many fans as possible. EdgeRank might count clicks to other websites, but we don't know that for sure.

---

8. http://www.facebook.com/SportsCenter/posts/107630972660174

Incorporating Selling the Dream

Chapter 7, "Selling the Dream: Going Beyond Benefits to Arouse Your Fans' Desire for What You Offer," laid a foundation that carries through what you target with your advertising and what you talk about in your posts. If you read that chapter and went through the steps to figure out what dreams you're selling, you should have topics, words, places, and some of the 12 "things people dream about" written down somewhere. If you used this in your FaceHook work getting fans (see Chapter 10), you saw which interests got the best CTR. You know what interests brought in your most passionate fans. Now all you have to do is get them talking about it.

Here are some examples based on interests and demographics:

- **Turtles (photo of turtle)**—"Click Like if you love turtles! What's your favorite thing about them?"

- **Marketing**—"Click Like if you love marketing! What's your favorite kind of marketing? What's your least favorite?"

- **Jazz (photo of Charlie Parker)**—"What's your favorite jazz era, and who was your favorite musician from that era?"

- **Kayaking**—"Click Like if you're kayaking this weekend!"

- **Home decorating**—"Click like if you love furniture with storage!"

- **Parents (25–44 years old)**—"Click like if your kid loves the *Cars* movies! And comment below who her favorite characters are."

Any of these can be photo posts. Just make sure the image is a good representation of the topic. All the same things go into choosing good photos here that go into choosing advertising images, so reread that section of Chapter 9.

Here are examples incorporating some of the 12 "things people dream about."

Let's say you've grown an audience of men who are 35–54 years old for a page that teaches financial success or sells retirement or insurance. You know that this audience dreams of security. You can therefore post things like "Click Like if want to grow your IRA. Comment below what your biggest obstacle is to doing that."

If you have built an audience of women between 25 and 34 years old who dream of connection, you can say "Click Like if you love your family and friends! Comment below: Who do you feel closest to and who would you like to be closer with?"

If you have an audience of men and women who are 55 and older who dream of freedom and choices, try a post like this one: "Click Like if you're going to mark something off your bucket list this year! Comment below and tell us what it is."

The following are qualities of successful posts:

- Has 1% feedback rate or more
- Has 50% or more impressions compared to fans
- Is attention-grabbing
- Is something 95% of the audience cares about
- Asks for a Like or asks a question
- Fits the demographics and geographic location of your fan base
- Contains no-brainer text
- Sells the dream
- Is based on what you learned from ad testing

Bad posts have these qualities:

- Feedback that's below 0.5%
- Impressions that are less than 30% of fan base
- Not understanding audience
- Posts that 95% of the audience doesn't care about
- Promotes things that very few people will care about
- Photos without captions or calls to action

Learning from Your Previous Posts

Administrators of pages can view some pretty cool insights, and one of them lists your last 10 posts, how many impressions it got, and the feedback rate you got from them (see Figure 11.3). You can use this (and of course you can also scroll through your page's Wall and look at more of these) to look for patterns in which posts got better feedback rates and why. Pick out a few of the ones with the highest and a few with the lowest feedback rates, and see if you can tell what you did right or wrong. After you develop a theory about which posts are best for your audience, test it by trying another post along those lines to see whether you get similar results.

Message	Posted ▼	Impressions	Feedback
	June 12 at 10:50pm	34,625	0.10 %
	June 12 at 11:33am	9,148	0.11 %
	June 12 at 11:31am	6,966	0.43 %
	June 11 at 7:03pm	5,239	0.076 %
	June 10 at 10:37pm	12,254	0.16 %
	June 10 at 7:18pm	279,392	0.43 %
	June 10 at 6:08pm	5,408	0.17 %
	June 10 at 2:28pm	20,467	0.12 %
	June 10 at 1:24pm	13,347	0.20 %
	June 10 at 12:04pm	8,000	0.14 %

Figure 11.3 *Page posts (blanked out due to nondisclosure agreement).*

Engagement Milestones

Here are three milestones that will tell you you're making great progress with getting your audience to interact with you:

- **Getting 1% feedback regularly**—If you're using the formulas from this chapter, this is easy to achieve.

- **People posting spontaneously on your page**—When people are really excited about your brand or page, they'll go back to the actual fan page and post there.

- **Fans seeing and posting on fan page posts**—If you have a lot of fans going back to your fan page and it's set by default to show fan posts, too, then some of them might comment on each others' posts. This is one way to know you've really got your fans stirred up. When they have that much enthusiasm, they'll tolerate more sales messages.

Guiding Your Community

Because you administer the page or Group, you have ultimate control. You can subtly guide the conversation with your posts and comments.

Giving Fans Some Room

It's a good idea to step back and let conversations take their course. On blog posts and Facebook I've noticed that when the administrator is too involved, discussions don't evolve. Don't think you need to respond to every post. I've also noticed that if you post something, get one comment, and then comment on that first comment, you are less likely to get more comments. Let 5–10 people comment before you comment. If you can, don't comment at all and see how many you get.

The point is that you create a space for discussion and then leave room. Imagine you're sitting in a circle with 10 people and bring up a topic. Would the people in the group want you commenting after each person? Or would they prefer to have a normal conversation? Let something evolve out of the fans themselves, and see where it goes.

Dealing with Difficult Fans

You can remove or block troublesome people (but let's hope it's because they're actually weirdos and you're not just blocking all the people who are bringing to light real problems with your business).

And by the way, if you do have issues with your business that customers complain about regularly, fix them! If you make a small mistake in social media, apologize! I've seen businesses take other approaches, and they don't work. One decided to delete a customer concern rather than address it—this converted an irritated customer into an angry one who pledged to post everyday and everywhere her displeasure with the company. Nestle got in trouble back in 2010 for responding snarkily to customer comments, and a number of brands have had this problem. The way to deal with these situations effectively is to listen, acknowledge the feedback, validate and thank the customer, and then fix the problem.

Because your customer service is public in social media, dealing with problems well or badly is amplified. If it happens in the comments of one of your posts, people are witnessing it. If you do a great job hearing and satisfying an irritated customer, other customers will trust you more.

How to Avoid PR Nightmares

Just breathe.

Most people have learned not to write an email reply while angry. It's even easier and quicker to shoot off a negative Facebook comment. When you read something distressing, step away from the computer, take a breath, and do something else for a while. Remember, if they posted it on your Facebook page's Wall, it does not go out to all your fans. Only the few that come back to the page will see it. It is not an emergency. If you feel defensive, worried, or upset, absolutely FORBID yourself from posting a response without getting someone else's opinion, taking time to relax, and even having someone else edit your response.

Also, if we're talking about comments that fans see, one of your most loyal fans might respond with a more fair view. It's much more powerful and believable when a customer comes to your aid. It can be worth the anxiety to wait 30–60 minutes for one of them to chime in.

Just as people try not to email when angry or drinking, it's best not to do social media when drinking. This is up to the individual—if you're a rock star or comedian maybe you *should* post while drunk—but just keep in mind that what seems like a great idea right now might not later.

Balancing Engagement and Selling Types of Posts

Some readers of this book might only care about creating interaction and remaining visible to fans, but others want a direct profit from their Facebook efforts. So, how do you combine conversation with sales? Do they fit together? Yes, a number of companies have found that they can alternate interaction-oriented Facebook posts with more direct offers, discounts, and other types of sales-oriented posts. You can see examples of these two types of posts in Table 11.2.

Table 11.2   Engagement Versus Sales Post Formulas

Engagement Formulas	Sales Formulas
Click like if…	When are you going to…?
Ask a question	Are you ready to…?
Share this	Check out our…
Photo post	Discount
Guess what/where this is	Contest

So how do you meld together these two Facebook posting approaches?

Ratio and Frequency

There's no hard-and-fast rule for how many of your posts should engage or sell the dream versus how many should actually sell your products or services. Some go with this rule of thumb: four engagement posts and then one sales post. Your audience might be okay with more sales posts than that, or they might want less. One business I've previously mentioned does four engagement and one sales post *per day*. Another business sells one homeware per day, and almost all its posts are sales-oriented and no one has a problem with it.

But if you're not sure, start with one post per day, mostly engagement oriented, and do one or two sales posts per week. You can look at your sales records to see which days of the week you sell best on, and do the sales posts that day or the day before.

I think you're missing an opportunity if you don't post every day, but there are exceptions. If you really run out of post ideas, it might be better to wait a day or two than post something inane. On certain holidays, almost nobody is online, so it might not be worth it to post then either.

Some businesses are seasonal and the customers aren't buying all year long, so you might not be able to sing the same tune all year. But I would advise against taking weeks or months off posting because of EdgeRank's time decay factor—otherwise, you might come back to posting and be reaching fewer people. Find things to talk about in the off-season. Even a summer vacation spot can show its fans wintertime photos and possibly get them to visit twice a year instead of once. If you know when people buy, you have a big advantage. For example, I know that most people who go to Myrtle Beach, South Carolina, book their vacations in January and February. The resorts there can start selling the beach dream while everyone in the Midwest is stuck in their cubicles and sick of the snow.

Ideas for Posting

Some businesses with fans see good sales right away. Others have to work at it, especially those with longer sales cycles.

How often do regular customers buy from you? If they buy every three months, then expect new fans to take three months until they're ready to buy. Your goal in that three months is to build awareness and a relationship so that, come decision time, that relationship and their knowledge of your offerings will be a strong influence to purchase.

Some of your fans might never have bought what you offer online. So, follow these suggestions:

• Post why it's good to buy online.

• Post why you're better than other online stores.

• Find previous customers with positive feedback whom you can quote.

Put a link to your website in more of your posts. If you get more likes and comments, you'll get more impressions. Let's say you're getting 15,000–20,000 per post. You should be able to get 1%–2% of those to click to the site if there's a link. That means you could get perhaps 200 site visitors per day and 1,400 per week. So create posts that give a reason for people to like, comment, *and* click. Here's an example:

"Click over and check out this product: [link]. Do you LIKE it? What would you do if you owned it?"

Here are some posts that get people thinking and talking about products:

• "What's the most important product for...?"

• "What _____ products do you like or dislike?"

• "Do you have trouble finding products for...?"

• "Do you buy _____ online?"

• "Are you ready to...?"

Another clever way to bring business into the picture without being so in-your-face that you turn people off is to talk about what's going on in your business. Not all companies are willing to be this transparent, but it can be a big advantage.

Here are some examples:

> German shepherd puppy breeder: "Essie seems to be stalled with her labor... recommendation for a C-section tomorrow morning...." More than 1,000 fans had been following Essie through her pregnancy. Daily photo posts remind potential buyers every day that new puppies are coming. (Essie was fine and gave birth to eight pups.)

> Vacation rental company: "We are almost all booked up for May and June. We're actually looking into buying a couple of other properties to meet demand. If you haven't booked yet, you can call us at xxx-xxx-xxxx." This bragging post creates urgency due to scarcity. If you've been watching this company and thinking about booking but haven't yet, you'll probably jump on the phone at this point.

> Attorney: "Great settlement in one of our cases today. A very happy client!"

> Chiropractor: "Trying out our new massage table myself today, and boy is it nice. Next time you come in, you can use it, too!"

> Association: "Just over 5,000 people attended our national conference this weekend. Great time! We're going to be putting on a bunch of local get-togethers over the next few months, too. Click here to check them out: (link)"

Feedback Rate and Sales Posts

Anytime you ask people to click on a link in a post, whether you're sending them to a blog post or to a product on a e-commerce website, your feedback rate will look low. The feedback rate only counts like and comments. Facebook doesn't say they count clicks on other links you add to posts, but I wouldn't be surprised if they do, or will in the future. Anyway, don't freak out that your sales posts have lower feedback rates—that's normal.

Engagement just asks people to participate around shared interests. Sales formulas try to get people to give up their money. There is definitely a gray area because you can get people to engage around your products and services, and you can send people to innocent-looking informative blog posts that are surrounded by sales messages.

Whenever you're in doubt, you can ask your fans whether they like some of your approaches better than others. Just take the feedback with a grain of salt, though, because some of your fans might never buy from you. You can phrase it more specifically like this: "If you've bought something from us because of our Facebook posts, tell us what you bought and why." That way, you've eliminated the opinions of those who aren't really your customers.

12

FaceMessage: Achieving Other Corporate Goals on Facebook

I'm an impatient guy. I constantly want to know if I'm on the right track. That's why I like to see results from what I do. I think I was drawn to direct marketing for the same reason I love doing stand-up comedy and improv theatre for audiences: The feedback is instantaneous. Throughout my marketing career, I've been drawn more to marketing where the performance is measurable, and I regularly innovate situations to improve measurability. So it's no wonder my specialty is Internet marketing, where metrics abound. I love being able to quantify persuasion and influence tactics. Best of all is matching the perfect metric to guide a specific client to their particular goal. That's a major theme in Chapter 6, "Facing the Facts: How to Continuously Get Better Results with the Five Steps of Optimization."

As my understanding of web analytics deepened, I realized that we actually can't measure everything. Some of the hardest things to measure, like public relations, networking, and TV commercials, still appear to have major effects. It's harder to track them as granularly as we can a set of Facebook ads, so even though we know they're effective, it's very difficult to optimize them to get better results.

In fact, measuring the effects of Facebook increased my esteem for the marketing disciplines of branding, positioning, and public relations (PR). At a Facebook conference in San Francisco, I saw a presentation based on a huge multicompany dataset confirming that, usually, Facebook is the potential customer's first step in a sales process that ends right after a Google search. Because of how most people do web analytics, Google gets all the credit for those sales and Facebook none of the credit. Unless you have an advanced analytics setup and an expert analyst, you probably aren't getting an accurate picture of how Google and Facebook each contributes to your bottom line.

Similarly, when I have done search engine optimization (SEO) and AdWords for the same company, we find that the AdWords exposure can increase how many people search Google for the company and that the conversion rates for each are higher. A profit-increasing marketing synergy occurs when you can afford to run more than one type of campaign at the same time.

The upshot is that almost all marketing and PR is good, especially when the same potential customer hears about you more times, in more ways, and from more places.

With that in mind, let's take a look at how Facebook works with some of these harder-to-measure strategies.

Non–Revenue-Oriented Facebook Goals

Not everything in social media is about money! Some of you say "Duh!" to that, but I come from a direct marketing background, where all that counts is profits I can prove I produced. I've learned by talking to other types of marketers and PR people that there are other valid business functions for social media. I felt this book would be unbalanced without at least a quick look at how else you might use Facebook (see Figure 12.1).

Although we've talked about other subgoals throughout this book, such as Likes and web traffic, it's usually been in the context of trying to ultimately achieve profits. In this chapter, however, we will talk about situations where the ultimate goal is not revenue or profitability.

Branding and Positioning

Branding has many definitions, but in the context of this discussion, it means increasing consumer awareness of your company, increasing interest, and perhaps arousing desire for your offers, but foregoing explicit calls to action. That means you're doing the first three phases of attention-interest-desire (AIDA) with emphasis on the first phase. Your goals are to get consumers to know who you are fundamentally (your brand) and who you are compared to your competitors (your positioning).

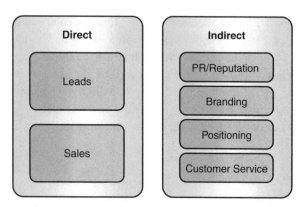

Figure 12.1   *Direct versus indirect marketing and communications activities.*

Before you brand your company or product, you need to answer questions like

- What are your company values?

- Why should customers be loyal to you?

- What promises do you make to customers?

- How do you describe your company in just three words?

Then that brand needs to be expressed creatively, visually, and conversationally. This all sounds rather conceptual, but there's a reason Coca-Cola's brand is worth more than $60 billion.[1] That's the value of *just the brand*, apart from any other physical property, apart from the formula for Coke, and so on. Coke's brand is everything we think we know about Coke, how we feel about Coke, and the psychological power Coke has over the people of the world.

Put another way, if you don't have a brand, what sets you apart from the competition? What makes your marketing consistent? What should customers expect from you? Are you confusing your potential buyers? Are you resigned to competing only on the basis of price?

Getting Your Brand into Purchase Consideration

From a bottom-line perspective, the point of branding is to fix your offerings as a strong or favored option within the mind of your potential customer so it's waiting there when it comes time for him to choose. If you have a strong brand and have done well to communicate that brand, and your positioning sets you apart from your competitors, you have a much better chance of getting that new buyer's business.

---

1. http://mashable.com/2010/11/06/value-of-brand-names/

If you already have a brand book that specifies how the company is represented creatively, you can use it on Facebook and expand it within Facebook. If this is the first time you've tried to nail down parameters that make sense for your brand, then gather all the people who should have a say in these decisions and begin to come up with the specifics. After reading Chapter 7, "Selling the Dream: Going Beyond Benefits to Arouse Your Fans' Desire for What You Offer," you might want to include ways to creatively portray the dream your company promises through its offerings.

Positioning

What advantage does your offering have that none of your competitors do? Do your competitors make comparative claims? For example, do they say they're the fastest or biggest or newest? What you come up with here could become a slogan, like Avis's, "We're #2. We Try Harder." And your positioning statement can be said and demonstrated in many ways. For example, Avis could do a commercial demonstrating how hard its employees work to make customers happy. Or they could show a funny balding white guy dancing with a voiceover, "We're Avis. We're #2. We're Sweating for You."

I take it back. That sounds like one of the Geico fake commercials. Don't create that one.

How Do You Do It on Facebook?

How do you extend your brand onto Facebook, and how can you better position your company with Facebook? What kinds of decisions are involved, and what are the limitations of Facebook?

After crystallizing your branding and positioning, answer these questions:

- How does this affect your choice of images for the page and ads?
- How does this affect your targeting of potential buyers?
- How does this affect what you ask your page fans?
- How does this affect how you portray yourself in posts and comments?

Customer Service

Social media websites are great places for customers to get help and for companies to solve their problems. Customers contacting companies through Twitter and Facebook has become more and more popular, especially in companies whose other customer service options are set up like brick walls. You know the type: companies you can contact only by phone and that have complicated phone menus

designed to keep you from talking to a human being. Websites like
DialAHuman.com and GetHuman.com have sprung up to provide tips on how to
get customer support from big companies.

And social media users have taken to contacting companies via their Twitter
accounts or Facebook pages. In other words, after you have social media accounts,
you will have to do customer service via them. Make sure you've given some
thought to how you'll do social media customer service. Many companies started
getting customer requests before they realized they'd need to handle them. Just
ignoring them isn't an option because it's a very public customer service failure.

Another situation that can come up, along the lines of crisis management, is dealing with abusive page fans or group members. As I've said elsewhere, my experience is that when you are actively engaging page fans or group members with
positive topics, negativity is extremely rare. But the bigger the page or group, the
more chance there is you'll get a few bad apples.

You should respond to abusive people with increasing levels of severity, depending
on how bad and frequent the abuse is. First, you should have a policy. For example,
"This is a positive community, and we do not tolerate abuse of any kind. We are
reasonable people, but if you engage in a personal attack you might be banned
without warning. We reserve the right to decide what comments are serious enough
to lead to a ban. Please be respectful to other group and page members." It's easier
to display this on a page because you can put it in the page info or on a custom tab.
Groups can create "Docs," and I recommend you create one called "Group
Policies—PLEASE READ."

Keep in mind, though, that not all criticism is out of bounds. A critic with a real
beef is not the same as an abuser. If you have a real customer experience problem,
thank her for helping you see it and work on fixing it. Customers appreciate a company that is always working to improve customer service. And social media is an
opportunity for companies in this regard—it's a great way to learn more about how
customers experience your brand, products, and services. If you have great offerings, you'll hear about it. If have problems, you'll hear about those, too.

Keep in mind the lessons the social media world learned from Nestle's Facebook
mistakes in March 2010. The page administrator was sarcastic and berated a user,
and not only did the community respond on Facebook, but the company received a
large amount of negative press elsewhere (see Figure 12.2).

In a big group, you might not be able to read every post and comment. You can
appoint a moderator from within the group to alert admins about troublemakers.
You might want to offer this moderator a discount or some other reward for doing
the job. I would suggest you do not make her an admin because any admin can
remove the others.

Figure 12.2   *If you Google "Nestle," you might see an article at the bottom of the first page about this, and if you Google "Nestle Facebook," it's still one of the top results.*

Public Relations

Public relations is a discipline at a crossroads. Traditionally, PR people dealt with journalists, who created media (news programs, articles, and so on), which communicated with the public. PR's public relations, in other words, was indirect. With the rise of social media, companies have been able to talk directly to the public. PR people I've spoken with admit they were slow to adapt to social media, but now some of them have come to it quite aggressively.

I attended one conference panel where a PR person from the audience angrily claimed PR people should be in charge of all social media because they "control the message." A marketing person on the panel replied that Internet marketers had more experience with digital marketing and they should be in charge. Then a journalist in the audience stood up, pointed at the PR person, and said that they—journalists—controlled the story, not the PR people. It was a bit contentious. What makes social media so much of an obstacle is that it crosses corporate department lines. It's a bit of direct marketing, a bit of PR, and a bit of analytics. We need all of that in social media, so we need to collaborate more than usual, and it would be best if we all expanded our skill sets into the other disciplines because every company can't always assemble a team of three superstars from different marketing disciplines.

I haven't been above the fray myself. I wrote a purposefully controversially titled blog post called "How PR People Are Destroying Social Media" in April 2011 in which I said that a certain type of PR person might inhibit the growth of effective social media. And I made the point that social media can be used for PR, market research, customer service, advertising, direct marketing, sales, and reputation management. PR people really have experience with only two or three of these seven functions.

PR people face yet more adaptation. You can't merely push messages in social media—you must learn to lead communities and create conversation. You can't control the message; you can *maybe* guide conversations. In 2006, Edelman revealed they had created fake blogs to help Wal-Mart improve its image.[2] They were skewered by bloggers. This kind of deception is the opposite of the transparency and authenticity people demand in social media. But inevitably, scouts return with arrows in their backs, and we should salute the early efforts taken by the PR folks with initiative.

Press and Blogger Relations

From what I can gather, one of the most unique and valuable things PR people do and can help us learn to do better in social media is build constructive relationships with journalists and bloggers. I asked a group of PR people for some tips on this topic, and here's what they came up with:

- Give them information and add value.

- Read journalists' writings (you can set up Google alerts on their names to keep up with their writings), and write something like they would write.

- Check out which questions journalists are asking via Twitter or Facebook, and answer them.

- Serve the journalist. You must first focus on helping them if you want them to care about helping you.

- Remember that everything you say is on the record.

- Don't send out a big BCC press release via email. It's not personalized, and journalists receive so many of these, they're likely to just ignore it.

- Be easy to find.

- Make the journalist's job easier by thinking about what they need and giving it to them, and be available via phone at anytime. Sometimes they have tight deadlines and if you wait, you'll miss your opportunity with them.

- Determine if the topic is worthy of discussion. Is it controversial?

- Appeal to journalist's vanity—make the journalist the hero.

---

2. http://www.mediapost.com/publications/?fa=Articles.showArticle&art_aid=49883

- When you read one of their current pieces, email them some information they didn't know—this cements you in mind as an expert for future use.

- 70% of journalists have to find content, videos and so on, so almost all will take completed video if you send it to them—only TV stations won't.

- Journalists will shape the article, so leave them their autonomy.

Thanks to Sally Falkow, Carrie Bugbee, Adele Cehrs, Li Evans, Chase McMichael, and Chris Brubaker for the previous tips.

I see a pattern in there, don't you? It's similar to the anti-"me me me" concept I talked about in Chapter 6. Help the journalist get what he wants, and you have a better chance of getting what you want.

Here are some more Facebook PR suggestions:

- You can add a custom News/Media tab to your Facebook tab and put information there that journalists can use.

- You can advertise to people who work at specific magazines, newspapers, TV stations, TV shows, and so on.

- Watch out for controversial writers, and know how they write before you talk to them.

- If there isn't really press for smaller niches, create your own audience— that means growing page fans and group members.

- It's not about the big hit (getting picked up by the media); it's about the right hit. You need to target the right media.

Crisis Management

Another thing PR people are good at is crisis management. The key thing they do here is plan for various crisis scenarios so they know what to do and stay ahead of time. But usually, the biggest crisis on a Facebook page is negative feedback, and an organized protest of posting would be the biggest form of that.

A crisis is an opportunity. Retreating into the turtle shell is only one response to bad publicity, but it's the most common for those without PR experience.

Making Related News Your Own[3]

Making news your own is a way to co-opt things people are paying a lot of attention to. As long as it's relevant to your company or organization, you can provide

---

3. Thanks again to Adele Cehrs of Epic PR Group for ideas on this section.

interesting information to the media while they're focused on that story. This strategy requires staying on top of both mainstream and niche news and then making a statement about it in relation to your brand. For example,

- If you're Southwest and other airlines are getting bad press for bag fees, you can make the relevant statement that you don't charge extra.

- If you're the Child Abuse Prevention Society, when there's a highly charged public trial on that topic, you can prepare statements ahead of time—one in case the verdict is guilty and one for a non-guilty verdict.

- When news comes out that a man died of a stroke after a chiropractic adjustment, the American Chiropractic Association can explain its safety record, the facts, and the research.

In each of these cases, a series of Facebook posts are in order. The bigger your Facebook reach, the better, but hopefully you have a significant number of your biggest supporters as Facebook fans, and you can get the message to them and ask them to pass it on.

To keep up on the news, you'll have to read daily headlines as well as set up some Google Alerts. Before you set up the alerts, search Google a few times to find the best phrases to use. Which ones bring up the most relevant information? Then go to www.Google.com/alerts and create an alert for each search phrase (see Figure 12.3). I suggest getting all types, delivered once a day to your email. I have 19 Google Alerts set up at this time.

Everything	Volume	How often	Deliver to	
"brian carter"	Only the best results	Once a day	bbcarter@gmail.com	Edit
"facebook fans"	Only the best results	Once a day	bbcarter@gmail.com	Edit
"facebook marketing" OR "marketing with facebook"	Only the best results	Once a day	bbcarter@gmail.com	Edit
"facebook profits" or "facebook roi"	Only the best results	Once a day	bbcarter@gmail.com	Edit
"facebook statistics"	Only the best results	Once a day	bbcarter@gmail.com	Edit
"like button"	Only the best results	Once a day	bbcarter@gmail.com	Edit
"social media marketing	Only the best results	Once a day	bbcarter@gmail.com	Edit
"social media trainer"	Only the best results	Once a day	bbcarter@gmail.com	Edit
"social media"	Only the best results	Once a day	bbcarter@gmail.com	Edit
"twitter marketing" OR "marketing with twitter"	Only the best results	Once a day	bbcarter@gmail.com	Edit
briancarter	Only the best results	Once a day	bbcarter@gmail.com	Edit

Figure 12.3   *Some of the Google Alerts I use to monitor my own brand and keep up to date on news in my niches.*

While you're at it, set up Google Alerts for your brand and product names, just to stay up on what people are saying about you, unless you already have a more advanced social media monitoring system in place. Andy Beal, author of *Radically Transparent: Monitoring and Managing Reputations Online* and creator of the social media monitoring service Trackur, told me in a 2010 interview that 95% of companies would get the reputation monitoring information they need from Google Alerts.

Journalistic Best Practices for Interaction

Facebook conducted a study[4] of people interacting with journalists' Facebook pages[5] that underlines many of the tips we discuss in Chapter 11, "Talking Till You're Blue in the Face: How to Get More Likes and Comments," but also puts some numbers to how important these practices are. If you're a journalist, you can use them. If you're in PR, you can help your journalist friends by sharing the research with them to improve their effectiveness (that falls under helping the journalist to build the relationship):

- Posts that included the journalist's analysis and reflections received 20% more referral clicks (clicks to your website from posts) than their average post.

- Photos received 50% more likes than non-photo posts.

- Including a thumbnail image with a link resulted in 65% more likes and 50% more comments.

- Posts with questions to the reader received twice as many comments.

- Calls to read or take a closer look increased response by 37%.

As you can see, it pays for journalists to foster interaction on their own page and include direct-marketing style calls to action. Sometimes journalists use Facebook to get reader input or find experts to interview.

What should journalists post about, if they want more responses?

- Posts about education received twice as many likes than average.

- Posts on politics received 70% more likes and 60% more comments.

- International news posts were clicked on 70% more than average.

---

4. http://www.facebook.com/notes/facebook-journalists/study-how-people-are-engaging-journalists-on-facebook-best-practices/245775148767840

5. https://www.facebook.com/journalists?sk=app_201416986567309

And what about policies to ensure that the big media companies don't run into problems due to public employee statements or inaccurate reporting? In 2011, the British Broadcast Corporation suggested the following to their journalists:[6]

- Say that you work for the BBC and discuss your work publicly, but don't put BBC in your name or title and clarify that your views are personal and not those of the BBC.

- Don't state political views that compromise your impartiality.

- Have a senior editor review tweets and posts as they go out.

The Canadian Broadcasting Corporation also has discouraged journalists from using Facebook posts as sources, encouraging them to look deeper for more reliable sources.[7]

6. http://thenextweb.com/uk/2011/07/14/bbc-publishes-its-social-media-guidelines-for-journalists/

7. http://www.allfacebook.com/bbc-cites-facebook-in-new-social-media-policy-2011-07

13

Face-alytics: Analyzing Your Facebook Results

Knowing is half the battle. Hopefully I'm not the only one who watched way too many G.I. Joe cartoons as a kid. Every episode ended with a public service announcement like "don't swim in thunderstorms" or "don't try to jump your bikes over a downed power line"—yep, so obvious that there are bunches of parodies of them on YouTube. After the G.I. Joe character taught the lesson, the kids would declare "Now I know!" and the soldier would add, "And knowing is half the battle!"

Neglecting analytics is a mistake I cover in Chapter 5, "How Not to Fall on Your Face: Six Mistakes That Block Facebook Profitability." Analytics tools of all types give you knowledge and insights, and that's half the battle to getting profitable results. The rest of the battle is taking action on that data—optimizing—which I explained in Chapter 6, "Facing the Facts: How to Continuously Get Better Results with the Five Steps of Optimization." In this chapter, I show how you can use Google Analytics as well as an advanced Facebook page analytics service to get a better picture of what's working and what's not.

Which Web Analytics Package Should You Use?

Most companies already have some kind of web analytics in place, and everyone with a Facebook page has access to Insights, so it should be easy to get started. Most people can quickly navigate through the information available for your Facebook pages in Insights and quickly discover this doesn't help them track what Facebook users are doing on their websites. It doesn't tell you anything about revenue or business leads. You need web analytics for that.

For those of you not yet familiar with analytics, let's talk about the basics. There are a number of kinds of web analytics packages (these are for activity on your website, not on Facebook itself). Here's an overview and my recommendation of what you should have:

- **Page tagging versus logfile analysis**—Current enterprise-level analytics packages such as Google Analytics, which I recommend, use page tagging (JavaScript code or pixels). Logfile analyzers such as AWStats are the oldest kind of analytics and not the most useful for marketers.

- **Click analytics**—These packages, such as Clicky, CrazyEgg, and ClickTale, give you more information about where visitors are clicking on your website. Some even allow you to monitor visitor actions in real time. They typically don't give you a lot of other web marketing information, such as where your web visitors came from. I recommend you add this later if you need more information.

- **Lead generation metrics**—Companies whose new business begins with lead generation often have trouble tracking phone calls back to specific web sources. How will you know if that call came in from Google or Facebook or Bing or the Yellow Pages? Companies like Mongoose Metrics have solutions for this. A customer relationship management (CRM) platform such as SalesForce helps you track your leads and sales back to web sources. What if Google gets you more calls but you close a higher percentage of sales from Facebook? Do you have tracking that will tell you that?

Because Google Analytics is free (until you hit 5 million pageviews per month) and has almost every feature its expensive competitors have, I recommend that most companies consider it. It's relatively easy for beginners to use and understand. And it is the most popular—used by more than 14 million websites[1] and estimated to be used by 49%[2]–57%[3] of the top 10,000 sites on the Web.

---

1. http://trends.builtwith.com/websitelist/Google-Analytics

2. http://metricmail.tumblr.com/post/904126172/google-analytics-market-share

3. http://trends.builtwith.com/websitelist/Google-Analytics

Other enterprise-level solutions you can choose from include Omniture, WebTrends, Coremetrics, and Hitwise. Each has its strengths and weaknesses, so be sure you have your analytics personnel review them thoroughly. The implementation and use of each of these can get involved, so if you don't have a dedicated analytics person, stick with Google Analytics.

Google Analytics Overview

When you first log in to Google Analytics, you are presented with the dashboard (see Figure 13.1).

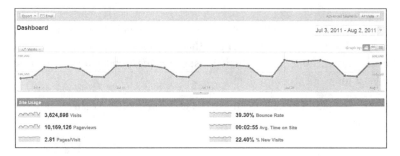

Figure 13.1   *The Google Analytics dashboard.*

The dashboard shows a chart of the most recent 30 days of traffic, as well as the following:

- **Visits**—Number of visits or sessions by all users in that time period

- **Pageviews**—Number of times a page was loaded by all users

- **Pages/Visit**—Average number of pages viewed per session

- **Bounce rate**—Percentage of visits in which the user left the website right after viewing the entrance/landing page (the first page he saw on your site)

- **Average time on site**—Amount of time the average user spent on your website per session

- **% new visits**—Percentage of visits that came from people who had never visited before

You can modify the dates in the upper-right corner, and you can compare two time periods, as in Figure 13.2, to look for changes in specific metrics.

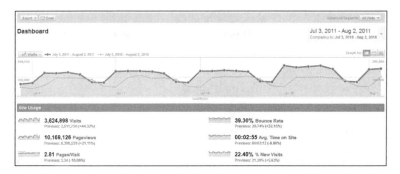

Figure 13.2 *Comparing results for two different date ranges.*

Before we go any further, let me tell you that you can get lost in analytics, especially if you don't know why you're looking at them. You should browse around, initially. But in the future, come to analytics with specific questions you want to answer and you'll get a lot more accomplished.

In the left navigation under "Dashboard" (see Figure 13.3), you'll see a few more main sections.

Figure 13.3 *The main left navigation options in Google Analytics.*

This list briefly covers what you might learn from each:

- **Intelligence**—Keeps an eye on your analytics and alerts you when anything abnormal happens.

- **Visitors**—Gives you deeper info on your visitors, including visitor loyalty, absolute unique visitors, languages, browsers, screen resolution, mobile usage, and more.

- **Traffic sources**—Tells you more about where your visitors come from. How many came from search engines? From Facebook? From other websites? Which keywords did they use to get to your site from Google? This is an important section because you'll frequently go here to find out what Facebook visitors did on your website.

- **Content**—Lets you see which pages on your website people went to most, which pages they first visited in your site, and which other page they came from to arrive at a specific page.

- **Goals**—You can set up conversion tracking in your Google Analytics Settings and then see in this section what percentage of visitors accomplished a goal you wanted them to reach. It's critical to separate this kind of Analytics Goal from the goals we talk about in Chapter 6. Goals in Google Analytics are simply web pages you want web visitors to reach. These may be reflections on your overall corporate goals, or they may be smaller goals that users will reach along the way to getting you the bottom-line goal you're after. For example, I helped a radio network use AdWords and Facebook ads to launch a station in each of three new cities. The bigger goal was to increase Arbitron ratings, but we couldn't track that with web analytics. We could track whether visitors played the "listen online" music player and how long they stayed on the website, so we made that our Google Analytics goal.

  Here's another example: If you wanted web visitors to give you their email, you might track the thank-you page (which appears after an email is submitted) as a Google Analytics goal and find out that 11% of visitors are completing this task. You might also learn that Facebook users are converting at 13% while AdWords visitors are converting at 10%. These details help you make decisions when you optimize.

- **E-commerce**—You can plug Google Analytics into your shopping cart to get info such as conversion rate, number of transactions, average order value, and number of purchased products. Then, just as you can with goals, you can further segment to analyze your conversion rate and per visit value for different traffic sources, keywords, and so on.

Taking Analytics with a Grain of Salt

After you begin to understand the benefits of analytics, you go through the "I'm in love with these analytics" honeymoon stage, which eventually leads to the "I'm disillusioned with analytics" stage. Here are some of the downsides of analytics, which we dive into in the next sections:

- **Untrackables**—Not everything is easy to track, and sometimes it's your key metric!

- **Uneven accountability**—Marketing channels that can be tracked, such as Facebook and Google, can be held to a higher standard than other channels that are harder to track, such as TV ads.

- **Last-Click bias**—If you only track the source of the last click before a sale or other conversion, awareness channels don't get enough credit.

- **Inconsistencies and inaccuracies**—When you compare data from two analytics packages for the same website, you might see very different numbers, and some of the numbers inside one analytics package don't always match up.

Let talk about each of these problems and how you can deal with them.

The Untrackables

The easiest thing to track is AdWords for E-Commerce. You have AdWords data, web analytics data, and probably even data inside your e-commerce system.

Here are a few things that are not so easy to track.

Complicated Real-world Multiple Interactions with Your Multiple Marketing Channels

In reality, most customers see your offering more than once and in more than one place. Each time they interact with your website or company from a marketing channel, that's called a *touchpoint*. Without web analytics that track multiple touch-points, you won't know how much credit to give to awareness channels such as TV, radio, and Facebook versus how much to thank the buy-now channels such as pay-per-click (PPC) advertising—which can also be Facebook. If you don't have analytics that sophisticated, you'll have to go on industry findings like these:

- **Synergistic lift**—Generally, marketing channels *lift* each others' results. That means that a lot of the metrics in each channel perform better because of the other channels. For years, search marketers have had to answer this question from clients: If they already ranked naturally via search engine optimization (SEO), did they really need to advertise for the same keywords? It turns out that usually, when you eliminate one or the other, sales, searches, and conversion rate all decrease.

- **The first and the last click are both important**—Often, a customer's first exposure to you is via a different channel from the one she came in just before she made her purchase. Using only last-click analytics leads you to believe you should turn off the awareness-generating channels, and companies often find that when they do turn them off, leads and sales drop much more dramatically than they expected.

You might be thinking that the bigger question is does the lift produce enough profits to justify the extra expense? You can't answer this question for your company without multiple touchpoint analytics. At this time, Google Analytics doesn't have that capability. I've seen multiple touchpoint analysis from Omniture web analytics, but this kind of effort requires a dedicated analytics person as well as a programmer who works on implementing special analytics code. Sorting through all the data to figure out what's actionable is no easy task—you'll need a full-time analytics person with significant experience. If you have the budget for it, do it. If not, prioritize your marketing budget and use as many channels as you can afford.

Phone Call Leads

Without multiple phone numbers, you can't credit a sale back to its traffic source. The cheapest way is to get your own phone numbers, but if you want to do the best job possible, use a company like Mongoose Metrics. They can dynamically use thousands of phone numbers to give you extremely granular data.[4]

Lead Quality Analysis

If you're involved in lead generation for a sales team, to do the best job of optimizing your marketing, you need to figure out which traffic sources bring you the best quality leads. This means finding out which leads you also need the salespeople to note in your customer relationship management (CRM) platform and which leads turned into sales. For example, if you are running Facebook ads for several demographic targets, what if the 25–35 age group gets you more leads, but the 35–45 group gets you a higher average revenue per lead? Without this data, you can't optimize your Facebook advertising for better profits. This level of optimization requires a CRM such as SalesForce. The upside is that you can also find out which of your salespeople produces the most profit, and even which salespeople work best with which traffic sources.

Marketing That Brings People into Physical Stores

Without a coupon (called a *return device* in direct marketing), you'll never know exactly how successful your promotions were. You definitely won't be able to track them granularly. For example, if you promote an in-store sale via Facebook ads and Google ads, without two different coupons or coupon codes, you can't compare those sources.

---

4. https://www.mongoosemetrics.com/blog/2011/08/10/from-%e2%80%9clike%e2%80%9d-to-lead-how-to-integrate-call-tracking-into-your-facebook-campaign/

Public Relations

Public relations (PR) is notoriously strange when it comes to return on investment (ROI). To be fair, most of the best PR folks I've spoken to do speak the language of profits, but you have to watch out for the subset that doesn't. There's a type of ROI calculation native only to PR called *ad equivalency* where the profit is calculated by comparing a placement (an article written by a journalist as a result of PR efforts) to the cost of advertising the same amount of space in the same media. This isn't true ROI—it's a theoretical advertising cost savings. However, it's spurious to compare the two in the first place because you have control over your advertising, whereas the journalist and editor have control over his writing. And if the mention is only a few lines in a longer piece, the size of the entire piece shouldn't be counted.

In my experience, you can get a press release onto thousands of websites, but tracking the web visitors from those websites is not easy. There's no easy way to group all those websites while you're looking at your web analytics. If you're lucky, you might find you get a large amount of traffic from one or two placements; then you can check out the value of those in your analytics or in terms of e-commerce results. For example, you might compare the bounce rate, time on the site, sales, or other metrics for visitors from the PR to your other traffic sources.

Uneven Accountability

Because not every sales or lead source is equally trackable, sometimes the most trackable sources are held the most accountable. If a company can see that AdWords or Facebook is producing a 200% ROI, you might think that is too low and decide to stop doing it. That might be the right decision, but these channels are easier to optimize to higher ROIs. But if that company has no data on Yellow Pages or billboards, it can't see that the ROI might be zero or worse. It might be incredible; it might not. But if you don't have hard proof of ROI either way, you'll probably just keep on advertising. Unfortunately, if the ROI wasn't great, it would be extremely difficult, or impossible, to optimize.

So what's the solution? Again, make everything trackable if possible. Keep these points in mind:

- A billboard can use a different website address from your main one, which might help you track some of its results. Keep in mind, though, that people might Google your businesses name instead if they can't remember the URL.

- In the Yellow Pages, you can use a unique phone number that forwards to your main number. You can do the same for radio, as well.

But what if you can't track everything? How do you make decisions about allocating budget among marketing channels? One approach is to divide your budget according to what you know and don't know:

- Spend 25% of your budget on untrackable channels.

- Spend 25% of your budget on trackable channels, not yet tested but that can be optimized.

- Spend 50% of your budget on proven high ROI channels, especially if they can be optimized.

Last-Click Bias

If you don't have multi-touchpoint analytics, you have to expect that Google is going to get more credit than it deserves and awareness channels will get less credit than they deserve. That means that just because you don't see awesome Facebook ROI in your analytics, it didn't necessarily play a role in the customers who ultimately bought from you right after searching Google.

If you do need multi-touchpoint analytics and a better sense of how to attribute revenue to multiple sources, check out Omniture. But keep in mind, it quickly becomes too complicated if you don't have someone devoted full-time to analytics.

Inconsistencies and Inaccuracies

After you start to measure things, it's not uncommon to assume that all your measurements are accurate. This bubble bursts the first time someone at a company finds an inconsistency. In reality, there are many ways analytics can be wrong:

- Not every Internet user has JavaScript turned on.

- Some people delete their cookies (estimated at about 12%).[5]

- Metrics-based cookies can also be off by 12%.

- People can go to another website, come back to yours a short time later, and still only be counted as one visit.

- Some webmasters accidentally fail to install the tracking code on each and every page.

- If you have a very popular site with a lot of traffic, Google Analytics doesn't even claim the reports are accurate. It estimates the degree of inaccuracy. You cannot accurately compare web log tools to JavaScript-driven tools.

---

5. http://www.marketingvox.com/iab_research_cookie_rejection_at_12_percent-021885/

- Different analytics packages have different ways of defining the same metric.

- Time on site is always under-accounted for because web analytics doesn't know when a user leaves. It doesn't know if he has gone to another site or closed his browser. It can only track things that happen onsite. There's no onsite event to end the session timer. Dynamic sites with URL parameters can serve unique pages without your analytics package knowing it; in this case, you will have to specifically exclude certain parameters in your analytics settings.

- If you use parameters for marketing purposes, likewise you might have to teach your package what they are to get accurate reporting.

- If analytics code is located at the bottom of the page's code and the page's file size is large, the code might not execute analytics code before the user clicks to the next page.

I know, the wizard behind the curtain is more complicated than we care to deal with. What's the solution? Take your analytics with a grain of salt.

Tracking Facebook Visitors with Google Analytics

If you want to know more about the effects of your Facebook marketing, especially on your website and bottom line, you're going to need a couple more tools:

Google URL Builder: This tool, which is found within Google Analytics, is really just a simple form that helps you create URLs with parameters in them (see Figure 13.4). These parameters go into Google Analytics and enable you to better segment and analyze both Facebook ads and Facebook posts. To use it, either go to http://www.google.com/support/analytics/bin/answer.py?answer=55578 or just Google "url builder" and you'll find it.

A shortURL service: To guarantee Facebook doesn't cause the loss of any analytics referrer data[6], you might want to encase your URLs inside a shortURL. ShortURL services became very popular with Twitter because you only have 140 characters for your tweet, any @reply, and any link you want to tweet. ShortURL services have created—wait for it—shortURLs that redirect automatically to the long-form URL. Bitly (see Figure 13.5) and Tiny URL are the best-known such services.

---

6. There's been speculation in the blogosphere about why Facebook traffic seems to be undercounted by Google Analytics. Some believe that the redirects that Facebook uses before your visitors leave Facebook for an external site are to blame for lost referrer data. I have not found an authoritative answer on this issue, so use of the shortURL is just an extra precaution.

Tool: URL Builder

Google Analytics URL Builder

Fill in the form information and click the **Generate URL** button below. If you're new to tagging links or this is your first time using this tool, read How do I tag my links?

If your Google Analytics account has been linked to an active AdWords account, there's no need to tag your AdWords links - auto-tagging will do it for you automatically.

Step 1: Enter the URL of your website.

Website URL: *   http://www.example.com
                  (e.g. *http://www.urchin.com/download.html*)

Step 2: Fill in the fields below. **Campaign Source**, **Campaign Medium** and **Campaign Name** should always be used.

Campaign Source: *	facebook	(referrer: google, citysearch, newsletter4)
Campaign Medium: *		(marketing medium: cpc, banner, email)
Campaign Term:		(identify the paid keywords)
Campaign Content:		(use to differentiate ads)
Campaign Name*:		(product, promo code, or slogan)

Step 3
Generate URL   Clear

Figure 13.4   *The Google URL Builder helps you create a URL tagged with more information to help you better track your tests.*

Figure 13.5   *The homepage of bitly.*

Tracking Visitors from Facebook Posts

Suppose you want to determine which type of post does best for you—for example, do photo posts get you more results on your website? Here's what you would input into the Google URL Builder:

- **Term**—Post type, such as photo, link, video, and so on

- **Content**—Description of post content, such as puppypicture, blog02042012, or runningvideo

- **Name**—If you're subtargeting your post to a language or geographic region

You can use these fields however you want. An example from one of my clients is in Figure 13.6. These are just suggestions. But be consistent in your usage because when you look at months and months of data, that data won't make sense if you used Term for one thing one month and then switched and put that same info in Content.

	what to put in the boxes
source	facebook
medium	cpc
term	interest target
content	image and copy
name	demographic

Figure 13.6 *Keep track of what type of data you're putting into each URL Builder parameter.*

Or what if you want to test different ways of writing posts? There are many ideas for this throughout the book. Let's say you want to post longer text versus shorter text. Use the Content field and add *long* or *short* to your description. For example, try longer text with a puppy picture (long_puppypicture) one day and then shorter text with a picture of three dogs (short_threedogspicture) the next day.

You can test all kinds of things, including

- Call to action or not

- Type of call to action, such as comment versus click

- Post approach, such as event versus selling the dream versus controversy

Another interesting tool for tracking Facebook post tests and ROI is available from http://www.campalyst.com/. Their tool does the job of marrying Facebook data and Google Analytics data.

Tracking Visitors from Facebook Ads

You'll test a number of ads and set up a URL for each with Google URL Builder. I suggest when you set these up, you use a table in Word or Excel to keep track of what you're testing and tracking (see Figure 13.7). What info are you putting into term, content, and name? Here's how I like to do it:

- **Term**—Interest target; if it's none, put "nointerest" in it

- **Content**—Name of image tested

- **Name**—Demographic; if it's none, put "alldemos" in it

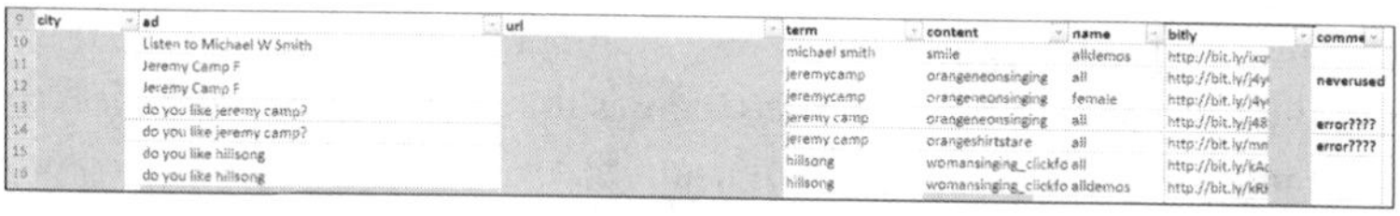

Figure 13.7 *Keeping track of your tests in Excel is critical if you want your tests to produce reliable data.*

You can create a number of ads targeting to demographic segments of your interest targets, send them to your site, and then see how those different ages and genders behave on your website. For example, you might be targeting people who love tennis, but you want to know whether the 35–44 demo spends more or less time on your website than the 25–34 demo.

In Figure 13.8, we can see how likely people in several demographics were to complete various goals and the respective per-visit value of each. This client, as shown, has four goals set up in Google Analytics.

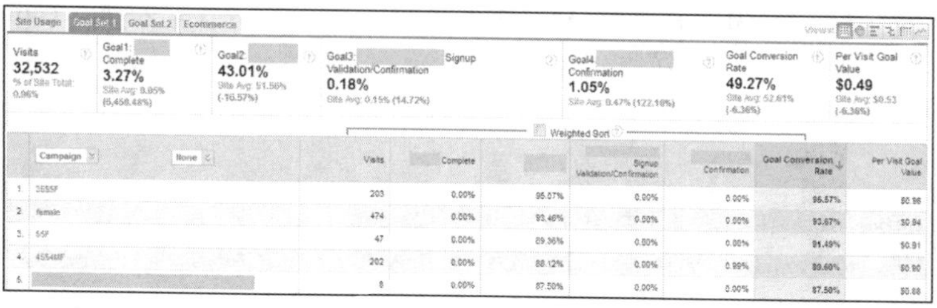

Figure 13.8 *Here's how test results look in Google Analytics.*

You can also compare the behavior of visitors from different pay-per-click sources, such as Google versus Bing versus Facebook. Google Analytics will automatically give you Google/CPC, which is traffic from AdWords (although you should enable auto-tagging inside AdWords to be sure it's accurate), but you can use the URL Builder to specify Facebook as the source and CPC as the medium, and end up with data like that in Figure 13.9 for comparison.

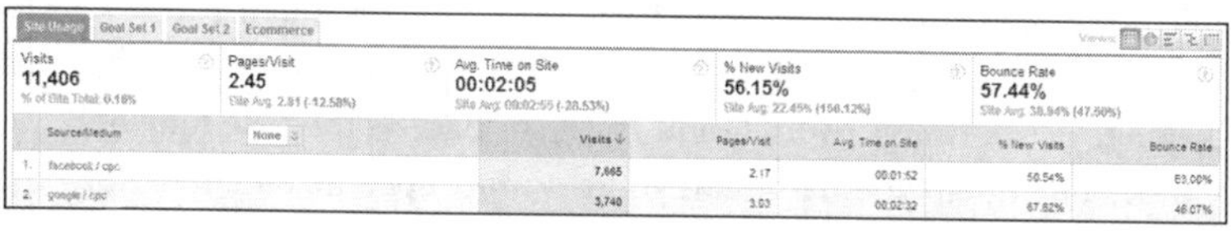

Figure 13.9 *Comparing Google and Facebook advertising traffic in Google Analytics.*

Incidentally, it would be useful for you to understand some of the particular metrics in Figure 13.9 because you'll see this a lot when you bring new visitors to a website. The numbers in the biggest font size show the average for these two PPC sources, and the red and green percentage numbers show how the PPC traffic compares to the site average. What you see there is that PPC visitors spent less time on site, were more likely to be new visitors, and had a higher bounce rate compared to the site average. This looks bad, but it's reasonable to expect that from new visitors. Some of these people will become your customers, and some won't. You're comparing them to the site average, which is web visitors who come to your site without seeing advertising. These are more likely already customers, loyal users, and people who use the website already. It's sort of like saying a regular watcher of a TV program is more likely to watch the whole episode than someone who's just checking it out for the first time.

There's going to be some attrition with the people who come from advertising—a percentage of them will not buy or take whatever action you want and might never return. That's normal. The key is to find advertisements that get you quality customers or leads at an acceptable cost per acquisition. Figure 13.10 shows that by using Google Analytics' Ecommerce functionality, you can actually get the revenue per visit for each traffic source. As shown in this example, every visitor from Facebook was worth $5.87 in revenue.

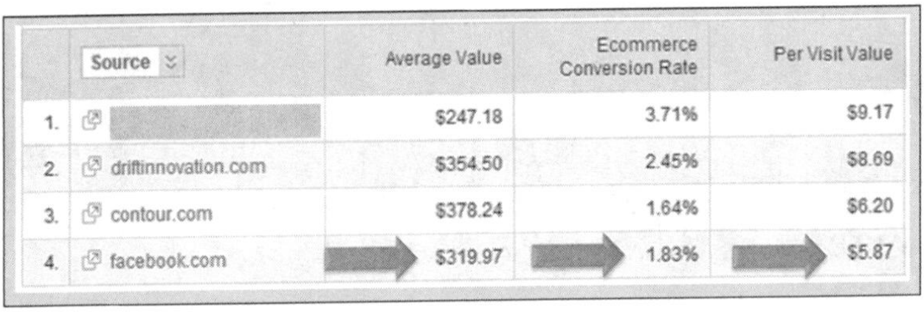

	Source	Average Value	Ecommerce Conversion Rate	Per Visit Value
1.		$247.18	3.71%	$9.17
2.	driftinnovation.com	$354.50	2.45%	$8.69
3.	contour.com	$378.24	1.64%	$6.20
4.	facebook.com	$319.97	1.83%	$5.87

Figure 13.10 *Comparing ROI from Facebook visitors to that of people from other websites.*

How to Get Advanced Facebook Page Insights

Let's talk about analytics for pages on Facebook now. Although Facebook's free Insights are interesting, the data isn't easy to use for optimization. I often come away saying, "Well, things overall look good (or bad, as the case may be)." Generalities don't help you. How can you get more specific data to help you get better results? The Facebook analytics service PageLever[7] (which is used by YouTube, Nike, Microsoft, and other companies) just left beta and is now publicly available. Much of the data comes from Facebook's API but isn't available in Facebook's free Page Insights.

---

7. http://pagelever.com

You might recall that I suggest you have a question in mind and then go to analytics for the answer. Here are five key questions you can answer with PageLever to help you get more likes and comments, thus increasing your posts' visibility to your fans.

1. How Often Should You Post on Your Facebook Page?

A lot of people assume it's best to post at the same frequency all the time—for example, once a day. Should you post again if your last post is still getting new likes and comments? And how do you know if you're not posting often enough? In PageLever, you can check on a specific post to watch for when its engagement levels off (see Figure 13.11).

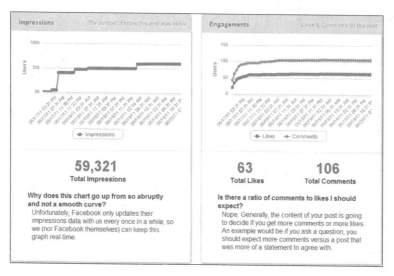

Figure 13.11   *Impressions and engagement for a specific Facebook post over time.*

If it flatlines and isn't getting more impressions or feedback, then the post is basically dead. It's time to post again. If you wait too long after this, you're missing an opportunity. If you post too soon, you can clutter your fans' newsfeeds with more than one of your posts, which could lead to them unliking your page or just being annoyed with you, which hurts your chances of getting their business.

2. What If the Demographics of Your Most Engaged Fans Is Different from Your Average Fan?

Facebook Insights tells you about your overall fan base but not the demo of your most active fans. PageLever gives you both.

Comparing the demographics of active fans to all fans helps you target your post content and think about whether your posts are written in a way that doesn't engage more people. Are you accidentally posting in a way that appeals to men but turns off your female fans?

This demographic comparison also helps you think about whether you want to change the ad targeting you use to get new fans. Is the active fan demographic telling you that you actually should be getting more fans with the demo of the active ones?

3. What Types of Posts and Post Content Get You the Best Feedback Rates? Which Get the Worst?

PageLever's Posts By Page makes all your posts available for analysis, whereas Facebook Insights only shows the last 10 posts. If you wanted to analyze more, you would have to go through all your posts by hand. PageLever collects all the information about your posts into a sortable chart. The first thing you should do is sort by engagement rate (ER), which is the same as what Facebook calls Feedback Rate, so that the highest ER is at the top.

Now look at the top 5–10 posts and note the type of post (photo versus video versus link and so on) and of course the content. Then sort the other way, putting the lowest ER at the top, and note the same things about those posts. Do you see any patterns? Are photos best? Are links worst? Do posts with calls to action get better results?

This kind of analysis can help you come up with ideas for new posts. Then you can go back a week or two later and see whether your theory about what gets the best engagement worked for you.

4. What's the Best Time to Post to Your Fans?

Use the same post analysis from the previous tip to see how time of day affects your engagement.

Be sure to look at the same post types because failing to do that could throw off your analysis. If photos get you the best engagement, check out how photos posted in the morning versus the evening fare in terms of engagement rate. If you currently post only once a day and always at the same time, you'll have to switch this up before you'll have the data with which to compare.

5. Which Sources Get You Fans Who Will Ultimately Unlike Your Page?

Facebook's free Insights tell you where your fans come from but not the origin of the ones who unlike your page later. PageLever tells you both.

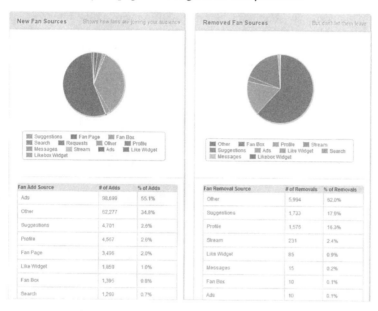

Figure 13.12   *PageLever shows top sources of new fans and the biggest sources of fans who later unlike your page.*

For example, if you incentivize fans to suggest a page to their friends, what percentage of the fans you get from that source ultimately unlike your page? In a number of the pages I've looked at, this percentage is rather high. Here's an example where about 1/10,000 fans from ads unliked but almost 1/3 of fans who came from friend suggestions unliked. Fan retention looks to be much higher when fans come from ads.

How to Use These Tips to Get Better Results from Your Posts

Here's how you turn all that intelligence from PageLever into more likes:

- Post at exactly the right frequency, which maximizes both exposure and weekly number of post likes.

- Post in a way that appeals most to your fan base demographic.

- Identify which demographic likes your posts most often and build more fans with ads targeting that demographic.

- Switch to favoring the post types that get you the best results.

- Find the best time to post to maximize likes.

- Avoid costly fan sources by identifying those with a high rate of eventual unlikes.

Now you know! And knowing is half the battle!

14

FaceFluence: Turning FaceBrowsers into FaceBuyers—13 Sales and Influence Tactics

When Influence Comes into Play

There are many potential pitfalls along the way to Facebook profits:

- **Distribution**—If you can't reach people through ads or as fans, no one hears your message.

- **Quantity of audience**—If you don't have enough fans, you won't get many website visitors or sales.

- **Quality of audience**—If you get the wrong fans, they won't care about your message.

- **Persuasion**—If you write your messages poorly, even good prospects won't respond.

This chapter is primarily concerned with the lack of persuasion pitfall and how to get better results. For the purposes of this discussion, we will assume that:

- **Your messages will reach a sufficient quantity of people**—You have enough fans and they're seeing your posts.

- **Your messages will be reaching the right prospects**—You've gathered the right fans.

- **Your offering is something that these prospects need and will at some point want**—The fans and your offering match.

So, assuming you have a good audience and a good offering, what can you do to increase your conversion rates?

Sales and Influence Tactics for Increased Facebook Profits

Marketers and researchers over the last 90 years have discovered powerful ways to influence prospects to buy. These principles can be applied on Facebook to dramatically improve your results.

Isn't it strange that, through most of the history of marketing and advertising, so few people have approached it scientifically? Perhaps it's not surprising because tracking marketing results has never been easy (and some of the ways TV and radio have been tracked are downright inaccurate). But for years, many marketing and advertising investments were made on faith. A notable exception I can think of in TV are the ads that direct you to a website and the web address starts with a number. These advertisers use a different number for each city in which they advertise, or even different ads, to see which ones get them the best results.

The best known pioneer in scientific marketing is Claude C. Hopkins, who wrote *Scientific Advertising* in 1923. Hopkins advocated research and sampling and used key-coded coupons to track which headlines and offers got more sales. His results were unparalleled, which is why he earned anywhere from $52,000 to $185,000 per year, depending on bonuses. In 2010 terms, that's equivalent to between $1.2 million and $4.2 million.

This scientific approach is the foundation for the kind of advertising I learned to do with Google AdWords in 2005. The ability to track the return on investment (ROI) of each keyword and each ad is why I was able to take accounts that made 200% ROI and turn them into 900% ROI accounts. For each keyword we targeted, I would test 3–5 different advertisements. The difference in results using a testing approach is amazing, and it's almost always a surprise as to which approach works best. I once saw a study that proved that even experienced marketers couldn't predict which ad would do better. Similarly, we can track each Facebook post and each Facebook ad to see which ones perform and which don't and then learn something from that and do a better job in the future.

All Internet marketing is a boon to anyone who wants to take a scientific approach to marketing and treat it as a laboratory to get better results and learn about their prospects. Why in that order? Often we test several marketing ideas, and when we see which one works better, that teaches us something about our customers.

Researchers including Robert Cialdini, Steven D. Levitt, and Stephen J. Dubner have conducted small- and large-scale tests in the fields of social psychology and microeconomics. *Influence*, *Freakonomics*, and *Superfreakonomics* are popular books that explain the insights of these experiments and how we can apply them to marketing and sales.

First, we'll discuss influence principles and then sales tactics because many sales tactics rely on the influence principles to some degree.

Applying Influence Principles to Facebook Marketing

Influence, or persuasion, is a powerful area of study for marketers. The fact that there are some scientific studies to give us guidance about what works and what doesn't adds more weight to the discipline. Learning the following will help you in all marketing, but of course we'll discuss them specifically with regard to Facebook.

Reciprocity

You've got to give to get. Give and ye shall receive. Don't be a taker. We hear these messages over and over in this world. Are they just platitudes, or are they truths that marketers can use to get better results?

It turns out that reciprocity is a powerful way to get a response from your potential buyers. People really do tend to return favors. Who hasn't heard or joked about the drug-dealer tactic, "the first one is free." Like any influence tactic, this one can be used for good or ill. As they say, guns don't kill people, people kill people.

When I first began teaching Facebook marketing, I followed the advice of a number of Internet marketers to create a free course first. I called it Facebook Marketing 101 and put it online at www.FBM101.com. It contained nine free videos. If you gave me your email, you got the free course. The idea was that not only would you get a sense of what my teaching was like before you had to consider buying the full course from me, but also that you'd feel obligated to me because I gave you something for free. More than that, I wanted to show people how to achieve some of their Facebook goals, to get them started. If they made some progress and liked my teaching style, then they would probably get value out of buying a full course from me.

Since then I've modified the free course, added more videos, and every so often send other free info and teachings to that original email list. How well did it work? More than 5,000 people have signed up for the free course, and hundreds of those have bought the full course. And what's more, some of those FBM101 subscribers became my clients. Rather than learn to do it, they preferred to have someone do it for them. I had demonstrated my expertise in the free course, and in line with the idea of reciprocity, any sense of obligation they felt to me would make it more likely they'd select me for that work.

During a few of the years my wife and I lived in San Diego, I had a home office and our next door neighbor was an elderly Italian woman named Maria. Maria was a master of influence, and I mean that in the scariest way possible. She had some things that needed doing, like fixing her fence, weeding her backyard, and mowing her front yard. And for some reason, she thought I was the best man for the job. She also thought my name was Jimmy, and she called my wife Mary (which is not her name). I think once you reach a certain age, you can only deal with the idea of a certain number of people and so new ones get the old ones' names. No idea. Anyway, Maria would arrive at my door with a bowl of pasta she had made and then ask if I could help her with chores. I once spent three hours in her backyard hacking down overgrown cacti. Eventually I learned to say no if she asked if I wanted pasta. What made it even more ironic, and underlines the power of reciprocity, was that her pasta was horrible. She used the cheapest canned ingredients and her pasta was overcooked. I rarely ate it and ultimately ended up throwing it out. But was I going to tell a nice elderly Italian lady that I didn't think she could cook Italian food? I'm not that crazy.

Some people call this a "freemium" model. Many online services have free 30-day trial versions of their offerings. Bloggers use this technique, too—all of their blog content is free. The information has some value—some blogs more than others—and although it may not make you buy anything from them, it does increase your affection and esteem for them.

Reciprocity doesn't happen just online; anytime you're in the grocery store trying a free food sample, you're experiencing the pull of the reciprocity principle. There's a much higher chance of you buying the food you sampled because of the obligation you feel for having gotten something for free. In a way, you could consider dating the freemium approach to marriage. Even more so when premarital sex is involved.

There's another interesting type of reciprocity that comes when you allow people to reject your first request. Let's say I ask all readers of this book to pay me $5,000 a month to coach them in their business and improve their Internet marketing profits. Many would say no.

So, I'd say, "Okay, how about you come to my Two-Day Digital Marketing Summit in Miami for $999?" Research by folks like Cialdini has shown that more people would go for the seminar if they first rejected me on the monthly coaching. It turns out that when people say "no" and you accept it, people feel obligated to you for letting them off the hook. Experts on pricing have likewise found that when you give people three options, from most to least expensive, they are most likely to choose the middle one. They want a deal but don't want to appear to be cheap.

So, how do we use reciprocity in Facebook marketing? It's going to take a lot of different forms, depending on your goals, your offerings, and what you have that you can give away. When done in combination with fan marketing or email marketing, you're giving yourself an excuse to make repeated contact with potential buyers, and you're building up equity in their "Bank of IOU."

Whitepapers

I've used reciprocity many times to help business-to-business (B2B) marketers get more leads. For an electronic medical records (EMR) company, we sent people from ads to a page that explained the value of a free whitepaper they'd get in exchange for entering their email. The whitepaper was called "The 5 Biggest Mistakes to Avoid When Choosing Your Electronic Health Record." Notice, the title also plays on fear.

Whitepapers should be very familiar to those in the B2B space. They're the most commonly used incentive for generating online B2B leads. Whitepapers are a very specific type of writing; they are reports or guides that help people solve problems or make decisions. The idea is to demonstrate authoritative expertise in your field to accomplish your other goals.

For example, the title of the previously mentioned electronic medical records whitepaper implies that it was written by those who are familiar with all kinds of EMRs and their pros and cons. It helps hospital and medical practice administrators decide which service to use. Obviously, if the whitepaper was written by a provider of that same service, even if they don't recommend themselves in the whitepaper, they're going to highlight the things that they do well. If you start with your competitive advantage in the field, play that up, and play down your competitors' advantages, you have a whitepaper as a sales tool. As you can see, these whitepapers are not the most objective of their kind.

Videos

The options here are pretty limitless. Your video could be informative, entertaining, or both. It might answer a frequently asked question (in fact, answering FAQs or explaining your niche's jargon in short 2-minute videos is a great way to start if you're stumped for other ideas) or show the consumer how to do something. It could cover recent news. If the video provides value to the consumer, you'll activate reciprocity.

These days, a video doesn't need to be professionally produced and, in fact, the way that many video experts produced videos as recently as the 1990s looks dated now and isn't interesting enough. People simply won't watch more than 15–20 seconds of the old-style videos. Think about movies like *Cloverfield* that use hand-cams and how many billions of amateur YouTube video viewings happen these days. The standards have changed, and the power of affordable video production programs has increased. You can even use your own green screen to make it look like you're in some exotic location without paying a video expert at all.

If you haven't seen the "Will It Blend?" videos, they are an inspiration. They reached millions and millions of people. Although few video campaigns succeed at this level, if you are having trouble thinking of ideas, I suggest you Google them.

Blog Posts

Blogs are powerful and pervasive because they're easy to write, they help you rank well in Google, and you have no editorial process except your own. You can dash off a 200-word idea post or a list of 15 points and publish. There's no one to stop you from doing it the way you want to. And then you can post it to all your Facebook fans or group members.

But to activate reciprocity, your blog post has to be or appear to be valuable. For it to really be valuable, it needs to either move the consumer's understanding forward with an insight or help him achieve something. Even collecting, distilling, summarizing, or comparing other people's content can be valuable.

I'm a firm believer that many people will share a blog post on Facebook or tweet and retweet it on Twitter simply because it looks valuable, even if it isn't. There are a few specific things you can do to increase the perceived value of your blog posts:

- Use a catchy, dramatic, shocking title.
- Bold headings for sections of the post.
- Use bulleted lists (isn't this ironic?).
- Employ fascinating, impactful, beautiful, dramatic images.
- Break up blocks of text—paragraphs should be different sizes and the occasional paragraph should be just one sentence.

If you do all the preceding, even if you say nothing new, I guarantee you that you'll see more shares, tweets, and readers for the post than your normal blog post gets.

For example, in May 2011 I wrote a post on AllFacebook.com called "The 7 Biggest Fan Page Marketing Mistakes." As of July 2011, it has been shared by 2,603 people on Facebook[1] (estimated reach of more than 38,000 people)[2] and retweeted by more than 1,000 people (no idea how many saw it, but I'm going with at least 10,000).[3] The WordPress stats show it has been viewed 49,152 times. This is probably one of my top-five most read blog posts of the last few years, and as time goes on, because it will rank in related Google searches, it will continue to get more and more views. (I wrote an article on ezinearticles.com six years ago that has been read 34,000 times.)

WHY DID THIS "7 FAN PAGE MISTAKES" POST DO SO WELL?

The nature of news is warning. People watch the news and read newspapers to know what evil is coming down the pike and how to avoid it. When it comes to mistakes, they want to at least double-check to make sure they're not making any of them. If they didn't at least skim the post, they would be wondering in the back of their minds if they were screwing up in some way they didn't know about.

The number of mistakes is defined. If there are seven mistakes exactly, then the writer really knows what he's talking about. In reality, I could probably come up with a few more. But number-oriented posts do well. Just take a look at the cover of any magazine and tell me how many magazines have articles like "9 Tips to Make Her Behave Like a Crazy Hamster in Bed." All of them? Okay, then. And how many points you cover is important, too. If you use too few, people may not think your article is authoritative. Use too many, and it sounds like too much work to read it.

If you saw the post on the AllFacebook.com home page the day it came out, it had an intriguing image of a homeless man holding a sign next to it. Curiosity makes you click.

The post itself contains three charts outlining processes, two Facebook screenshots (one with interesting data in it), and of course our beloved and likable-looking homeless man whose sign I Photoshopped to say "WILL DO ANYTHING FOR FANS!! (EXCEPT ADS)."

Images help us increase perceived value in a few ways. First, people hate reading. That's the big secret of blogging—people don't like taking a lot of effort to read. If you make it easier to read or more fun-looking, you'll keep their attention longer. And if those images are charts with interesting data, or they're infographics that make data easier to grasp, people are going to share and tweet your post with wild abandon. In fact, I believe that some of the people who share and retweet frequently do so without fully reading what they're sharing. If it looks valuable, if it looks impressive, then it will impress the people they share it with. These people are content curators, and they derive their value from passing on valuable (or valuable-looking) content.

---

1. http://www.allfacebook.com/7-biggest-fan-page-marketing-mistakes-2011-05

2. Estimates vary on how many friends the average Facebook user has, from 150 to 229. Because there was likely overlap among friends, I went with 150 people per share. Other research has shown that 10% of your friends see your posts, so we have 2564 × 150 × 10% equals a little bit over 38,000 people.

3. http://tweetmeme.com/story/5088627263/the-7-biggest-fan-page-marketing-mistakes

Free Samples, Almost Free Trials, X-Day Trials

This will not be possible for all businesses. For services, you can offer a short consultation, an audit, or a quote. For products, you can let people borrow it…this isn't as crazy as it might sound. Consider these examples:

- Many car dealers let you take a test drive car home overnight.

- Amway sales reps would leave a sampling of their products for homeowners to try for a day and found that it dramatically increased their sales.

- With FanReach courses, we let people try them, not for free, but for a very low fee—for example, the full FanReach course is $5 to try for 5 days, and if you decide you like it, then we bill you the rest of the cost. If you don't, you get the $5 back!

- Some fitness centers offer guest passes or free 7-day passes.

- Many web services offer free 30-day trials.

One warning about these sorts of enticements: For some potential buyers, trials are annoying. If the prospect wants to buy it outright, right now, and your trial makes that more difficult, you can be losing sales. Make sure the trial is either optional or doesn't create any extra steps for people who are already convinced.

Cheaper Product That Helps People Use Your Main Product

You can give something cheap either to prospects or as a bonus to people who buy from you. For prospects, you probably want to get them to do something in exchange for the freebie, like sign up for your email list. If you're daring, give something away for every like—but to redeem it, people have to give you their mailing addresses. Could you use that info?

Here are some examples:

- For lawyers and insurance agents, give people a branded pen.

- For web service providers, give them a branded flash drive.

- For a shoe e-commerce site, offer a set of comfort inserts.

Have you noticed that some airlines give away branded headphones while others make you buy them? Neither approach is right or wrong, but the branded one is exposed to more people, and the airlines that charge you for everything don't typically gain your affection, do they?

Facebook Group

A Facebook Group is a gift? It really is to the most enthusiastic participants. I've seen a number of cases where Facebook ads for fan growth revealed the most passionate interests—I would see one particular ad get a really high click-through rate (CTR) or, in some cases, an entire niche had a high CTR. Businesses that create groups based on those interests suddenly have administrative control over a vociferous, positive, neverending discussion. What's more, the participants frequently express gratitude for the Group. For example,

- "This group has been a place for me to make new friends, share my accomplishments, vent, get good advice, and receive support during difficult times and best of all LAUGH. And even get in a few arguments! I moved to a new area recently and so, I don't know many people. This group has helped keep me grounded and connected out here in the desert. Good or bad, I take these girls for who they are, and I feel they do so in return."

- "It means the world to me without these lovely people I would have panic attacks. And the laughs I get out of here are GREAT!"

- "It is a cyber family that you can laugh with and share the adventure you just took. It is a place to tell stories that other people would never understand. It is a cyber country and we are the residents."

- "To me it started as being able to chat with people with like minds and same interests and exchange ideas, etc. It has since become so much more. I feel I have made some genuine friendships on here. Being able to come into a group and ask opinions etc. is a wonderful option as you usually hear options you hadn't considered before."

- "I love this group. It is a great way to meet [mutual fans] and share what we know and to learn what we don't. Each person in this room is special."

- "I don't really 'do' groups much, but this one is a gem. Whenever you have a group of strong-willed women, you have wondrous conflict, but with a common love and interests in so noble a beast, we cannot help but find common ground from which we can work."

You might want to communicate to them that you paid to create that group and remind them that if they love it, they owe you. They need to understand that you created value for them; then that may activate their sense of obligation to buy from you. Rephrase the following into your own brand's voice:

"Wow, we're grateful we spent extra money advertising to get you fans into this group because you really seem to love it! It's so cool to be a company that doesn't just sell stuff but also creates community. Click Like if you love this group!"

You might be able to get the group to help moderate itself for you. Why not offer a group member something in exchange for helping? This is smart in some cases because the group becomes so tightly bonded that if you're not really one of them in spirit, you can seem like an outsider and not be listened to as much. If you really want to create a response to the moderator idea, instead of just asking for one, ask for a pool of applicants.

For example:

"Do you love this group we created for you? We're looking for applicants from within the group, real _____ lovers, who would be interested in acting as a community moderator in exchange for a discount on our products. If you're interested, comment here and tell us why you'd make the best moderator!"

I would not give moderators admin access, though, because they could remove you as admin and own the group. Instead, have them report to you if they think someone needs to be removed.

Also, remember that Facebook pages can't join Groups or participate in them. If you want to like posts and comment, you'll need a profile to do that. Don't be afraid to let someone in your company be the face of the brand for these purposes. But as with page administrators, this is a position of great trust and responsibility, so choose your brand representative carefully.

Commitment and Consistency

People like to be, or at least like to appear to be, consistent. A man is only as good as his word. My word is my bond. James Bond. (Bad joke. I have a million of them.)

If you can get someone to say he'll do something, especially in front of other people, there's a good chance he'll follow through. You can get clever with posts and say something like, "Click Like if you would buy x (product or service) this week if you had the spare cash." Then the next day, say, "Click Like if you sometimes spend money on frivolous things." Or reverse the order of those two posts.

You can also nibble away at the things people need to internally agree to before they buy your product or take an action. For example, let's say you're a chiropractor and you're talking to some new fans you grew through ads. They're mostly guys who love sports, played sports, and are now getting a bit older (you targeted guys age 35–55 with your ads). They're probably experiencing some aches and pains. But

you know they have some internal obstacles to going to the chiropractor for the
first time:

- Tough guy syndrome, not wanting to seem weak or old

- Fear of getting hooked into lots of money and care over a long time

- Fear of the unknown and not knowing what chiropractic care is like

- Ignorance and not knowing what worse pains and problems lay down
  the road if they don't take care of their bodies

So we can use innocuous page posts to get these guys to agree to reasonable things
that eventually make them pushovers for a first visit:

- Post a picture of Michael Jordan (or another athlete known to use chiropractic care). "Did you know Michael Jordan gets chiropractic care?
  Click Like if you love MJ!" or "Michael Jordan gets chiropractic care
  because it helps him play golf more comfortably and with less pain.
  Click Like if you think that's smart!" Those who click Like have agreed
  that it's okay for tough athlete studs to get chiropractic care, and by
  extension, it must be okay for them, too.

- Post something like "The best chiropractors make treatment affordable
  to their patients. Click Like if you'd do chiropractic if you knew you
  could afford it!" Now they can call and find out it's affordable, and
  they've already committed themselves internally to doing it.

- Use a video overview of chiropractic care. "Chiropractic is safe and
  makes you feel better. It's easy. Click Like if you want less pain and
  more comfort!" This alleviates the ignorance and commits them to the
  benefits.

- Post a picture of two spines, one pointing out painful areas with red
  lines. "One of these guys got chiropractic and he's active and pain-free.
  He's in his 60s and playing golf twice a week. The other spine is a guy
  who came in once but didn't continue with chiropractic care, and he's
  now homebound and taking pain medications. Click Like if you'd
  rather be the happy, active guy!"

Take a minute to think through the internal objections your prospects have to your
service or product. What agreements do they have to make in order to make it easy
for them to buy? Walk them through these, step-by-step, with posts that are easy to
like.

People are also consistent with their self-image, so if that conflicts with your offer
somehow, you'll have to help them change their self-image through the same series
of easy-to-agree-to likes.

Social Proof

We look for cues from others to see what we should do. It's called *conformity*, and although our pride says we aren't it, the research (and our inner voices, if we're honest) tells us we are very influenced by it.

Television continues to employ canned laughter in sitcoms because even though we don't think it should work, experiments show it causes more laughter, and it also tends to protect a show against our judgment when the jokes are really bad.

What I learned when doing stand-up comedy is that if you can get some people in the audience who really like you and laugh loudly, you can kickstart the rest of the audience to laugh and get them to laugh more. The commitment principle works here, too—if you invite someone to a show or you've bought the comedian's CDs, you're more likely to laugh harder and lead your friends to do the same. Some clubs actually employ people to come in and laugh on purpose, just to get the crowd to enjoy the acts more. One comedian admitted publicly that a TV show had extra laughter added to his recorded performance because he had an off night and people weren't laughing. They had already invested in getting the crowd there and record-ing it, and normally people laughed, so they figured why not put in the laughter where it should be? Why represent his show with one really bad night?

Ever notice how tip jars at delis and coffee shops always seem to have money in them, no matter how early in the day it is? We're more likely to tip when we see that others already have. We're more likely to stop and listen to a street musician when others are already listening. We'll even look up in the air if several people already are doing so. We see a restaurant with a line of people waiting out the door and decide we'll try that restaurant the next time we're out. We have to experience what other people think is so good.

Testimonials in marketing work the same way, though they have been faked so many times that they've lost some of their credibility. Ever see someone out in pub-lic who seems like she might need help, but no one is helping? Sometimes we think this means she doesn't really need help, and we hesitate and decide not to help. Want to make it easier to talk to women you don't know? Find a way to have a pub-lic conversation with other women. Women who don't know you see that you're entertaining and safe, and they become more open to you.

It makes sense because we have limited time and capacity to judge each new thing for itself, by ourselves, so we look to what other people have done and how they view things.

How does social proof work on Facebook? The most obvious way is in how many fans you have. When people see your Facebook page and tens of thousands, hun-dreds of thousands, or even millions of people have liked it, well, it must be worth liking! The same thing happens when you have a like box on your website that shows how popular you are. If someone has never been to your site and the first thing she sees is that 15,000 people like your business, that's a strong statement of quality. It creates trust and leads to more likes.

All of this is similar to the physics concept of momentum. You know how it's harder to get something started than it is to accelerate it? Did you know that cars and bikes in lower gears are exerting more force than in higher gears? The same is true with people. A canned laugh, a planted audience member, a few one dollar bills in the tip jar all mean you're going to get more laughs and more money quicker. A whole bunch of Facebook page fans could help your business quicker than one page, if you have the time to keep all the fans on each engaged.

Another kind of social proof is how many people like or comment on your Facebook posts. This is a function of both your fan count and how good you are at getting interaction. Edgerank accentuates this social momentum by showing more interacted-with posts to more fans.

How can you use this to get more revenue? Here's one way: figure out which thing your new customers most often buy. What's the best entry product? Tell your fans that. "Hey, did you know that 78% of our first-time customers buy Product X? Check it out here: (link to the product's webpage)." Do you have any sales numbers or new customer numbers to brag about? Tell your fan base! Although some people try to avoid bragging, if you don't tell potential buyers about your success, you won't harness the momentum of your popularity, and if you don't tell existing customers, they eventually might wonder if things are going well for you.

I've found this in my consulting practice—when I email my customers that I'm going to speak in San Francisco or that a blog post was recently viewed by 49,000 people, it's very effective. And I've found that if I don't tell the people I do Facebook ads for that I also have been succeeding with SEO, they might hire someone else to do it despite their satisfaction with my work. When you have success, let people know, and it leads to more successes.

Liking

There's a common saying that we buy from people we know, like, and trust. Tupperware parties exploit the power of someone who's already a friend to increase the pressure to buy. Who are you more likely to help or buy from: someone you like or someone you don't like? So, likeability is a big factor in succeeding at getting people to do what you want.

Research shows that most of us like a specific bone structure in people, and we will vote for candidates based solely on the most vain of attributes. Good-looking people (as defined by this strange consensus of ours, strange because in other historical times, fleshier folks were regarded as more rich, powerful, and desirable) are also treated more leniently in the justice system. Let me ask you this: Why do you think Go Daddy, Carl's Jr., and a high proportion of Facebook advertisers use sexy women in their marketing? Why did Old Spice use a bare-chested former football player? Why do movie executives choose traditionally attractive men and women to be movie stars? We buy and help based on our likes.

We are also influenced by people we have things in common with and people who say they like us or who compliment us. Sounds like brown-nosing, doesn't it? Evidently it works. We also like things we are familiar with. Have you ever heard a political candidate considered a good bet because they had "name recognition"? Do you think Arnold Schwarzenegger or Sonny Bono's political successes had anything to do with their previous fame and voters' familiarity with them? Without question.

Authority

Robert Cialdini discusses amazing examples of how obedient we are to authority figures: Almost all in a study obeyed a researcher's command to repeatedly harm a subject who pretended to scream in response to fake electrical shocks; millions of consumers bought decaffeinated coffee on the recommendation of an actor who was not a doctor but played one on TV; TV audiences estimated a guest's height to be taller if he was more of an expert.

People respond to titles and uniforms. Random people are more likely to obey commands coming from someone wearing a security guard uniform. People are more likely to follow a jaywalker if he's wearing a business suit.

Ever wonder why people continue to wear expensive watches even though most rooms contain at least one clock, computers have clocks, and so do mobile phones? They are a form a jewelry and they convey a kind of success and authority. Similarly, drivers are less likely to honk at a new BMW than a 20-year-old Honda.

How can you use this in your Facebook marketing? If you market yourself, use marks of credibility to differentiate yourself. Third-party associations help. For example, I created an image for my Facebook page that included a list of well-known and trusted periodicals that had interviewed or profiled me. If your product has won awards, mention those. If your restaurant has been positively reviewed, post those reviews. Are there well-known experts or celebrities in your niche, well known to your audience? Can you get them involved? Have you ever been to one of those restaurants where the walls are covered with autographed pictures of celebrities eating there? This is an example of establishing quality through authority.

Scarcity

You don't know what you've got till it's gone. And you might not value something until you realize you could lose it. In sales, this is called a "take away." It's similar to playing hard to get. After you have attention or interest, if the product or service is unavailable or exclusive, people want it more.

This arouses desire (in the AIDA process), and if you wait until the prospect has reached maximal desire and only then make the offering available, you're more likely to get a commitment or sale. This is also why pickup artists will teach guys to get phone numbers and then not call a woman for eight days. If you call her the next day, you're too easy. If you wait, she starts to wonder. You create mystery. Your lack of availability makes you seem more valuable. The grass is always greener, and if you can't get over that fence, you really want that grass. Speaking of unavailability, this also explains the married man's appeal—as soon as someone is "taken," he appears to have more value. This is both scarcity and social proof in action.

I discovered this accidentally while selling our FanReach Facebook marketing courses. We had never sold an infoproduct before, so we had no idea how to price it. I felt that it was info that could help any business, but in particular we wanted it to be affordable to small businesses, so we chose a price we thought would make it a no-brainer decision: $47. Almost every customer was ecstatic about the value of the information compared to the price. But one customer told us he almost didn't buy it because it was so cheap. He thought for sure we must be saying $47 per month. He urged us to charge at least $500 for it. We were torn because we wanted to be affordable for everyone. We decided to compromise and increased the price to $97. Here's where we learned a big lesson about scarcity. We emailed the thousands of people who'd taken our free course and told them the price was going up to $97 on such and such date. The day before that date, we got a deluge of sales.

We discovered later that some people never even logged in to the training—they may not have been ready to learn, but they didn't want to lose the chance to learn at $47. They were motivated by what they perceived as a potential loss of $50 (the difference in prices). Price hikes seem to activate a scarcity response that makes people buy.

Scarcity is also behind all those "limited time offers."

Scarcity is one of the harder principles to apply on Facebook, but here's one: Don't comment constantly after you post on your Facebook page. Start the discussion and then make yourself scarce. Let fans fill in the conversation. And don't like every comment by every person. Make your likes selective so that people know they mean something.

If you're marketing yourself in a service business, scarcity can help you in many ways:

- **Don't handle all your leads**—Do what you do best in your business and let your assistant or salespeople deal with prospects. If people can talk to you before they pay you, your time is less valuable.

- **If you speak with prospects, limit the time you spend with people before they've decided to pay you, and keep the focus on them**—Try to withhold advice until you're being paid for it. You don't have to squander your gifts on people who don't value you. And when this is made clear ahead of time, if you do volunteer advice or spend extra time, make sure you point it out by saying something like, "I'm doing this because I like you and I think I can help you."

- **Be clear about how and how often you communicate with customers**—If you're hired to do a specific service, you might offer consulting advice when it pleases you, but you also should have an hourly consulting rate and be clear when you're donating your advice. If you're giving more than you have to, tell people so they know they're receiving a gift. This activates reciprocity.

- **Get indecisive prospects to choose**—First, tell them that you have a policy not to string out decisions because your best customers have always been the decisive ones, and your business manager (that's me now) has told you that you can't afford to talk to prospects again, at least not for 3–6 months. Tell them they can come back and speak with you again in 4 months if they're not sure now. That's scarcity. And use reciprocity; tell them if they decide now, you'll give them something (whatever you want—sometimes it's something extra for free or you can require a shorter commitment than normal). You show you're willing to meet them halfway, so this often is the tipping point that gets them to say yes.

If you're like me, you're naturally generous (as well as gorgeous and fascinating), so these boundaries seem weird at first. But scarcity makes complete sense for service professionals because there is only one of you. There's a limited supply of your time. By nature, you are scarce. If you don't act accordingly by setting boundaries, you will give yourself away and won't be able to take care of yourself. You'll probably also become resentful of the people you're being generous to.

Another way to view scarcity is that it's stuff you can't have. Forbidden love. Banned books. Illegal drugs. Things your parents don't want you to do. Inside most of us is a terrible two-year-old and a rebellious teenager who don't want to be chained, excluded, or dictated to. Is there an authentic way to add a "forbidden fruit" story to your products?

Applying Time-Tested Sales Tactics to Facebook Marketing

Now that we've talked about influence principles and how to apply them to Facebook, let's look at some other sales tactics that have worked online and offline for years.

Discounts

Discounts are one of my least favorite tactics because they can put you into a price war. Price wars are bloody and lead to situations like Wal-Mart's retail leadership and the death of K-Mart. But they also lead to adaptations such as Target's new positioning—its response to the Wal-Mart challenge was to position itself as "Cheap Chic."[4] Target focused on selling quality products in squeaky clean stores at a competitive price. But discounts are powerful. They might be the only excuse some potential buyers need to buy from you the first time.

Facebook Fan Discount

You can offer a discount for Facebook fans only. This may get you more fans, and it can make those who chose to be your fan happier about that decision. It also affirms their usage of Facebook, another decision they keep making. This is something you can remind fans of in a post. If you're getting a lot of new fans weekly, post this weekly.

Some people recommend using a discount to incentivize more likes, but this only works when non-fans come to your welcome tab. If you get fans through ads or a like box, they probably won't see the welcome tab.

Facebook Discounts with Time Limits

Although this might not be combinable with the Facebook fan discount, one thing we've learned about discounts on Facebook is that they're more effective if there's a time limit on them. Post something like "Here's a discount for you...but it's only good today!"

Facebook is real-time (or close to it), and people's attention spans are short. Don't rely on them remembering that your discount ends in a week. And this also keeps you from having to post a reminder every day about your expiring discount, which can annoy fans and keep you from posting engagement posts that get more likes and comments.

---

4. http://hbswk.hbs.edu/archive/4319.html

Need More Discount Ideas?

Create a poll to ask people what kind of discounts they'd like. Remember how much of engaging your fans is about getting them to give their opinion? Here you can do some market research and get fans engaged at the same time.

Bonuses

Bonuses are free gifts people get when they buy. This not only makes it easier for them to decide to buy, but also makes them less likely to ask for a refund since they don't want to give the "gift" back. When you give bonuses, people perceive you as being generous, and that activates reciprocity, which makes them want to give you something in return—namely, their money.

Upsells

An upsell is another thing you try to sell people after they've decided to buy the main offering. This could be an add-on or helper offering that makes using the main offering even easier. For example, when you buy a car, they try to sell you a service warranty. You just bought the car so of course you want to keep it in new-car shape and don't want to pay extra to repair it. The consistency principle makes us unlikely to reconsider the entire purchase at this point, and self-perception comes into play: Are you cheap? Do you want the best, or just the good? Fear also comes into play. We don't want to risk losing what we so clearly want to buy.

Selling the Value

There's an interesting relationship between price and value. The value of a product or service is often subjective, but sometimes it can be quantified in terms of the monetary value of its benefits. For example, if a Volvo is really better at saving your life in a car accident, what's the value of your life? Or your spouse's life? Priceless. But you can't sell a Volvo for $1,000,000, can you? If this book helps you get fans for $0.50 less than you would have, and you need 20,000 fans, it saves you $10,000. But obviously we can't sell the book for $10,000.00, can we? I've heard it suggested that if something seems to have 5–10 times the value of what you pay for it, the customer will feel like she got a great deal, be satisfied, and won't return the product.

Value also is related to benefits. We have a Dyson vacuum, and although it may be better at sucking than our last vacuum, its real value is in durability and ease of use. There are no messy bags, and it's easy to empty and keep going. No matter how strong its suction power, we would feel worse about it if it broke easily with normal usage. So your product or service has to appear to have great value in the benefits that your customers care about the most.

The point of this sales tactic is to actually communicate the value that your offering has. You know way more about it than the customer does, so you have to get that information out of your head and into compelling words. Don't underestimate telling the story. There was once a beer manufacturer who took out a full page ad and described the details of its brewing process. It sounded impressive and diligent. It made people believe in the company, the beer, and its quality. It turns out that all that beer's competitors used the exact same process, but they hadn't told the story to the public.

Here are some questions to help you pull out what you know about the value of your offering:

- Do you do it better than anyone else? How?

- What are the benefits, and can you quantify them?

- Does it save people money? How much?

- What went into creating it?

- How many people have bought it?

- How is it different from other solutions for the same problems?

- Does/did it require expertise within your company? How much?

- Does/did it require distinctive education of your employees to make it happen?

- Do any third parties review or approve it?

- Has it won any awards?

As you go about answering these questions, consider this—even after someone purchases, it helps to give him ready-made logical reasons why his purchase decision was a good one.

Testimonials

Similar to social proof, these are case studies of or reviews from happy customers. Often, there's some audience skepticism about testimonials, especially if they're in a paid advertisement or on the company's own website. But Amazon.com reviews are a great example of seemingly unbiased testimonials. Still, if the reviews are all five out of five stars and no one's ever heard of you, it smells a little fishy.

What makes a good testimonial? If you ask customers to post stories or videos, ask them questions like this:

- What did you love about our offering?

- How did it help you?

- What was life or business like before you got it?

- Did you try other competitors, and what did you think?

- Would you recommend this to other people, and why?

Truth and Consequences

There can be downsides to our potential customers not buying from us. Do they know them?

Although many of us don't want to be fear mongers or to manipulate our prospects, this shouldn't keep us from helping them realize the risks of the customer not buying their product. Let me ask you this: If you sell something you really believe in that helps people, aren't you concerned about what will happen to them if they don't buy from you?

Some of us have come to believe that selling is selfish and that if we gain something from the transaction, the other guy loses. But if you're a tax accountant who legally saves people money, you're helping them. If people don't do their taxes, they could lose money or go to jail. And if you're one of the best in your area at federal and state taxes, if someone goes to your competitor, she might lose money she could have gotten from a refund you engineered. So if you really care about these potential clients, you should convince them they're better off going with you, right?

Some of this, I say for my own benefit because I always hated sales and felt manipulated by salespeople even when they were selling me something I really needed. I was almost more afraid of losing the money than losing the benefits of the thing I needed. It took me a long time in life to be okay with buying things I wanted. And once that happened, it was easier for me to market things to people besides the bare necessities.

So, let's put it this simply: It is honorable to help people buy things they need and want. It's certainly not honorable to sell drugs to an addict or booze to an alcoholic. It's a little harder to say that Krispy Kreme shouldn't advertise donuts because there are so many sugar addicts in danger of diabetes. If it's not illegal, we have a harder time making a moral judgment about it.

So, let's assume you want to help people decide to buy an honorable product from you. Here's how to navigate this technique. Answer these questions in order:

1. What are the benefits of your product?

2. What are the opposites of those benefits?

3. What are the dangers of not getting those benefits?

4. Are there reasons why there's a built-in urgency for buying and a danger to waiting?

5. What alternatives and competitors are out there?

6. What are the downsides of those alternatives?

7. Do you know of any stories of people who've suffered these consequences?

After you've answered all of these questions, you have some powerful stories to tell. As I've said elsewhere, the reason news grabs attention and the reason news is usually negative is that we're hard-wired to listen to warnings. If you can build case studies (we could call these *reverse testimonials*) that serve as cautionary tales to your prospects, you can move people toward purchase. This is similar to the scarcity principle. Let prospects know what societal and internal forces and tendencies might be pushing them toward these disadvantages of not buying.

15

FaceBusiness: Seven Principles for Success

The last chapter of many modern business books is called, in the publishing industry, a "Save the Whales" chapter because it's a forward-looking narrative. It's supposed to send you away with a sense of possibility and inspiration. Too often, though, today's brilliant and plausible predictions sound utterly ridiculous next year, and even worse in 10 years.

I'm not going to write one of those. I believe that life is what happens while you're busy making plans. "But you've got to plan, don't you?" Yes, you should know where you want to go and should plan your next steps to get there. Chapter 6, "Facing The Facts: How to Continuously Get Better Results with the Five Steps of Optimization," talks about finding optimal routes to clear quantified goals. But can you tell me for sure that, halfway to your original goal, you won't learn something that might change your goal? What if your marketing tests reveal a huge new opportunity, much better than your original plan?

I think humans are extremely bad at predicting the future. Even crackpots who believe God has spoken to them about the exact date of the apocalypse find themselves issuing retractions and corrections—or just hiding in embarrassment. As you might have gathered from the rest of the book, I'm not a shiny object syndrome guru who runs from new social network to newer social network, screaming with excitement that this latest thing is going to change everything. Having seen this happen over and over, I know it's easy to be wrong in this regard.

Here are some areas where, in the last few years, pundits have been guilty of sensational and ulimately inaccurate predictions:

- Twitter was predicted to change the business world. It has in some ways, but it's not popular enough, and the text-only format is too limited to replace email or make Facebook irrelevant.

- Some said Google Buzz would steal all of Twitter's users. As it turned out, too many people were attached to Twitter and Buzz wasn't different enough to make people switch.

- Google + could fail to rival Facebook for the same reason Buzz couldn't beat Twitter.

The problem with the futurist is that everything sounds great while I'm listening to him, but as soon as I get down to work, I'm lost. Rarely if ever does the vision include a practical method that I can apply now. Mapping out a viable path to a better future is a lot harder than just describing that future.

Being a big believer in efficiency and repeatable systems, I naturally approach any new technology or website with skepticism. They call new technology "the cutting edge," and many companies indeed come away cut and bleeding. But as soon as I see the latest and greatest opportunity get results, I work to discover if it's optimizable, and if so, I'm all over it. Facebook marketing has proven to be one of those opportunities.

So, we're not going to save any whales right now. For me, this last chapter needs to be about two things: summarizing the material and focusing you on putting everything I've taught into action.

I also want to point out how a lot of what this book teaches can be applied beyond Facebook and beyond social media websites. If in five years there's no more Facebook, you'll still be able to apply a good 60%–70% of this book's lessons to whatever comes next. As you might remember, the principles I've found to work on Facebook come from traditional networking, sales, copywriting, and marketing. If this is the first time you've seen some of them, I encourage you to try them outside of Facebook and social media as well. For example, try them in your business emails or at social functions.

Thus, the rest of this chapter is a discussion of the principles underlying this book, combined with encouragement and calls to action. Here are the principles:

1. Harness the Power of Positive Marketing

2. Embrace the Entire Sales Funnel

3. Leverage the Facebook Advertising Platform Now

4. Map Out and Optimize Your Revenue Model

5. Know Your Customers Much More Deeply

6. Test, Track, and Optimize Your Marketing

7. Start Fascinating Conversations

Harness the Power of Positive Marketing

This book is about making a shift in your approach to marketing—away from "the company's marketing ideas are always right" to "through testing, we figured out what our customers love and now they love us back even more!" To get from here to there, let's consider a judo-like saying from Tai Chi: "use four ounces to defeat a thousand pounds." Tai Chi isn't just those peaceful people from the park. It's a martial art, too. Done correctly, when your Tai Chi opponent resists you, you yield so they "feel like they're falling into a hole." On Facebook, when you discover what your customers like, you should reflect and amplify that. Empower their passions. Then they'll fall into the hole of loving your brand. Okay, so the hole thing isn't such a great analogy. Work with me here.

Our own marketing ideas can actually run counter to where our fans and customers want to go. Figure out the direction of the force they're already applying (likes) and push them further that direction. It might be impolite to think of the customer as an enemy, but until they pay us for what we offer, they're not really a partner.

Another principle within the Tai Chi metaphor is flexibility. As you test your ideas in posts and ads, keep an open mind. Be flexible about your tactics and strategies so that when you discover something that customers love, you can put your momentum and theirs into it. I suppose in our analogy, we're both falling down onto a mat of awesomeness, laughing and singing "Kumbaya." Maybe the martial arts analogy breaks down here, too, but you get the point, I hope.

Positive marketing feels better for everyone. What kind of emotions would you like to experience at work? Fear that you'll fail or be found out while trying to take advantage of customers? Or laboring to support and make them happy? Wouldn't you rather be interested in your customers, support their enthusiasm, and help them achieve their goals and dreams? What a positive business to be in! If this kind of thinking infects your entire company, you have a positive company. It's not that stress disappears—life and work always involves struggle—but at the end of the day, positive marketing is more satisfying and healthy for everyone involved.

Embrace the Entire Sales Funnel

As several chapters have pointed out, business on the Internet is a multistep process. You understand now that more than one website or marketing tool is involved—usually more than one roleplayer—and maybe even several consultants.

You know that even our best analytics doesn't always give us a clear-cut picture of how much credit each marketing channel deserves. Sometimes analytics raises more questions than it answers! You've learned that you can't just rely on the highest return on investment (ROI) last-click services such as Google AdWords; you also need marketing channels to raise awareness, arouse desire, and educate the customer. And following a purchase, how do you leverage the customer's satisfaction to pull in her friends and business associates? Your happy customers are Facebook fans who help convert new customers (see Figure 15.1).

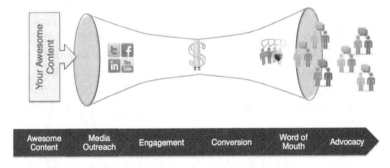

Figure 15.1 *The two-sided conversion funnel. (Image created by Kristy Bolsinger and included with her permission.)*

Develop a plan that embraces the entire sales funnel. The plan can be based on one of the revenue strategies from Chapter 4, "FaceBucks: Five Ways Businesses Achieve Profits with Facebook." You will most likely be using additional marketing channels to Facebook, so your plan will be more complicated. Map it out with your team on a whiteboard and take a picture of it. Get analytics in place at every step of that funnel. Review your results weekly or no less often than monthly.

The multichannel marketing team has to be on the same page for this to work and be focused on inclusiveness and growth. When everyone works together, you increase sales more quickly and more efficiently.

Leverage the Facebook Advertising Platform Now

Hopefully I've convinced you that the Facebook advertising platform is a remarkable marketing tool. It allows you to reach more people, more affordably, with more customization and control than any marketing channel in history. And, at this point in history, it is still cheaper than its major competitors: Google's AdWords and Bing/Yahoo!'s AdCenter.

The most important thing to understand about Facebook advertising is that right now it's one of those golden windows of opportunity that comes along every five years and lasts only a few years at most (and we're about a year into that already). In 2000, that infrequent opportunity was search optimization. In 2003, it was AdWords. Those are still both great marketing options, but the degree of advantage they gave people when they were new was 10 times what it is now. Facebook advertising is in that sweet spot now, so take advantage of it now.

If you're a student of marketing, you know that the first-to-market advantage is hard to overcome. If you're the first in your niche, or in your locale *and* niche, to use Facebook advertising, you're staking a claim that will be hard to unseat. The benefits of getting in now could be as clear as extra profits you'll be able to reinvest in your business, giving you even more of a leg up on your competitors. Yes, getting into things early means not every best practice is nailed down, but the little bit of experimentation it requires is well worth the outsized gains you'll achieve with it.

The choice here is whether you'll spend a little time learning and a little money testing or whether fear and inertia will keep you from trying it. If you prefer struggling and fighting your competitors on equal ground, don't try Facebook advertising. But if you prefer business situations in which you have a decided advantage, get a move on!

Know Your Customers Much More Deeply

Customers are real people—not composites, not demographics, not search keywords. Facebook marketing works much better if you understand your fans and customers on the human level.

After doing search marketing plus working with traditional marketing folks and then working with client after client exploring Facebook marketing, I've come to the conclusion that you have to become a better marketer to do Facebook well. Experienced marketers can fail in Facebook marketing because some of the easier tactics from other channels don't translate. For example, in search, sometimes all you need to know is the search phrases your customers use. The search marketer's insight into customers is very indirect—they only know how customers behave in relation to their searches.

For Facebook marketing, you have to understand your customers in depth and keep getting to know them better through the following:

- Qualitative information from your conversations with them
- Quantified feedback from advertising reports, web analytics, and Facebook page analytics

Facebook provides a huge amount of intelligence about your customers and fans. What you learn about your target customers, you can apply in Facebook, and that gets you more engagement, more enthusiastic customers, and more sales. What's more, this information can be supplied to web designers to reconsider their images and website copy, PR folks to improve their messaging, and so on.

You can learn in a few days from Facebook what in the past took market researchers months and tens of thousands of dollars to learn. This kind of information just wasn't available to most companies. Now that it is, those who take advantage of it will connect more and sell more. It's a major opportunity for you to beat your competition and grow your business.

Test, Track, and Optimize Your Marketing

If you approach marketing as a scientist, you can make consistent improvements. This trips up some of the more intuitive, creative folks. To me, it's not a question of science *or* art. We need science *and* art. You most definitely need intuition and inspiration to create good ideas, write good copy, and choose the best images, but you also need the discipline to test and track multiple ideas.

No, we don't always feel like approaching marketing in an organized, systematic way. No, that doesn't matter. Do it anyway. Steven Pressfield wrote a book called *The War of Art* to teach artists and entrepreneurs how to persist when you don't feel like it. Read that. You'll thank me later when you optimize and get your stellar results back...and after you discover that at least half of your favorite ideas didn't resonate with your target audience.

Before the Internet, scientists could easily laugh at the idea of scientific marketing. But now we have an amazing amount of data about how people respond to words, images, and ideas. You can learn exactly what turns your customers off—and on. You can turn persuasion and sales into a science, thus increasing your profits and sales.

Start Fascinating Conversations

Your goal is to know your customers well enough to be able to stimulate conversation whenever you want. What makes someone the most interesting person at a party? Either she is remarkable or she is incredibly skilled at drawing people out. Not many of us are remarkable, and if you talk too much about yourself, you risk being labeled a bore. More of us can benefit from learning to draw people out.

You know people's loves and their hates, their dreams and their fears. You get them talking about what they're proud about. You get them fantasizing about their dreams. You create a virtual party on Facebook where like people can share and amplify each others' passions. Who wouldn't want to go to that party? Who wouldn't go back? And who wouldn't love their host for making it all possible?

Become the beloved host, the company that cares, and the business that makes its customers happy.

Index